AT THE HEART OF THE DEVIL
DISCRETION ADVISED

BALTHAZAR RODRIGUE
NZOMONO-BALENDA

Also by Balthazar Rodrigue Nzomono-Balenda:

The Depth of My Soul

The Struggle for Power & The Fight for Survival

Freedom of Press: The Sitting Duck

Silent Talking

Far Beyond the Horizon

DEDICATION

This book is dedicated to the victims of human trafficking, women who are oppressed in Muslim countries and elsewhere. I also dedicate this book to the victims of the Rotherham Scandal and those who are going through similar situations in other parts of the word. My thoughts also go to those who are genuine victims of racism for the color of their skin and where they happen to come from; apostates who fear for their lives because of threats from religious fundamentalists and those who are are victims of other evil deeds. I address myself to those who are alive, and those are no longer with us; you are winners in your own rights, regardless of what anyone tells you, you are also winners in the eyes of those who appreciate you. To anyone else who thinks otherwise; if you believe that this book is about enabling victimhood, let me make it clear to you - this book is not for you, if you feel that this book is anti-white, then this book is not for you; if you believe that I am trying to conceal internal feelings of racial inferiority, this book is not for you. If you are someone who does not approve of Islam being criticized or Muslims being challenged, this book is not for you, the same goes to you who could play the anti-Semitic card on me, when I mention Zionism; we want to confront evil, no matter what clothes it wears, we must be prepared to identify it and prepare for the battle at any cost. Sometimes it can cost you your job; it can cost you your relationships and to the worst case scenario, even your life. If you want to defeat evil, you don't have time to think about being popular, nor do you have the time to seek for other people's approval

INTRODUCTION

Throughout the Western world, many people don't feel like they recognize their societies at all due to Globalism and uncontrolled immigration; another factor that we cannot ignore is that human trafficking is wrong for both migrants, as well as the host countries. Another denominator that we need to address is many individuals in much of the Western world do not feel like they have control over their lives anymore, especially those who are living on public assistance, whether we're talking about locals or new arrivals.I would like to be harsh and say that some Western countries struggle to recognize their lack of experience when it comes to integrating migrants of color, countries like Denmark, Norway, Finland, Iceland, Austria and other homogeneous societies. Those are the same nations that grumble about the amount the amount of immigrants they have and the kinds of immigrants they're welcoming, instead of finding workable solutions, race and religion play a role in that. On the other hand, even experienced nations like Germany, the Netherlands, United States, Sweden, Canada, Australia, France and other countries that have a history of coexisting with people of different backgrounds struggle to deal with Muslim immigrants and Muslim immigration; it is very critical that we address this issue because we're kidding ourselves if we choose to pretend that those problems are going to go away. There are questions about the role that Muslim immigration is playing in mainstream Western societies and elsewhere, in the rest of the non-Muslim world. Many people in the civilized world are tired of the Left and the far Left protecting Islam and Muslims from criticism; there are just as many individuals who are also tired of Far right extremists, bullies, anarchists, Kosherfascsits who use political incorrectness as an excuse to belittle other people because of their race, gender, sexual orientation, and other reasons. Not every Western country is meant to be multiethnic; some are intended to be as homogenous as they are. When it comes to Black Africans, we need some serious self-examination; we don't place enough value on the individual, we place value on a group. We don't question our traditions, our customs and the compatibility of our cultures and this is contributing to our demise, especially when we are governing over 50 countries worldwide and most of them are unsuccessful. We expect to be respected, but we don't even respect and value ourselves. This book is going to set some of you on fire, but I am not here to run for a popularity contest; I am here to confront evil in all of its uniforms. Even if it means challenging the Scandinavians, Africans, Muslims, Jews, the Far Left, the Far Right, Mid-Easterners, etc.; I can promise you that it is going to get gruesome, but in the long run you'll understand. I am also looking forward to focusing on topics like illegal immigration, poverty, the WTO, the treatment of non-European migrants and domestic workers in Middle Eastern countries and the demographics of the Western world. Especially when it comes to the Muslim Brotherhood's plan to destroy the West from within and establish and Islamic government on Earth. If we don't deal with Muslim Brotherhood front groups and surveil mosques, then we are in a losing battle. Calling it racism is idiotic; Islam is not a race, Muslims are not a race, just like Christianity and Judaism are not a race. When both Liberals and some Conservative call it racism whenever Muslims are criticized, they do an injustice to the victims of honor killings and those who can no longer walk free in streets for threats they face from Muslims all over the world. We talk about crimes committed in the name of Christianity, Judaism, Hinduism and other religion, but when it comes to Islam, we want to avoid it, just like the Danes and other Nordics avoid talking about hatred in their societies. When we do that, we are not doing Muslims any favors, nor are we doing the same to ourselves. Islam is responsible for over 270 million deaths for the last 14 centuries, including the slavery of Blacks by Middle-Eastern Muslims, but these are not taught in schools out of the fear of not making Muslims happy, by the way, many Muslims always come up with excuses. Another thing contributing to the destruction of the world is those who wage unnecessary wars in the name of money and power; let me make something clear here, I am not against the wealthy and the super wealthy who love their countries, nor do I believe that money is the root of all evil. However; we cannot ignore those who are using their wealth to establish the New World Order by conquering to divide through any means that they have; we have to address that and come up with some ideas about what needs to be done differently. Money does not tell us to go and destroy lives; we make the choice of doing those things through our own behaviors and the way of thinking we decide to implement in our lives. Once we realize that we are in charge of our own behaviors, then we can begin to embrace processes that can change our nations and the rest of the word.

CONTENTS

PREFACE

This book contains some of the most controversial statements that I have ever made on any group of people, whether it is a statement about Scandinavians, Muslims, Africans, Arabs, Turks, Jews and other groups of individuals. The purpose of this book is to addressing one of the most important challenges that the Western world is facing, it is facing the largest migration crisis since WWII and struggles to cope with it. Since the moment of time, migration has always been part of our history and the entire animal kingdom; we migrate for a search for better territories, better lives, better environments and for various other reasons that I can explain. From the early moment of our existence, we have either expressed welcoming or hostile attitudes towards those who are different from us, for the following reasons: Race, tribe, ethnicity, religion, nationality, culture, norms, political persuasion, social class, status and looks. We feel the need to defend what we have and protect ourselves from the unknown; we want to support what we believe our ancestors built, fought and died to preserve, this is not just an issue in White majority countries; it is also a problem in majority non-white countries.In many of those places, you even have more problems because things there are more complicated when it comes to the issues of national identity because of tribe, ethnicity, religion, etc. You, the reader could ask me about the point I am trying to make in this book, and I do not blame for that.

However, we need to take a look at the situation from various nuances; the subject of immigration is a theme we can no longer afford to ignore, and there is a particular kind of immigration, which is worth the debate these days. I am talking about immigration from Muslim countries. Unfortunately, we cannot ignore this problem anymore; if we do not address this issue critically, then I am afraid that we are giving power to the extreme right wing political parties and any other far right associations. If we continue to be politically correct towards this subject, the people who are going to end up paying the biggest price will be all minorities of color like me, whether they're Muslims or not, I am focusing mostly on minorities of color who live in any Western country. There are also some Western nations that have not been honest with themselves and their abilities to integrate newcomers from different backgrounds, and when it comes to their national identity. They force themselves to incorporate those newcomers in one fell swoop, without even questioning their experience and their abilities to do it. For some people, this is a bitter pill to swallow, but the fact remains that those are the same countries that struggle and complain about why integration is failing in their world. Another thing that gets to me is that those countries fail to recognize that they have never had any experience of integrating minorities of color, nor have they ever had power colonial histories. Some populations in those countries portray their societies as "multicultural," yet have never had a history of diversity, this might surprise some of you, but I am going to go further. I am talking about countries like Denmark, Iceland, Austria, Norway, Finland, the Faroe Islands, Slovenia, Croatia, Poland, Ukraine, FYR of Macedonia and Czech Republic. Those countries are not diverse, even if they have amounts of immigrants from non-Western countries, just because your country has a significant number of people from non-Western backgrounds that itself does not make your it diverse, just because you're sitting in a garage for six years that in itself does not give you a car; it is all about historical ties and the willingness to give those newcomers opportunities to live their dreams, rather than encouraging them to live on welfare, it is all about giving them a sense of belonging and a sense of patriotism. I am well aware that some of the things that I am saying in this book might seem inflammatory to some people, but again, you cannot change what you don't acknowledge. Let me give you an example: In Denmark many people from the Greenlandic minority do not have access to the labor market; I am not saying that all don't, but a significant amount of people originally from Greenland do not have access to the Danish labor market, that is why there are many people from that background who end up being trapped in alcohol addiction, drug addiction, etc., this problem has been going on since Denmark discovered Greenland in the first place. There are much Greenlandic People who live in Denmark who have never identify themselves as Danes, even if they have Danish passports, the same can be told about many immigrants from non-

Western countries who live in Denmark and fail to find careers that match their qualifications. As far as I am concerned, the majority of the Danes do not view Greenlanders as Danes either. Just like I said recently, you find many Greenlandic people struggling with alcohol and drug addiction as a way for them to deal with alienation from the Danish society. I am not saying that all Greenlanders deal with isolation from the Danes the same way, on the other hand, some Danes are struggling to figure out what they are and what they country is becoming; they wonder if they are a diverse or a homogeneous society. Seeing a person of color waving the Danish flag in Danish streets could get some interesting attentions from the mainstream Danes themselves

ACKNOWLEDGMENTS

I would like to take this opportunity to thank my family, my friends, my acquaintances, my fans and my subscribers on different social media channels. To my parents, I would like to thank you all for being very supportive of me, and I also would like to thank you for believing in me and this project. To the reader who is probably reading this book, whoever you are, whatever your race, ethnicity, religion, tribe, political persuasion, nationality, sexual orientation, gender and social class; I would like to thank you for taking your time to read this book, I cannot promise you that both of us are going to see eye to eye on many subjects that I am going to cover here, nor can I guarantee you that you will always laugh when reading this book because there are some things that are going to make your mind boil, that is something that I can warn you about. Not to be negative here, but there are going to be some of the statements that you're going to find in this book that is not going to be pleasant to you, but once you read the whole book, you will discover my worldview about many things that I care about. If you believe that I am making generalizations, let me tell you that when I generalize, it is because there are general problems and sometimes you have to send a

1

tough message to get your points across, when someone knocks you down, you've got to push back and sometimes you have to do it in a way that will create an awful memory to the individual for the rest of his/her life. That is why this book is called "AT THE HEART OF THE DEVIL" because you when you will read this book, you will feel like you are in hell with the hell with the Devil, but take a deep breath, and you're going to be ok. Discretion was Advised to you, my reader.

CHAPTER 1

CULTURAL INTEGRATION INC.

Like I said in the preface of the book, some countries are better than others when it comes to integration and assimilation. If you take countries like Norway, Finland and other similar countries where you have Sami minorities and other immigrants of color, the ideas of those societies being diverse and multicultural are debatable in my opinion. Politicians in those countries and elsewhere use these normative concepts on how to handle minorities in their countries. In one way or the other, they know that their countries are not diverse, and they do not want to allow their countries to be dominated by foreign culture, let us take another example, many immigrants from non-Western countries identify themselves as citizens of their countries of origin, the countries where they or their parents come from. They are also defined by the Danes as first generation immigrants, second generation immigrants, third generation immigrants, etc., you get my point. They feel the sense of realism because they are usually reminded that they're not Danes, but outsiders by the mainstream Denmark. It is also a problem some other countries worth mentioning. I can understand that that some immigrants in Denmark, Norway, Finland, Iceland, Austria and Estonia might see themselves as Danes, Norwegians, Finnish, Icelandic, Austrian and Estonians, however, they need to realize that

3

subconsciously, those societies are either not ready or not willing to be diverse communities, that is something that they need to deal with unfortunately; it might mean that they might not feel welcome or my opinions are controversial, but the fact is that those societies are not diverse and they are not multicultural. I am sorry that I have to disappoint some people reading this book, if you're an immigrant living in Finland or Denmark, you are a guest, whether you have had the Danish/Finnish passport, you are still a guest in one of those countries where you live. They are still highly homogeneous societies and they do not want to give up on their high amount of homogeneity, if you do not open your eyes and mind by realizing it, you will continue to set yourself up for disappointments and the only person you're going to fool is no one, but you. If you want to continue to define yourself as a Dane, a Finn an Estonian, a Norwegian, etc., while you're an immigrant, that is also your choice, and I am not going to impose my thoughts on you, all I can say about is...good luck on that.Countries like: Germany, France, Australia, Netherlands, Belgium, Britain, Canada, United States, Brazil, Portugal, Sweden, Switzerland, Spain, New Zealand, Russia, Greece, Argentina and Uruguay have far more experience with new arrivals because they have had a history of planning long term have had history with parts of the world, which they "successfully" colonized that is something that they have used to their advantage for better or worse, it is still open to debate, that is why integrating newcomers in their societies is not as much of a new thing as it is in for instance: Poland, Denmark, Norway, Finland, Slovenia, Hungary, Czech Republic, Bulgaria, Romania, Faroe Islands and some other countries. These countries in my opinion have still a lot to learn, but they see themselves as homogeneous societies and still want to keep their monocultural existence. An immigrant of color or an Eastern European living in Germany, Britain, Netherlands, France, United States, Canada and Australia does not have much explaining to do when he/she travels with the German passport, the British passport, the French passport, the Dutch passport, the American passport and even the Canadian passport overseas, if you take an immigrant originally from a Third World country who lives in Norway, Denmark, Poland, Czech Republic, Iceland etc., and you add to the fact that that individual has let us say for instance the Norwegian passport, the Danish passport or even the Polish passport. The individual has to make twice as much effort to convince overseas authorities that he/she is a Danish citizen, i.e., or a Polish citizen because of the way the individual looks, especially if that person looks Middle

Eastern, African or Asian. A couple of other examples that I would like to give you is that on my Youtube channel, bnbalanda I started a controversial debate about a Black football (soccer) player of South Sudanese descent who now plays for the Danish football (soccer) national team. To get into more details, the individual in this case plays for a Danish domestic football club, FC Midtjylland, which is one of the best football clubs in the country, his name is Pione Sisto. I started a debate about Pione Sisto playing for the Danish national soccer team, to me it did not make any sense to see a Black soccer player playing for Denmark, a country that is not known to have Black football players in its national team. I went on to say the following, I quote: "Pione Sisto is not Danish, and I wonder why he does does not play for his own country, South Sudan or even Uganda where his parents moved after the civil wars broke in Sudan, when Sudan was still a single country". I went on to say that the average Dane does not see Pione Sisto as a Dane, but just another Negro from Africa because the majority of the Danes, the Norwegians, the Poles, the Finns, the Faroese still call Blacks or any Mixed person with an African blood drop Negroes, even if they have the word "black" in their own languages, they still refer to Blacks as "Negroes" or "Niggers", both of which are derogatory names used on Blacks, also something we, Blacks use to dehumanize ourselves and each other. Many things that I said about Pione Sisto on Youtube ended causing some stir, as many Danes responded by calling me a racist, I responded by saying this, I quote "Don't you guys call Blacks Negroes in your country? Now who's the racist here? Is it me saying that Pione Sisto is not Danish or is it you guys?" The statements that I made about Pione Sisto ended up causing a lot of offense from other Danes who were commenting on Youtube. I ended up debating with many Danes about the problems in their societies and those who believe that Pione Sisto is one of them, I decided to talk to them about their failure to integrate minorities, I decided to speak of the extreme right wing parties like the Danish People's Party, the Danish Party and other hate groups and their hostile views on migrants from non-Western countries, whether they're Muslims not not. I went on to say that many people from those parties alone do not view Pione Sisto as a Dane, nor do they view Jores Okore as a Dane either. But those Danes still believe that they are a "multicultural" society and fail to take a look at the history of their own country. One of the persons that I was debating against was a Danish White Supremacist who actually lived up to my prejudices went on to call me a "Negro" for telling him that calling someone names has nothing to do with a culture; it is stupidity. I went on to call him and his countrymen, I quote "Welfare parasites", "Viking morons", "Honky", "Northmen", "Rotten Potatoes", "Spirits Swines" "Potato Daner", "Filthy Scandinavians" I even went to to talk about the humiliation his countrymen faced in 1864, when they were crushed by the Prussians at Dybbøl, in the Southern part of Denmark etc. You guys might wonder why I responded like that, I just felt like I had to be extreme because I had to make a point and I do not feel the need to apologize for it by the way. If I could go back in time to do it, I would do it again. I know that some people who are probably reading this book are shocked to hear statements like that from me, but I would like to say that when someone attacks me with racial slurs, i will make respond

forcefully to the individual responsible for that message and it is not going to be pleasant. That is why I have to say that I have no guilt about it; you are what you give. The debate ended fiercely and I ended up going on with my daily routines. The next example occurred in 2001; A Congolese woman went to Germany with her Danish passport, she was planning to travel from Germany to another country. When the Congolese immigrant faced a German policeman, that German police asked her to show her passport, and the passport she showed was her Danish passport. Then the German police looked at her passport and asked her if she is Danish, the woman replied that she is Danish because she is a Danish citizen. The German police stirred at her and went on to tell her, I quote: " Even God in Heaven knows that there is no such thing as a Black Dane." Personally, I do not know what happened afterwards, but you get the point, I hope. My personal take on this situation is that these examples indicate that you can be a Danish citizen, but you will never be a Dane; you can be an Estonian citizen, but you will never be an Estonian; you can be a Polish citizen, but you will never be a Pole; you can be a Norwegian citizen, but you will never be a Norwegian; you can be a Finnish citizen, but you will never be a Finn; you can have the Czech citizenship, but you will never be a Czech, and you can have the Latvian citizenship, however; you will never be Latvian as long as you are an immigrant in one of those countries, whether you are an immigrant from a Western country or a Third World country living in one of those homogeneous societies. As long as you do not have any historical or cultural ties to one of those countries, you will never be a Pole, you will never be a Dane, you will never be a Norwegian, you will never be a Finn, you will never be an Icelander, you will never be a Slovakian etc.; someone will always remind you that you're not one of them because you either are not a Caucasian or you do not have any historical or cultural ties with one of those countries, especially if you are from the Middle East and Africa, even if you were born in one of those countries. Although I am not a religious person myself, you cannot deny that religion and culture play important roles in the existence of any state. You need to realize that the way a people from China, South Korea, Senegal, Russia, FYR Macedonia, Croatia, Japan, Thailand, Vietnam or another country views nations like Norway, Denmark, Iceland, Latvia, Finland, Estonia, Lithuania, Slovakia, Poland and the Czech Republic as White homogeneous societies, although their aspects are different. In their worldview, which is different from White Liberals from the Left, you cannot be black and Norwegian, you cannot be Asian and Czech etc. because when they think of a Norwegian person, they think of a White person of Northern Germanic or Scandinavian descent. When they think of a Pole, they think of someone who is a White person from Eastern Europe with Slavic lineages. Things are different when you have a passport from a country that is a melting pot, let us say for instance America, France, Germany, Italy, Brazil, Netherlands, Belgium, Sweden, Switzerland, Argentina, Australia, South Africa, New Zealand, Great Britain and Russia. Chances are that you could end up not having lots explanation to do when you say that you're from one of these countries, unless you have a fake passport of course, then you have huge big problems ahead of you. Mark my words: I am not saying that there isn't any form of racism in those countries, but you as an individual who plans to migrate to another country, you need to do your homework about the country where you expect to stay and ask yourself these questions: What do you want, both for yourself and your family? Do you want to live in dignity by getting a job, starting your own business ? Or Are you just planning to migrate to a wealthy country for the sake of life on social security/welfare? Have you made a research about the country where you want to migrate, and its ability to integrate newcomers? Do you know if that country can offer the job that you're looking for? If not, what do you plan to do instead? Will you and your family be able to cope with the nature of the society where you expect to be? Either way, you have a choice and your choices do not just affect you, but your loved ones as well. The society that took you in, your country of origin and people who have the same background as you could benefit from your answers in one way or the other. It can also have an influence in other immigrant communities, think of it like this: Immigrants from non Western countries, whom I usually refer to as immigrants of color living in advanced countries are often looked down on, judged, insulted, bullied for living on welfare, and they are viewed as a burden to the societies where they live, especially illegal immigrants who are mostly from Third World countries. I would also like to add that some immigrants from Third World countries enjoy living on welfare, instead of getting a job and provide for themselves and their families. I guess you're going to notice it; I am going to be harsh again in countries such as Denmark, Norway, Sweden, Finland, Netherlands, Iceland, France(my birth country), Belgium, Switzerland and some other countries worth mentioning on this list, they have created a system where they have encouraged both immigrants, refugees and their-their less fortunate citizens to embrace welfare dependency, robbing them of their lives, their dreams, their aspiration and their purpose. In some of the countries that I have just mentioned, I have heard about people who have been living on welfare for five, six,seven; eight; ten; eighteen; thirty, even 40 years and some have done it longer than that. My question about this madness is this, who on Earth is profiting from such a situation? At whose expense are we allowing this to happen? Excuse my language and terminology; this is what I call a Socialist utopia; you are destroying people's lives, dreams, hopes, aspiration and their willingness to take their destinies into their hands, but on the contrary, the individuals are responsible for their lives. Yet you are the same people who end up grumbling about the percentage of immigrants living on welfare, you complaining about the amounts of illegal immigrants coming to your countries, you complaining about your governments not creating jobs, forgetting the fact that most of the jobs are caused by small businesses and the rest of the private sector, you are complaining about immigrants from non-Western   backgrounds, criminal activities, and I would like to finish by asking you, what on Earth are you doing about it?

CHAPTER 2

SINGING THE SAME SONGS

The same old, the same old again; you grumble about the integration of migrants from non-Western countries not adapting to your cultures and you wonder why there is so much crime in your countries, I am not justifying crime by any ways shape of form, on the other hand, many of you never questioned your abilities to integrate them, nor have you asked their customs, norms and philosophies before you took them in. You never asked yourselves if you need some labor in areas where there aren't enough people to hold jobs. You have encouraged companies to employ illegal immigrants at the expense of your citizens. Many of those people come to your countries with qualifications, Academies, etc., and when they look for jobs that match their skills, they are denied jobs because of what they are in most cases, even though some of you might not admit it. A person who comes from Egypt with a Masters Degree in Computer Engineering comes Denmark, looks for work and fails to get a job that matches his/her qualification and ends up driving a taxi or cleaning public toilets, now ask yourself how do you think that individual might think about his/her dignity? Another result is that many of those migrants end up doing ghetto jobs or living on social security. Now you keep making the same stupid mistakes again and again by taking more migrants without giving them any job offers; that adds more welfare recipients in your countries and more burdens on your taxpayers. You are going to sing the same songs about building parallel societies, but fail to recognize that you are as guilty as the fundamentalist Muslims who call for parallel societies because you have given your newcomers a false sense of hope. There are faults on both sides unless many politicians in Europe recognize it, then this cycle is going to bed for the whole Europe and the rest of the Western world. Moving on to another subject, personally I have never been a fan of the Jante Law, which is a is the idea that there is a pattern of group behavior towards individuals within Scandinavian communities that negatively portrays and criticises individual success and achievement as unworthy and inappropriate, something that I have always find sick, destructive and inappropriate. I guess the Jante Law mentality pumps up people with so much anger, envy, resentment, jealousy and then the hatred of those who strive to success and believe that they are special at what they do and pride themselves for it. I have never liked the Jante Law and I never will, this Nordic code of conduct with its so-called ten commandments is against the culture of success and people who believe that they are special. The Jante Law gives people a false sense of humility and negative view of themselves and their potential to inspire others to the paths success, most of the people who adopt this "code of conduct" are Scandinavians and I almost forgot to add that the Jante Law encourages mediocrity and the negativity of oneself and others.

Do you know what I think about the Jante Law? It is full of crap and I say proudly that the Jante Law is freaking rubbish. I do not care if it is politically incorrect or if any Jante Law lovers out there feels uncomfortable about the things that I just said. I care about other people succeeding as much as I care myself being successful. When you live on welfare, you are wasting your life , your resources and other people suffer as much as you. You might think it is your life and you get to choose, but remember that someone else pays so that you can life on social security, of course, you also pay taxes, but think about your own dignity, whether you are a refugee, an immigrant or just an ordinary average Norwegian, or someone from another country. You're better off getting a job, creating your economy, etc., unless you are physical, if you are mentally challenged, or you're dealing with similar problems, you can be on welfare or illness benefits. At the end of the day, you get to decide, you can do what feels right for you. We all have one life and the moment that you keep wasting are those you will never get back; days become weeks, weeks become months, months become years and years become decades, the question is when you are going to reach the end of your life, how are going to look back to the live you're on your way to leave behind? Are you going to look back to your life with pride, honor, dignity and think of the things that you have achieved in it? Are going to take a look back at the relationships that you've built, the opportunities you have responded to etc.? Or are you going to look back to your life with shame and disgrace? The decision is yours, yours alone to make, not your government, not your environment, not your problems, not your friends, not your enemies, not your family, not your job center, but you alone. What I know from experience is that when you are on social security, you are in a prison because you are living on someone else's money and the system controls you. Job centers steal your independence; you are made weaker like a child, and you're not a free person. It is your decision if you want to remain in chains or break free. I am proud to say that I enjoy the benefits of Capitalism and I am someone who loves expending, rather than losing my independence to the government, I create my own life, instead of just allowing life to happen to me. Integration is not about encouraging migrants and refugees to live on social security, the same should also be said the native born citizens who are struggling to find work in their own countries, whether it is the Danes, the Germans, the Americans, the Brazilians, the Australians, the South Africans, the French, the Italians, the Spaniards and so forth. Integration is about placing value on the individual and championing his/her path to success; when you do that, you lift the individual up and strengthen his/her desire to contribute to society, when you feel like you are part of society, you empower yourself to make a difference as your self-worth soars. I do not know if it is just me, but if I am wrong on this, then please feel free to correct me; I have never seen immigrants from Thailand, India, Hungary, Poland, Bosnia & Herzegovina, Slovakia, Croatia, Vietnam, China, Serbia, Armenia, South Korea,Albania, Russia, Iran etc. on welfare, at least they do not settle for it when they live in countries like: Norway, Sweden, United Kingdom, France, Denmark, United States, Netherlands, Finland, Canada and Australia. They always believe in the culture of working and when they don't work, they start their own businesses. I might be wrong about these types immigrants, but I have a feeling that they value the need to make it on their own. In Denmark Hungarian immigrants always work, not just them, but many other East Europeans as well and they work hard. On the other hand what frustrates me is that most of the immigrants who live on welfare in First World Western countries are mostly from the Middle East and Africa, as someone of African descent that breaks my heart because we can do a lot more than begging municipalities for money. My question is how on Earth Liberals, Conservatives, Libertarians from any

Western country can allow this to happen? Who profits when you have millions of people on welfare? Are doing many of those people a favor by letting them live on welfare and food stamps?We wonder why the amount of crime is concentrated in areas where you have social, challenging communities and tough neighborhoods; we wonder why many of those people are attracted to easy money, aka, drug trafficking, human trafficking, sex slavery, child labor, theft, homicides, etc. We wonder why children in much of those areas have some of the highest dropouts nationally in any Western country. We also happen to forget that in much of those communities, you have huge amounts of children who are fatherless, a high amount of teen pregnancy and the rise of single mothers struggling to provide for themselves and their children. I am not saying that single mothers do not do a good job for their children; the point I am trying to make here is that our society is ignoring the facts that in socially challenged neighborhoods and projects there are many children who are left by their fathers who should be real men and take responsibility for themselves, the well-being of their children and their partners. When this does not happen, it results in social conflicts in ways that girls begin to search for validation to men because they have never had a male guardian in their lives or absent fathers, unwilling to display affection, in other words, indication of value and those men use it to their advantage at the expense of those young girls, young ladies and later in life when they become women. This negative attention usually leads to domestic violence, child abuse, and child neglect because of the incapability of mature relationships on both sides. As for the boys who lack their father's affections, this results in them being desperate for love wherever they can seek it. When that goal is not reached, it even results in more anger, violence, crime and the need to get approval from a group. Another thing that can happen is that they can buy value for material benefits or in the worst case scenario(this is a taboo), they could also end up seeking for validation from other men. The impact can wage from revenge to envy, depending on the way the individual responds. Individually, people respond to such situation differently, whether you're a man or a woman, but the results are not pleasant. I can understand that when you have never been given any form of affection by your male guardian(your father in this case), and you female guardian(your mother in this case), you will do all sorts of things to get the affection you have been claiming since the time of your existence, although I do not justify robbery or any other illegal activity for that matter, that is why you need to question your methods of doing that. What I have personally learned in my life is that I had no influence over what happened to me when I was a child, and the things that I was facing when I was a child. I had no influence over the rejection that I encountered from my so-called biological mother, her family, some of my father's cousins and siblings and the neighbors who were living beside us. However, I have an influence over what I can do about the situation now as an adult; I can choose the way I deal with it as an adult, and the power that I have to get my life back and live it to its fullest potential. I know that your situation is probably different from mine, perhaps you went through a situation, which was far more worse than mine; perhaps you your situation was similar to mine or different, but I have a message for you; it is not your fault that you went through what you went through as a child, it is not your fault that you were never given love and affection and it is not your fault because you had no control over it. You didn't choose it; anyone who tells you That it is your fault is a bloody damn fool, believe me, I don't care where in the world you come from; I don't care if you are of a specific race or ethnicity; I do not care if you belong to a different religion or no religion at all, I just want to tell you that it is not your fault that you went through the things you did as a child, however; You have the power to influence the way you deal with it as an adult, you have the power to work within your values and do what feels natural for you. You have what it takes to change your life and live it the way you want, on your terms. Don't allow anyone else's negative opinion of you to become you living experience; just follow your path and trust your instincts. Don't use your pain as an excuse to bully others and don't put up with bullies either; use your common sense, when you're dealing with a bully and take a stand the way it feels right for you.

Domestic violence, child abuse, child neglect and other types of-of these evil virtues are not just things that happen in social, challenging communities, but also in suburban areas and other parts of society, but women and children are mostly who live in social challenging areas are more likely to be vulnerable from such bad cycles. You can always say that it is your municipality's fault, you can always say that it is your mayor's fault, you can always say that it is your government's fault, but remember this: Your municipality did not ask you to impregnate many ladies and leave their children fatherless, your government did not tell you to abuse your child/children, your government never prevented you from nurturing your children, your government did not do not stop you from giving child support, your government never told you to bring your child/children in this world; those are decisions that you made, and you need to take ownership for your actions at the end of the day. Your government did not tell you to get involved in selling drugs; you made that choice on your own, maybe your government could have done a better job dealing with problems in your community, perhaps your government could have been good enough to create jobs and fought crime in your community, but at the end of the day, you are accountable for your life. Coming back to the subject of welfare dependency, the more people you have living on welfare, the more you allow crimes to soar; desperate people do desperate things when they're in a situation where they have to do what it takes to survive. I am not saying that all welfare recipients are criminals; I have been in that situation myself, and I know how it feels like. Another example that I would like to give you is that most of the immigrants who live on social security for a long time, let's say for six years also happen to be those who face all sorts of temptations when it comes to criminal activities and illegal money trade in forms of drugs, human trafficking, sex trafficking etc., if you do not believe me, please make your own research and take a look at what is happening in Sweden, Denmark, Norway, France, Britain, Netherlands, Belgium, the U.S., Canada and the rest of the Western world. Most of the people who live on welfare live in multi-level concrete apartment buildings; those are also areas where you have people with the lowest incomes per capita, and you have in most cases immigrants from the Middle East and Africa representing those statistics. Those are also areas where you have massive amounts of riots, lots of injured people, burnt cards, clashes with the police and the vast majority of individuals who are involved in such riots are immigrants from the Middle East, Africa, Eastern Europe and even South East Asia these kinds of riots take place in many European countries and sometimes results in amounts of deaths. Those are also areas with the highest numbers of thefts, illegal activities, welfare fraud and the risk of Islamic conversion and radicalism.

Those are also areas where you see massive amounts of child marriages, arranged marriages, honor killings, polygamy, female genital mutilation and some women are prevented from having jobs where there are men. The question, which we need to ask ourselves is that how and why have we as a society allowed it to happen. In suburbs dominated hugely by immigrants and those some nations call second and third generation immigrants there are usually areas that are called No-go areas where only Muslim immigrants can be, anything that does not relate to their religious and cultural practices is not allowed to express itself there because there is the Sharia "police" controlling the areas. There are even areas where the police from the mainstream country is not allowed to enter because the there are groups who have decided that they want to create a state of their own within a state. In my opinion, there are faults on both sides; we need to look at the internal factors in those areas, as well as the external factors from the rest of society. First of all, let us look at the internal factors: In areas where you have a huge concentration of migrants, you will notice that the vast majority of those migrants are Muslims and among them there are many who do not have an interest in participating in the activities of the mainstream societies, another problem that we need to take a look at is the view that many of those migrant men have on women, especially Caucasian and other non-Muslim women; those migrant men see those women as filthy, whores and devalue them because of the way those women dress. Another factor we need to look at is the imposition of halal meat, I know that I might get on some people's nerves, but we need to raise this subject; when you impose such a way of life in a society that does not share your history, you're going to have a lot of resistance, one way or the other. We have already mentioned welfare dependency, we have also referred to the importance of taking responsibility for one's life. Another factor that is destroying those areas is the amount of mosques being built there and financed by Saudi Arabia, Qatar, the UAE and other rich Muslim countries, which contributes to radicalization and we all know what happens once an individual gets radicalized, he/she joins terrorist organizations like: ISIS, Al Qaeda etc. We also need to take a look at the amounts of students in those areas who drop out of school or no longer having any level of self esteem and self worth, that leads to a lack of self respect. There is also a huge amount of anti-White racism towards the Caucasians who live in suburbs dominated by immigrants of color; it comes in the sort of anti-French racism, anti-German racism, anti-Swedish racism, anti-Danish racism, even the Danes don't talk about it; anti-British racism etc.; those migrants put all of their anger, resentments and bitters towards the mainstream societies for the lack of equal opportunities, they being called derogatory names for instance: Camel Jockeys,Darkies Chung, Gypsies, Ragheads, Pakis, Sandnigger, Negroes and other kinds of vicious names by someone of that mainstream society, in the vast majority cases, done by a Caucasian person. Many migrants living in social challenging areas see themselves as victims because they're called names and feel racially abused to a point where they do no longer feel that they belong to the society that has taken them or their parents in. Many Muslim migrants in the areas fail to understand that no religion is above criticism in a civilized country; they take it personally when someone draws a picture of their prophet or makes jokes about their holy book, they also fail to understand that religion is an idea; you cannot change your race, because you did not choose your race, but a religion is an idea, which you can choose to accept or reject. Another problem with those areas is that many migrants do not question their system of values, their cultures, their norms, religions and their virtues, what I mean is that they do not examine the customs, virtues, norms from their countries of origin or the countries where their parents and grandparents came from. Don't get me wrong; there are those who do, but those who do face massive amounts of criticism from their own communities; sometimes they are even disowned by their own communities because they are seen as sellouts or uncle toms. There is also a high level of self-hatred and self-rejection in immigrant communities to a point where it becomes a trademark. Many Muslim immigrants living in Europe and other part of the Western world fail to understand in a civilized country you have the right to leave your religion; many Muslim apostates who abandon their religion live in the dark out of the fear of being beaten up, assaulted or in the worst case scenario, they are afraid to be killed by their fellow Muslim immigrants who cannot accept the fact that leaving Islam in a civilized country is ok. There is also a high amount of hatred between different immigrant communities; you find Middle Eastern Muslims, Albanians, South East Asians and other East Europeans who have a very negative view of Blacks by viewing us as inferior species; you find Blacks having negative views of themselves, other Blacks and people from other backgrounds; you find the Turkish community having negative views of the Armenian and Assyrian communities and I can go on and on, you get my point, I hope. Gang activities in social challenging areas are part of the norms. The idea that immigrants are all one united group living in a single space is an illusion, believe it is an illusion. Another possible internal factor is the hatred that many of those migrants have towards Europe and the rest of the Western world in general; they blame the Western world for wars in Muslim countries, they blame the West for slavery in Africa, they blame the West for the racial segregation in the U.S. and South Africa; they blame the West for everything that goes wrong in their lives. that experience, but it is not ok to impose your religious and cultural practices in a country that does not have a standard value to yours, it is not ok to treat women as second class citizens, it is not ok to treat non-Muslim women as natural meat, especially if those girls and females are white; it is not ok to kill someone for drawing a picture of your prophet; it is not ok to burn other people's things, and it is not ok to impose Sharia Law in a country that does not share its beliefs. Like it or not, if you're living in the West, you live in a society whose values have Judeo-Christian roots, and those are the same values that have made the Western world successful, secular, humane and tolerant; I am not saying that there are no problems in those societies, I am going to get to it later. You do not have the right to make the Western world a majority Muslim society; I am an Atheist myself, but I think I've got to tell you this: Christianity is the main religion in any Western country and if you feel like

Islam is being challenged, then go to a Muslim country, you will have a peace of mind there. You do not have the right to kill your daughter if she refuses to marry the man you have chosen for her, you do not have the right to kill your son if you find out that your son is a homosexual or even a bisexual for that matter; if you do not agree with his lifestyle, tell him that you don't, if both of you agree that it is wrong, then show him he can change his paradigm and focus on changing his mindset, but if he does not share your views about it, then maybe that is just the way he is and feels.This message is also for immigrants from other communities, not just Muslims. Remember that religion is a private matter, practice your culture in your home and don't impose halal food in continues, remember that a canteen is not a compulsory. Question your religion, question your way of life and challenge your norms. Bear in mind that someone will always remind you that you're a guest, believe me.Now let's focus on the external problems: There are many countries in Europe that have taken in migrants from Muslim countries and migrants from other non-Western countries without questioning their abilities to integrate those newcomers in their societies, I think you are familiar with those countries because I have mentioned them in this book, when they take in those refugees, they just take them in without making any research about their cultural norms, social constructs, tribal instincts and religious practices. You do not just important someone from another part of the world and expect that he is going to be Danish, Norwegian, Finnish, Icelandic, Faroese, Czech, and Austrian. You don't just assimilate like that; take a look at the kind of person you're taking in your country, ask yourself if your or your society has enough experience to integrate them, if not, then find other suggestions. Do you even prepare the individuals about the struggles, they're going to face in your societies? Do you prepare them for the fact that they might face rejection when they look for jobs because they happen to have the "wrong" name or they don't have the right qualifications. What kinds of work are you going to give them? Stop treating those migrants like children and stop asking them stupid questions, like for instance: "Do people celebrate Christmas in Africa?", "Do people drink Coca Cola in Afghanistan ?" , " Do you guys have diapers in France?", "Is your skin color able to tolerate the Sun?", "Do Africans have tails behind their bodies?", " Do you guys have underwears in Africa?", "Do you speak African?", "Can I rub your skin?; "What letters do you use when you write in France? , "Should I call you Gypsy or Romany?", "Is the Congo still a jungle?"; " In what kind of houses do you guys live?"; "Can people buy new cars in Hungary?", "Are all Muslims dark people?"; "Why are you so dark, what happened to you?"; "Do women give birth at hospitals in Africa?" , "How come you can speak such good Danish?", " Are all the dark people in the USA poor?", "I feel so sorry for the dark people in Africa, do they have food to eat?" ; " Can you become light?"; Do you, East Europeans come here to steal?" , I can go on and on about this kind of madness, you get the idea. When you ask such stupid questions, you make yourself look like a jerk, and you make yourself look like someone who just keeps making a fool out of yourself.

On the other hand, the individual/s to whom you're asking those questions might think that you are sending the wrong signal to them by treating him/her/them like small children. This can give them the perception that you and your countrymen/women are all ignorant and uneducated. Next time, be smart when you ask questions. If you recognize that your society is not equipped at integrating newcomers and has never had a history in doing it, then tell your government to stop taking more refugees and migrants in your country. If you want newcomers to be part of your society, learn from countries that have had a history of integrating newcomers for many generations, find out how they do it and create your model. I am not saying that all your country does is wrong, and theirs is the right way, but you cannot deny that there are other countries in Europe and the new world that had had more experience at integrating and assimilating peoples of color for hundreds of years before your country got into the game. If you do not know what the names of those countries are, please take a look at page 8 in this book. Not all European countries have the capability to integrate peoples of color in their societies, and not all of them were meant to take that road. Raise debates about discrimination on the labor market in your country, raise discussions about what kinds of people you're bringing in your country, raise debates Islam and ask yourself whether it is a threat or not to the existence of your country, the way you got to know it and ask yourself why is your government allowing Saudi Arabia and other rich Muslim countries to build mosques and madrassas in your country and what purpose do they serve. Encourage people to criticize any religion, even Islam, encourage people to criticize cultures and norms of any kind and help anyone who wants to leave any religion is welcome to do so. Raise problems with immigrants on welfare in the media and bring honest debates, what is their ownership in the situation, and what did your country do to contribute to the situation? Then find out what solutions you have that can benefit your country and your newcomers. Now I have a message for other Western nations out there who are probably facing more or less the same problems with different immigrant groups, especially Muslim immigrants; my message to you is that you need to say it out and loud that not all cultures are equal, you need to mention that i.e. the Western culture is superior to the Muslim culture, that is the way you're going to get rid of cultural relativism. You need to take back your authority and demolish the No-Go areas and give the power back to the police and the army to take control of those areas. Whose streets? Your streets, anyone who imposes Sharia Law or other forms of laws that are going to threaten your values need to be deported, whether the individual has the citizenship of your country nor not. You may say that it is against your constitution, then question your law and come up with better suggestions. You also need to put a limit on both Muslim immigration and other unsuited and uneducated migrants. Defend your nation without falling into the trap of bigotry and racism; if you do, then the other side will crush you like hippos crushing crocodiles. You need to call a spade for a spade; if Danish high school students are behaving like fools in Prague, then call it exactly as you see it; if you frustrated about China being a threat to the dominance of the United States in this world, call it by it name; if Swedish tourists are not respecting the Bulgarian law, then call it like it is and if there are Muslim migrant men involved in criminal activities and trying to spread Sharia Law in Western countries, tell it like it is; if there are East Europeans involved in theft in Western, whether they're Poles, Latvians, Lithuanians, Albanians, Hungarians or any other nationality involved, call them by their-their names; if you have done your research and believed that most drug dealers in France are Arabs and Blacks, then call it by its name; if you think that most of the financial crooks are Jews, call it like it is; and this message goes to the mainstream media in the Western world because the mainstream media in the West is distant from its audience and too dishonest; they do not seem to call things by their real name, yet they wonder why they're not so popular anymore. For instance when Donald Trump said that the Mexican government is not bringing the best of its people in the U.S., but rapists, drug dealers and criminals, the media was so quick to call Donald Trump a bigot. When Donald

Trump suggested a ban on Muslims coming the to U.S. until the authorities find out why there is so much hate from the Muslim community, hatred on America, the media was so quick to portray him as an "Islamophobe." The mainstream media is not doing minorities of any race, group, religion, tribe any favor by putting the head in the sand and ignoring that the problem is there. If you want to solve a problem, you need to identify it by its name first, otherwise, you will never solve that problem. The mainstream media is not doing many societies that have a hard time with illegal immigration when they see irregular migrants as victims and people who are against illegal immigration as hateful. If you break the law in someone else's home, you're not a victim; you are an intruder, and you need to be treated like one unless one can come up with valid arguments on why you arrived. It is not just the mainstream media, but also many human rights organizations as well; they are too quick to see illegal immigrants as an underdog, thinking that they have the right to immigrate illegally to another country when you do that, then is no longer about them, but about you and your ego. Yes, illegal immigrants have the right to be treated with respect and dignity, they have the right to be treated humanely, but not if some of them are involved in criminal activities and cheating the system. I hear this statement very often: No one in this world is illegal, that's rubbish; we have sovereign nations for a reason, and each nation has laws for a reason.

CHAPTER 3

THINGS THAT WENT WRONG WITH THE MIGRANT CRISIS

Illegal immigration from Third World countries to Europe, or even America, Canada, Australia, Japan, South Korea, Israel, Hong Kong, New Zealand and

South Africa has been an issue for decades and there are many governments and some people from those places that have not questioned the impact that it has on their nation's economy, the impact that it has on crime, the impact that it has on welfare dependency, the impact that it has on the ability for the locals from the working class jobs; by the way, they also have a responsibility to do something about their situations, instead of focusing on their limitations and blaming all their problems on illegal immigration, however; we cannot ignore that illegal immigration has serious impacts on the possibilities for the working class local populations to get a job because there are many companies that are hiring illegal migrants, then that happens, illegal immigrants receive lower wages than those from the local populations. Another excuse we hear from these enterprises, the media, Leftist groups, anti-racist groups and human rights organizations is that illegal immigrants are willing to do the jobs that the locals do not want to do, but the question they need to ask themselves is this: Have they asked the locals about their unwillingness to do the jobs that illegal migrants are doing? Illegal immigration is not just a problem in any Western country; it is also an issue in some emerging economies like India, Brazil, Argentina, Turkey, China, Taiwan, Egypt, Chile,

Uruguay, Panamá, México, FYR Macedonia, Serbia, Romania, Morocco, Algeria, Tunisia, Dominica, the Dominican Republic, etc.; most of those migrants come from poorer nations where they cannot seem to find opportunities back home, they usually come from countries in Sub-Saharan Africa, the Middle East Asia, and other Latin American countries. Illegal immigration within African nations, illegal immigration within Europe, illegal immigration within the Americas and Australasia always feeds to the fear of the strangers taking jobs from the locals, and this often results to a backlash. If we take the example of South Africa, where you have massive amounts of both illegal and legal immigrants from other Sub-Saharan African countries and other parts of the developing world, what we is that many South Africans, especially Black South Africans feel like their jobs and way of life are being taken away by immigrants from other Sub-Saharan African countries, the consequences of this situation lead to a high amount of xenophobia, in particular between Black South Africans and Blacks from other African countries, that is why you have witnessed many locals burning African migrants alive, setting fire and shouting derogatory slurs towards other migrants. This shocks many Africans from other countries because they tell themselves: "We have fought Apartheid for these people, how come they treat us, they fellow African brothers and sisters like this?" I can see your point, but remember that just because you are African and fought against Apartheid for your fellow Black South African brothers/sisters, that does not mean that they have a debt to pay to you. You also need to remember that South Africa is not your country; just because you are Black and African that does not mean that every African country is your home, you have have your own country and they have theirs. South Africa belongs to South Africans, whether they're Black, White, Coloreds (Mixed Race), Indians and other groups of people from that country. On the other hand the way many South African Blacks responded to that situation is animalistic and primitive, maybe you need to question your ability to keep a proper job, and you are set aside; many of those immigrants own companies, businesses and some of them have worked very hard to get where they are, of course there were circumstances under Apartheid that made things difficult for you, but don't use it an excuse for your animalistic behavior, by the way, maybe you need to claim solutions to your government, whom you have chosen to keep in power for more than 2 decades under the ANC; how is it working for you now? Maybe you also need to stop putting up with reckless Whites who call you Kaffirs, baboons and the use of the N-word on you, whether they call you Niggers or Negroes, it is all the same to me; it is still the N-word. Maybe you need to stop blaming Apartheid for all your problems and take ownership of your lives and your communities. Aren't you realizing that you're getting exactly what you are, and what you believe you deserve? This also goes for White South Africans, Colored(Mixed Race South Africans), Indian South Africans and all other groups; you're getting exactly what you are and it is only you who can change it, no one else will do it for you, not even your own government. As someone who has roots in both the Republic of the Congo and the Democratic Republic of Congo, I have witnessed the level of hostility between the citizens of the two Congos, especially from the hostility from the citizens from the Republic of the Congo who really have a negative view on their neighbor from the other bank of the Congo River, believing that the "Zairians" are thieves, criminals and are not good at speaking French. On the other side, the citizens of the Democratic Republic of Congo do not understand it, because in their worldview, they see both Congos as one single country, only separated by Congo River Mainstem. Brazzaville and Kinshasa are the second closest capitals on the planet, only surpassed by Rome in Italy,and Vatican City in Vatican. The point I am trying to make here is that this is something that happens in other African countries, as well as other parts of the world, when you have a local population feeling threatened by your presence, a backlash is inevitable. In my birth country, France, there are many French people who are tired of East European immigrants coming from: Poland, Hungary, Slovakia, Latvia, Serbia, Croatia, Bosnia & Herzegovina, Romania and other countries because they believe that those groups of people come to France to claim child benefits and other types of benefits at the expense of the French people and many French people believe that they tax funds must not benefit people who have no moral right to them: Whether, they're East Europeans immigrants or immigrants from Third World countries, the French people are not the only ones thinking that way; the Brits, the Dutch, the Germans, the Swedes, the Danes, the Norwegians, the Finns, the Icelanders, the Irish, the Belgians, the Italians, the Spaniards, the Portuguese and the Luxembourgians share the same concerns. Many East Europeans economies are not as successful as the countries of the Old Europe because they're still in the process of developing their economies; the standards of living in many East European countries have seen their economies and standards of living decreased after the fall of Communism, although governments in Poland, Romania, Hungary, Czech Republic and some other East European countries that have joined the EU in 2004 are making efforts to bounce back their economies, a large population seems to believe that their standard of living is deteriorating. Let's face it, although Poland, Romania, Hungary, Croatia and other East European countries have seen an increase in the life expectancy from their populations, although some people have rising incomes and a lavish life there; the fact remains that there are more jobs in Britain, France, Germany, Sweden, Denmark, Italy, Switzerland, Holland, Norway and some other West European countries, and those jobs have a better better than the average salary in for instance Budapest, Warsaw, Bucharest, Bratislava, Riga, Sofia etc. That is why many East Europeans come to the richer half of Europe to look for opportunities that they cannot find in their home countries, some even claim that they are entitled to receive housing and child benefits from the rich countries where they're going because they are as white as those from those from the Old Europe, but they don't look at cultural differences and the differences of mentalities as well; just because you are from another White European majority country in Eastern Europe, that does not mean that you automatically claim benefits from any West European country, mark my words: They do not owe you a cent; you need to respect their rules, else you have no business going there in the first place. If it was the Romanies, whom you call Gypsies did it in your countries, you would run after them to a point where you would even want to kill them. Just like you tell Third World immigrants to fix their countries; do the same by fixing yours, if we take a deeper look to this problem and remember that you will always be reminded that your part of Europe is more impoverished than the Old Europe.

The United States, Britain, France and some other Western powers have made tremendous mistakes with their foreign policies in the Middle East by thinking that they can somehow bring freedom and democracy in that part of the world, without questioning those people's mentality and their willingness to accept democracy and freedom the way we know it in the West. Western political elites have failed to understand that those countries are tribes with flags, aligned with old thinking and the lack of compassion for their fellow man. The Middle East is a place where governments keep their people ignorant and informed;

that's how they rule their masses. That is one of the areas where governments and religious organizations, which are mainly Islamic control the content of information that comes out of the media and the rest of society. A place where minorities of different races and religion are far worse situations when it comes to discrimination, racism, and anti-Semitism. We're talking about a part of the world where women are treated like properties, second class citizens, we're talking about a part of the world where leaving Islam is illegal and punishable by death, and we're talking about a part of the world where being gay could get you trouble or even killed, I wonder where the "gay right activists" from the Western world when that happens, but that's another subject for another time. They are used to be brainwashed to whatever religious authorities and dictators want them to believe, we're talking about a part of the world where they burn flags of civilized societies because someone from Sweden or Denmark, or France, or America draws a picture of their Prophet, we're talking about a place where religious leaders sent fatwas on those who have critical views of Islam and Muslims in general and we're talking about the part of the world that hates our way of life and our system of values. My question to many of these Western politicians and businesses that trade with countries like: Saudi Arabia, Qatar, the UAE, Kuwait and other similar countries, how on Earth do you think those countries are going to change their system of values and adopt ours, despite having populations that have been brainwashed for 1400 years? Another question that I have for you that what was your intention to include Turkey in NATO, and now what is your plan planning to give access to Turkey in the EU? The Third question that I have is that are you contributing to the destruction of the Western world as a whole by selling yourselves out to those wealthy Middle Eastern/Muslim countries? I can tell you that Tommy Robinson is not responsible for your naivety, Pamela Geller is not liable for your naivety, Robert Spencer is not liable for your naivety and nor is Brigitte Gabriel, you alone are accountable for your naivety, although I do not always agree with them. Those societies have their foundations in a one man religious based regimes who care about nothing more than power and the need to control their own citizens. Those societies do not even offer citizenships to refugees, even their fellow Arab/Muslim refugees. For instance, the Palestinian refugee problem could be solved if many Arab and other Muslim countries took their share of those refugees, until those refugees are able to go back and rebuild their country, but instead,

they use that situation against you, and against Israel to distract the public the public opinion in the Western world, throughout gaining sympathy from Leftwing activists and some idealistic Conservatives and those activists fall for that, they tend to see Palestinians and Muslims as a whole as victims. They see both America, Europe and Israel as oppressors who are threatening the Palestinian cause. That part of the world fails in its objectives of human
rights, it fails to treat migrants who are working as slaves and with no dignity at all as people; I am talking about migrants from Africa and South East Asia who are taken as slaves to build stadiums and other venues for the FIFA Football World Cup in Qatar 2022, I am talking about the same kinds of migrants who are treated like dogs when they go to that part of the world for domestic jobs by their Middle Eastern employers because they happen mostly to be of a different race, instead of integrating them into their societies. Instead of starting Middle Eastern student organizations in Western universities, high schools and primary schools and find some idealistic individuals who have no idea about what is going on in your world, in this case, the Middle East, why don't you want to acknowledge you guys are backwards and you have the unwillingness to fix your own issues? Why

don't you guys figure out why you and your mentality are not fit for civilization? Instead of putting the blames about your problems on the Crusades, Europe, America, Australia, Colonization and the rest of the non-Muslim world. You have had 1400 years to question your beliefs and your way of thinking, but you chose to be prisoners of your own systems, you chose to fail to think critically about your values and of. I am not interested in hearing about what you guys did during the so-called Golden Age; I am interested in knowing why do you have the mentality that you have, and what you can do to fix it? You have allowed yourselves create societies where religion is not a private issue, but a public rule for each single individuals, some of you might think that I am a racist, maybe you need to seriously take a seriously look at your culture of hatred. What many Western elites and idealists do not understand is that the Middle East consists of tribes that have kept to themselves and continue to follow revered rules that have existed for a dozen of centuries, until today. You cannot expect such a place to adopt Western values and become total democracies and it is not the job of the Western world to turn those countries into democracies; it is their job to question their values, ways of life, political and religious doctrines, we cannot do it for them. There have been tremendous amounts of trillions of Dollars, sacrificed lives and resources that have been spent in the Middle East for decades after decades, what have we gotten out of it? We have gotten rid of dictators in Libya, Iraq, and other places, thinking that we would succeed at turning those countries into democracies, but what we're getting is way worse than the dictators that kept those economies in control. We are now doing the same insanity in Syria, think about what are we getting now? Western politicians have given countries like: Saudi Arabia, Qatar, Kuwait and other rich Muslim countries too much power to a point where those countries are buying our governments, building mosques, madrassas and bringing hate-preachers in our shores. The only state with common sense in this situation is Russia in my opinion; at least the Russians know that those countries will never be democracies, while the West keeps holding illusions of a democratic Middle East, the only Middle Eastern country, which I know of is a democracy is the State of Israel. Israel is the only country in the Middle East where people of all races, religions and cultures are treated equally before the law, while the neighboring countries around Israel have system of beliefs that are at odds with Western values because of their negative views on women; their negative views on people who

50

are not Middle Eastern Arabs, Turks, Persians, Afghans etc, (Indonesians, Indians, Pakistanis, Nepalis, Thai, Chinese, Africans, Malays, Jews, Yazidis, Kurds and groups whom they still view as slaves, underclass, subhumans, apes, pigs, filths and inferior species.By the way, Midddle Eastern Muslims have a far more hostile view of Africans than the avarage Westerner does) ; Israel's neighbors also have a far more hostile view on peoples of their own who belong to other tribes, they have a hostile view on people from other religions; freethinkers; atheists; agnostics; homosexuals; bisexuals, and people who tell them what they do not like to hear. Western politicians have been so deluded to a point where I ask myself if I am living in a real planet Earth, sometimes I wonder if I am in another universe. You cannot promote democracy in societies that are still stuck in archaic system of values, you cannot expect them to be democracies because their mindsets are not fit to it yet. Although I justify the fact that United States and its allies bombed Afghanistan because of what happen during the 9-11 terrorist attacks in New York, just like I also justify the fact that Japan was nuked in the mid 1940's, the mistake that America and its allies have made were that they believed that they could successfully promote democracy in Afghanistan, just by encouraging people there to vote. Well, that does not work because it has to be up to themselves to decide to want it without our interference, I also want to add that the United States and its allies are not obligated to rebuild Iraq, Afghanistan and other war torn countries because it is not our responsibility at the first place; that is the responsibility of their own governments and their own citizens. The mainstream media and the Liberal Left will point out that Tunisia is a successful democracy, you know what? Ask yourself if apostasy is legal in Tunisia, ask yourself if you can be critical of Islam in Tunisia, ask yourself if minorities in Tunisia have the same rights as the majority population and if it is legal, then come and talk to me. Yes, Tunisia has been the only successful country so far emerging from the Arab Spring, but there are still lots things that they can do differently. When the media talked about the Arab Spring and its quest for democracy in 2011, I was laughing so hard to a point where I just said that those dictators will be replaced by Islamic terrorist governments. You cannot compare that movement to the movement for democracy that took place in Poland, Estonia, Hungary, Czechoslovakia, Latvia, Lithuania, Romania, Bulgaria and other East European countries that were fighting the Soviet Rule; these countries have populations that are able to question the system that rules them, and they have abilities to take a stand in opposition to a larger group and values they find medieval and outfashioned. That's what's lacking in the Middle East and many other Muslim countries from elsewhere, it is also lacking in many African countries unfortunately, but that's a subject I am going to cover in the coming chapters. That is why it has not taken East European countries long to become democracies and the idea that they're somehow different is just another excuse from others in my opinion; this has nothing to do with Poles being Europeans, it has something to do with their willingness to challenge the status quo and the commitments to change beliefs and values overtime, if the Poles can do it, people from other parts of the world can also do it. There are many non-European countries that have also been successful with the transition from dictatorships to bill of rights: South Korea, Japan, Taiwan, Botswana, Senegal, Myanmar, Thailand, Malaysia, Mauritius, Seychelles, Cape Verde, Kenya and not to forget that India is the world's largest democracy, so there is no excuse for others. That's why I believe that the Western world does not have a responsibility to promote democracy in other parts of the world that are still imprisoned by their medieval ways of thinking, if those populations want it, they have to take the initiatives on their own. That begins with them questioning everything about their beliefs and values. On the other hand the West has got to stop digging its own grave by treating countries like: Turkey, Saudi Arabia, Qatar, the UAE, Bahrain and other similar countries has its allies because those countries have values that are not aligned with enlightenment; let me be honest with you, in countries where Islam has a very powerful influence are radically incapable of embracing modernity .

We all know that the conflicts in Syria, Iraq, Afghanistan have brought a tremendous amount of migrants from the Middle East to Europe, since the German Chancellor, Angela Merkel opened the floodgates. It is not just those migrants who are coming to Europe, but also migrants from other countries like Pakistan, Palestine, Bangladesh, Eritrea, Nigeria, Morocco, Senegal and other Third World countries and many of those migrants are illegal. Many European countries are already struggling with huge amounts of illegal immigrants who have been on their shores for decades; the same countries are also struggling with Muslim immigrants whose values are in conflicts with the values of Europe. There are already social problems, where you have for instance some

Islamic migrants willing to murder anyone who is critical of their religion, their prophet and the Quran. This is happening in Holland, Belgium, France, Germany, Italy, Sweden, Austria, Great Britain, Denmark and Switzerland, when you have a society where you have a particular group of people refusing to adapt to the laws of their host countries, you have a parallel society, even in countries that have the experience of integrating newcomers. This problem also occurs in Australia, Uruguay, New Zealand, Canada, United States and other Western countries, yet the political elite is ignoring this issue out of the fear of being called "Islamophobic" and racists. Can anyone of you tell me how is addressing the problem with Islamic immigration a racist issue? Is Islam a race or a religion? Are Muslims a single race or groups of peoples who practice Islam? It is like saying that the fact that the Norwegians, the Danes, the Finns, the Latvians do not have the same level of experience when it comes to integrating peoples of color like the French,the Dutch, the Germans, the Americans, the Canadians and the Belgians a racist statement, you better come up with some valid arguments here, believe me. Another problem that many Western countries have not addressed critically when it comes to immigration from Muslim countries is cultural relativism; many trade unions, churches, schools, academies and different anti-racist organizations claim that all cultures and traditions are equal, may be in their theory, but the real word is different. They see themselves as oppressors and Muslim immigrants as underdogs who need to be protected from all forms of criticism from the other side, even if when they know that they're not helping Muslim immigrants or other minorities out there. Those institutions even defend illegal immigrants, people who do not have the right to stay in their countries because they do not meet the requirements need to live legally in Europe or another part of the developed world. Some Globalists claim that no one in this world is illegal and the entire world is their country, wow! I wish you nothing, but the best of luck with that one. Illegal immigrants who travel from one Third World country to another are treated much more worse than those who arrive in Western countries. It does not matter if those illegal immigrants to another Third World country, which could be on the same continent, they still face worse treatments,I guess there is no sense brotherhood and sisterhood in these kinds of situations; you are still viewed as an intruder. I do not hear anti-racist groups, trade unions, churches and other institutions taking a standing against that. Now, Europe is facing the most challenged wave of migration since World War II, it has seen amounts of migrants, mostly from Muslim and African countries arriving in its shores day by day, and the numbers keep increasing. Those migrants leave their countries by foot and they cross the entire Middle East, reaching Greece, FYR of Macedonia, Serbia, Hungary, Croatia and Slovenia. Some risk their lives, crossing the Mediterranean Sea from Africa to Europe, they are often taken care of by the Italian and the Maltese authorities. Unfortunately, not many make it to Europe alive to a search a better life here; there are many men, women and children who drown in seas and lose their lives in my opinion it is a sad situation for them and the loved ones who have to suffer with so much pain and loss. It is a sign of misery when you see so many people desperate to leave their nations to come to search for a better life in Europe, which they hope to find, but they end up being disappointed with the Europe from which they expected so much. Those migrants have different destinations in mind when they make plans to settle in countries where they expect a better future for themselves and their families. Those countries are: Germany, Sweden, Norway, England, Scotland, Netherlands, Wales, France, Italy, Finland, Austria, Belgium and Denmark. Not many migrants have a desire to stay in any East European countries, which they view as poor and more racists than West European countries. Some of those migrants want to come because they want to study, some want to work, but there is a significant number of them who just want to come to claim social security benefits, that to me is sick and crazy. There comes a time when you see an influx groups of people from other parts of the world with different values than those of your own coming to your country in massive uncontrollable numbers, you will feel threatened, and that is a natural response, like it or not. When the Hungarian government decided to build fences to protect its borders and sovereignty from migrants who were coming illegally through Hungary for destinations to far more richer countries like Austria and Germany, the European Union criticized for violating European values. But Hungary was doing what many other nations for the European Union should of done, had they had common sense; the European Union failed to find a solution for those migrants inside Europe and demanded that all EU countries must share the burden together, but many East European countries do not want immigrants, especially Muslim immigrants; they looking at the social and cultural problems that that situation in bringing in Western Europe and they are witnessing the clash of civilization taking place for instance people like: Geert Wilders, Pat Condell, Tommy Robinson, Kevin Carroll, Kurt Westergaard, Flemming Rose, Lars Vik and Ayaan Hirsi Ali living under constant protection by the secret services because they are likely to be killed by some Muslim immigrants who are not willing to face up to the idea that in a civilized country it is acceptable to be critical of any religion and that includes Islam and draw pictures of Muhammad in a newspaper. Many East Europeans are also witnessing the fact that many immigrants from Third World countries living on welfare for years, decades and some don't even learn the language of their host countries. There are also ethnic enclaves, parallel societies, clashes with the police, riots, more demands for mosques, more demands for halal meat anywhere, more demands for a ban on pork meat; gender segregation in swimming pools; special prayer room at work; laws on making it punishable for anyone to criticize Islam, Muslims and the Quran; Sharia courts; Sharia banks; Sharia Barbie dolls; Muslim study groups; the infiltration of the media; terrorist attacks, attacks on non-Muslims,especially White girls and violence. Another thing that cannot be ignored in this situation is the demography; Muslim migrants tend to have more children than non-Muslim migrants and especially the indigenous populations in Europe. Some Muslims use demography as a war to make plans to destroy the Western civilization from within with the hands of the Liberal Left and weak people on the Right. This is one of the tactics the Muslim Brotherhood, which is the oldest terrorist organization in the world, founded in Egypt, in 1928, 5 years after the fall of the Islamic Caliphate, which ended in Turkey. The Muslim Brotherhood has terrorist offsprings like: Hamas, Al Qaeda, ISIS and other terrorist groups and they have a plan known as the Project, whose goal is to turn Europe into and Islamic continent in decades or centuries from now. They also have a plan for America, which they want to destroy. When you have people with such beliefs, then you cannot blame Donald Trump for making the statements about Muslims, you cannot blame Ted Cruz for only wanting to bring Christian and Yazidi refugees in America, you cannot blame Stephen Harper for making it hard for such people to migrate and I am not saying all of those migrants are like that, but the idea that you're bringing in people you have no idea who they are, don't be surprised if there is a trojan horse among those "refugees". Other countries such as Uruguay, Brazil, Canada and the United States are making similar mistakes as well; they want to take in more Syrian refugees and there are even private citizens who are sponsoring their money to take in dozens of Syrian and Afghan families, giving them shelter, food and other necessities. One of the questions that I asked myself is this: Why don't rich Arab and other Muslim countries, such as: Saudi Arabia, Qatar, the United Arab Emirates, Bahrain, Kuwait, Oman, Brunei, Indonesia, Malaysia, Kazakhstan and Azerbaijan take in refugees who are their Muslim brothers, Muslim sisters; people with whom they share a common religion, people whom they can integrate in their own societies and given them citizenship? I guess it has something to do with civilization and barbarism, when they want Europe, America, Australia, Israel, New Zealand and Canada to carry the entire burden, while they are financing the destruction of the West with our own hands. They talk about their Muslim brothers as victims of Western oppression, yet when it comes to helping their fellow Muslim men, women and children, they seem to be absent and careless. The only vibrant emerging Muslim countries that have taken in Muslim migrants are Turkey, Egypt, and Jordan, the less fortunate of those countries that also has lots of its fellows Muslims as migrants are Lebanon. Imagine if this was another way around, imagine if we, non-

Muslims were refugees in Muslim countries, would they treat us humanely? Would they value our rights as minorities? Would they treat us with respect and dignity? Would they treat us equally before the law? Would they give us equal pay if we had jobs there? Or would they treat us like second class citizens, third class citizens etc.? Would we be allowed the exercise freedom of religion there, even freedom from religion? My answer to these questions is that I find it questionable they would do that because Islamic values are incompatible with those of the Western civilization. Instead of Muslims conforming to Western laws, Western societies keep mounting to conform to Islamic laws, as they wish to practice their religion the way it was practiced in their home countries for centuries. Many Muslim immigrants across Western Europe live in suburbs that are subject to violent clashes between gangs, high unemployment, clashes between the youths and the police, poverty and those are also areas that have faced what I call white flight, in other words many ethnic Swedes, ethnic French, ethnic Germans, ethnic Spaniards ethnic Brits etc., leaving those areas out of the fear of the unknown or out of the fact that those areas have become highly populated by minorities that people from the majority populations living in those areas feel like they have become minorities there, that leads to a situation where they make decisions to leave and go somewhere else. When you bring more groups of the same migrants in those areas without integrating and assimilating those who already are there, it adds to more problems and this could possibly lead to more ethnic enclaves and in the worse scenario, a civil war. It is worth mentioning that Muslim immigrants are not the only ones involved in criminal activities in Western Europe; you also have East European immigrants who are involved in crime, whether it's the Poles, the Latvians, the Lithuanians, the Czechs, the Romanians, the Bulgarians the Hungarians, the Slovaks, the Ukrainians, the Russians etc.; you also have uneducated non-Muslim Africans, unsuited native populations, Chinese and other non-Muslim Asians involved in criminal activities in Europe, but Muslim immigrants from the Middle East, Albania, Kosovo, Bosnia, Africa and other parts of the world are highly represented in criminal activities. Yet politicians from the mainstream political parties in many important West European countries have not raised serious debates about these issues, they have left it to the far right extremist parties like: The Danish People's Party, Denmark; the Danish Party, Denmark; the Golden Dawn, Greece; the British National Party, United

Kingdom, the Identity Bloc, France; the National Front, United Kingdom; the Progress Party, Norway; the NPD, Germany; the SVP, Switzerland; Vlaams Blok, Belgium, and other far right groups across Netherlands, Sweden, Finland, Spain and other European countries, which could result to the return of Fascist ideologies, which are not that different from Islamism. One of the points that I want to make is that people like: Geert Wilders, Pamela Geller, Robert Spencer, Lars Vik, Tommy Robinson, Frank Gaffney, Brigitte Gabriel, Wafa Sultan and Kurt Westergaard do not have to live under constant protection because their lives are in danger for being critical of Islam, Muslims and the Quran; you don't have to agree with them, you can las make your point across, but the idea that they have to live their lives under the protection of the secret services from: Netherlands, United States, Sweden, Denmark, Great Britain and other Western countries is really disgraceful. That shows that there are a group of Muslim immigrants in such advanced countries who are willing to murder those people because of critical remarks about Islam. Islam is an idea, just like any other religion is an idea; you do not take it personally when someone criticizes your ideas, and the truth is that Islam is a totalitarian political doctrine, masking itself as a religion. I do not agree with Geert Wilders when he says that he does not have anything against Muslims, but the ideology alone; an ideology is not created by itself, it is created by people with a certain view of themselves and others around them, in other words, Islam would not exist if it was not for Muslims; I have a lot against the Islamic ideology and Muslims who are imposing it upon those of us who do not have anything to do with their religion, but I have respect for Muslims who question their beliefs, I have respect for Muslims who have the willingness to reform their religion and my greatest respect is to those Muslims who make a decision to leave Islam and become apostates; they take great risks when they make such an important decision in their lives and they need my support and those of us who view such an ideology as a barbaric totalitarian doctrine. In 2004, a Muslim immigrant of Moroccan descent killed Theo Van Gogh because of the movie he made about Islam, together with Ayaan Hirsi Ali, France has witnessed two terrorist attacks in 2015, Denmark experienced a terror attack in 2015, and the list goes on, now we need, to be honest with ourselves here seriously: Who are the perpetrators of all the attacks? Are they Buddhists? Are they Christians? Are they Jews? Are they Hindus? Are they Jains? Are they Voodoo worshipers? To be honest with you, the answer is no, they're not, they are Muslim terrorists and it is not up to me to protect Islam and Muslims from criticism; it is up to Muslims themselves to keep their house in order, it is up to Muslims themselves to recognize that those perpetrators are following, much of the strict doctrines from their holy book. Islam is not a European religion, it never was and it is never going to be a European religion; there are Muslim immigrants in Europe and they bring Islam here, and in Western Europe we are seeing conflicts between the values of Islam and those of Europe. Muslims who choose to adapt to the values of Europe are those who are willing to be French, Germans, Swedes, Italians, Dutch, Spaniards, British, Belgians, Irish, Swiss and Portuguese. Muslims who choose to adapt to the values of other Western countries have the willingness to be Americans, Australians, Canadians, Chileans and New Zealanders, etc. Those who don't will never embrace the values of their host countries, that is a decision each one of them has to make at some point in their lives. That is why the Liberal Left and the Conservative Right are not helping Muslim immigrants when they are trying to protect them and Islam from criticism from other non-Muslim Europeans, instead of demanding them to take responsibility for their the deeds of their religion and realize that the values of the

Western world are Judeo-Christian and Humanistic values, values, which have given Muslim immigrants the freedom to practice their religion. The political elite and institutions in many Western countries are not demanding Muslim immigrants to know that there is a difference between demanding respect and intimidating others; it is not the European societies' responsibility to raise those youths from disadvantaged areas, it is primarily the responsibility of their parents. In Western countries, nuclear families are the foundations of the societies, which have made them what they are today; it is here their norms, their values and their beliefs are rooted. Western nations are also those that place much more value to the individual, than approving belief systems from a group, although in each culture you find families with problems. Human traffickers are responsible for the influx of economic migrants in Europe from Muslim countries and other Third World countries, they give those desperate people false promises on a better life in Europe. Human traffickers promise economic migrants betters jobs, better education, free money, villas, lavish cars and other false promises and the masses buy into it and pay human traffickers a tremendous amount of money, after receiving money from economic migrants, they put them in filled gummy boats and there are many who drown and lost their lives. Human trafficking is a crime and most of those human traffickers are Middle Eastern, Africans and Asians. I personally think that human trafficking should be punished either by death penalty or labor camp; North Korea would probably need more unsuited people for labor camps in my view, and human traffickers should be trafficked to North Korea and work there as slaves. I know that these statements are very controversial, but I do not have any sympathy for anyone who chooses to traffic another human being or even an animal for the sake of making easy money. I do not hold any sympathy for people who traffic others by lying to them and giving them false promises when it comes to living the misery from the Third World and reaching a better life in the West, that is why I believe that human trafficker has got to either work on labor camps for at least 30 years or face death penalty for robbing other poor people their lives. On the other hand, economic migrants are as guilty because they choose to believe all those lies, and many of them being Muslims have an agenda to destroy Europe from within. Europe needs to tell economic migrants that it has nothing to offer them and they have to go back to their countries, Europe needs to tell Muslim immigrants that it is a continent whose values are found on Humanism, Christianity, Judaism, Renaissance and Enlightenment; and it needs to tell Muslim immigrants and other kinds of immigrants as well that yes they're here and they have rights, but also have obligations and Europe needs to understand migrants as a whole that if they / we do not abide by that commitment, then they must penalized. Europe and the rest of the Western civilization have got to find out if some nations within those countries have the ability to share a collective future with peoples they have never had a common past or history for that matter, that's how various Western countries can figure if they're able to integrate and assimilate more people from other backgrounds or they want to remain homogeneous societies. That is why it is very important that you make a decision on, which kinds of migrants you want in your countries and which ones you do not want That's when the idea of Hungary building fences all around its borders comes into the debate; Hungary was heavily criticized by the international community for building fences around its borders with Serbia, Croatia and Romania. Hungary was also criticized by the international community because of the way it dealt with migrants from different parts of the world, but I think the international community is missing a very important picture here; first of all, Hungary is a sovereign country with its own laws and the Hungarian government has made it clear that it does not want to take in those migrants, nor does it want to let those migrants go to other European countries. The Hungarian Prime Minister, Viktor Orban believes that Muslim immigration is a threat to Europe's Christian identity and the values it holds dearly, to understand his views, let take a deeper look at the time when the Hungarians were invaded by the Muslim Turks in the 14th century. The Ottomans (the Turks) had an eye on Central Europe and their attacks on the Hungarians was something the Magyars could not avoid. Louis II who was the Hungarian sovereign that time attended the battle of the Mohacs in 1526, that battle was the result of the Hungarian sovereign, Louis II's rejection of the Turkish invitation to accept Islam. The consequences of that rejection lead to Turkey invading Hungary and subjugating the Magyar population, the complete surrender of Hungary lead to the Turks heading for Austria and Prussia. Those were times when Croats, Bulgarians, and Serbs suffered at the hands of the Turks. The goal for the Turks was to either tell the local populations to accept Islam, to treat them like dhimmis or second-class citizens, or wage a holy war against them. We all know what happened when the Muslim Turks and Arabs were trying to invade Vienna, the Poles kicked them out and taught them a lesson for life. We have got to realize that the battle of Mohacs was an eye opener for the Magyars who realized that the Muslim Turks were not just interested in their riches; the Turks wanted to force them to change their culture, their existence and they saw it as a threat to their survival. Many East European countries like Poland, Slovakia, Czech Republic, Latvia, Hungary, Estonia, Serbia and Bulgaria have those awful memories; that is why right now they do not want to have anything to do with Muslim immigration because of the negative impacts Islam has had and still has on Europe as a whole for centuries, and do not forget that many natives on the Old Continent were enslaved by Muslim Arabs and Turks. That's why the Crusaders were launched across the entire Old Continent, they did not just come up out of the blue and start killing a bunch of people; they have been initiated because their goal was to liberate Europe from the Islamic invasion, unless Muslims recognize it, they will never be at peace with the Western world in general. Why am I bringing up this subject? What does it have to do with refugees and migrants today in the 21st century? Well, if you're asking me these questions, I do not blame you; you need realize that each problem in life has its roots somewhere and the the best predictor the the future behavior is the past behavior, you may say that the "refugees" and the migrants are fleeing terrorism and poverty, but let me tell you something: Why aren't they migrating to to rich Muslim countries? Why is it that when they migrate, they bring their problems with them? Why are there 44 conflicts in the world between Muslims and non-Muslims anywhere? That's countries like Poland and Slovakia only want to take in Christian and Yazidi migrants, people who are mostly persecuted, discriminated against and killed by Muslim terrorists. You might say, but most victims of terrorist attacks are Muslims, well, although it may be true, you still need to remember that Islam in its purest form cannot coexist with values from any non-Muslim country; it wants to dominate, not to be dominated, that is why the problem with Islamic fundamentalism is the fundamentals of Islam itself as a religion. It is up to Muslims to recognize that, also do not forget that many East European countries are struggling to integrate different minorities, especially the Romanies and the Jews in their societies. Countries like Poland, Hungary, Romania are still homogeneous societies that have not had a history of integrating people from other parts of the world; they were under the Soviet rule since the end of the Second World War and got their freedoms again after the fall of the USSR in the late 1980's. Romanies continue to suffer prejudices and discrimination in those countries, especially in Czech Republic, Hungary, Russia, Romania and worst of all, Albania. Hungary faces another problem with its Jewish community whom they view as Zionists who are trying control the Magyar society. Although East European countries are emerging well economically, they still do not have the resources that West European countries have when it comes to vetting those migrants, and they do not understand why the European Union is demanding them and other sovereign countries to take the share of the refugee burden. Going back to the subjects of the awful treatments racing series of racism, hatred and attacks in Hungary and other East European countries, something that I condemn harshly, however; we must not forget that many Romanies still hold on to their nomadic way of life, they are also involved in gang activities and make things hard themselves also, not just in Hungary, but across the whole Europe. Romanies are also exploited in their communities by money lenders and persuaded to marry young, instead of getting an education and starting businesses, this situation needs to be addressed as well. In my opinion there needs to be a meeting between the Romany and communities from other East European countries, and there needs to be a moment of healing; in other words, truth and reconciliation. Going back to the subject of migrants, Germany has received more than 1 million refugees and economic migrants, Sweden has received more than 140,000 migrants, and other Western countries have followed suit. There have been many volunteers who have advocated their humanitarian causes with signs, such as: "Stop Racism!", "Refugees are welcome here!". The refugees and the migrants were welcomed with open arms in Germany, Austria, Sweden, France Italy, Croatia, Hungary, Greece, Serbia, FYR Macedonia and other European countries. As the influx kept growing, there were also voices in Germany and across the entire Western world that were against the idea of bringing in more migrants, the people who were concerned about more migrants were concerned about the rise of crime, violence, Islamic extremism, etc., but they were not heard by their government, especially in Germany and Sweden. We have seen groups of nationalists setting fire on asylum centers in Germany, Sweden, and other places. The PEGIDA movement in Germany made countless amounts protests against Chancellor Angela Merkel's immigration policy in Dresden and other parts of Germany, warning her about the consequences of those policies, not just in Germany, but the rest of Europe. Far right extremist parties across Europe were also profiting from the situation to promote their hateful and destructive agenda, I am not talking about PEGIDA, nor am I talking about the AFD(Alternative for Germany) and other parties such as: the UKIP, the Sweden Democrats and the Freedom Party; I am talking about Neo-Nazis who were/are using this situation to promote their evil agendas, both them and the Islamists are two sides of the same coin, as they both believe in the pure and the impure. On the other the consequences of Chancellor Merkel's immigration policy has lead to massive amounts of sexual assaults on German women in Cologne during the New Year 2016, at least hundreds of German women were also raped by a group of at least 1,000 Middle Eastern Arab men, who are Muslims, the same madness went on in other German cities, such as: Frankfurt, Hamburg, Hannover and elsewhere in the country. The German authorities and the media were trying to cover it up out of the fear of being labeled as racists and islamophobic, luckily for the Germans, there have been some independent online media that were covering that story on the internet. This is not helping Muslim immigrant men

75

who do not have any respect for German women because of the way they dress, who are those Muslim men to tell German women in Germany how to dress? When the this incident got reported in the media, there were protests from PEGIDA, protests, which I understand because many of those Muslim Middle Eastern and African Muslim migrant men ought to realize that they cannot impose their jungle desert laws in a civilized country like Germany and other Western countries. The story does not end there; it is not only in Germany that primitive incidents like these happened, they also took place in: Finland, Sweden, Austria, Switzerland and other European countries; let us take the example of one of the European countries that has had a history of integrating newcomers, the country, which I am talking about is Sweden; in Sweden there have been massive attacks on Swedish women by Muslim immigrant men, but the Swedish media and press do not want to point out that the perpetrators were Middle Eastern Muslims, in same cases African and Southeast Asian Muslims because it is racist and bowing down to the far right parties there. I think that the Swedes are making things worse for themselves in such a situation because it is very important to point out what kinds of people who were standing behind the assaults and encourage that community to keep its house in order, whether the perpetrators are Danes, Arabs, Blacks, Jews, Norwegians, Finns, East Europeans, Southeast Asians, Persians, Turks, Kurds, Hispanics, Mixed Race or even just ethnic Swedes; the point that I am trying to make here is that you have to call things by their name, that's how you begin the figure out what kinds of solutions you can find to these problems. You do not switch the problems under the carpet and expect them to go away on their own; you've got to confront them. It is not racist at all to portray the rapists by name; you are doing that community a favor, and you are also protecting the women, you might say that this could feed to more prejudices, but you know what? There are risks in everything we do in life, you can also say that that does not mean that every member of that particular community does it and let that demand them to corporate with the government and make requirements to them so that they can take responsibility for the things that go on in their neighborhoods and take a deeper look at themselves as a community. Let me give you an example, when two Black British men of Nigerian descent beheaded a British soldier, Lee Rigby; when I found out about it on the news, as a Black man, even though I do not live in Britain, I was so angry that I just felt like confronting those two imbeciles because they are a disgrace to my race. I made lots of comments on Youtube, and I even wished that those two men's British citizenship gets revoked from them and that they are deported from Britain back to Nigeria where they could face torture, in my opinion, I still think that it is a good idea that those two men face torture in their country of origin. It even aggravated more when those two idiots said that they were trying to defend the Islamic cause; those people were highly educated and had good jobs in Britain, if they were living in a Middle Eastern Muslim country, they wouldn't have those opportunities, and they would be treated like animals, then we will see how they would fight for the Islamic cause in Middle Eastern slave slums, where they would probably do the dirty works and face racial and physical abuse. There are many Africans who are risking their lives, wanting to come to Britain and other rich European countries to study, to get an education and to work, while those two retarded fools do not realize the opportunities they got in the UK; I wish that the UK gave me those opportunities, instead of those two idiots. That's the way a community needs to take a stand by recognizing that the problems are first of all internal, in other words from within, then they can focus on the external factors later. But it begins by the community confronting some members of its groups and calling it like it is, without mincing words and then saying, not in my name. Going back to Sweden's failure to call things by their name, this wonderful Scandinavian country prides itself as the champion of gender equality and the capital of the Feminist world has politicians, both on the Left and on the Right who do not have the courage to face up to the problems in areas concentrated with large amounts of immigrant populations,especially Muslim immigrants. Feminists in Western countries do not raise debates about sexual assaults done to non-Muslim women in Europe, most of whom are Caucasians by Muslim immigrant men from different parts of the world. Feminists do not raise debates about female genital mutilation, honor killings, gender discrimination in Third World countries and the cultures that are behind such beliefs and system of values; they focus mostly blaming men from the West for all the misery of women in the developed world, and other subjects that are irrelevant in my view. The only political party in Sweden that is dealing with these matters is the Sweden Democrats, a party that was once far right, racist, anti-Semitic, homophobic, etc., but now it has emerged as a significant populist force in Sweden that has to be taken seriously by other mainstream political parties. Just because the Sweden Democrats are against immigration from Muslim countries, that in itself does not make it a racist party; if the Sweden Democrats were a racist party, you would not find Assyrians, Jews, Blacks, Armenians and other non-Muslim minorities supporting that political party. What the Sweden Democrats want is the limit on immigration in Sweden because the country has taken too many people that do not have its best intentions; in my opinion, it is common sense, not racism. The Sweden Democrats want to integrate migrants who have the willingness to assimilate into the Swedish society, and the same party wants to focus on other policies that can benefit the mainstream Swedish people. Let us take a look at it from their perspective: Sweden has almost 10 million inhabitants, it is a small country by population, compare to Germany that has over 80 million people; Sweden takes in migrants from other cultures and offers them opportunities, but on the other hand unemployment in that country is high, especially among immigrant communities, yet that country keeps taking more and more migrants from areas whose customs are not compatible with Swedish values; when that happens you have more migrants living in social, challenging areas with no jobs, living on welfare, etc. In my opinion, no Nordic country has done more to integrate peoples of color, fight racism, the use of racial slurs and other destructive propaganda against immigrants of color than Sweden; does it mean that there is no racism in Sweden? No, does it mean that there is no discrimination in Sweden? No, however; the mistake that the Swedes have made were to take in too many migrants who impose their way of life and system of values in the the name of their religion, in a society that does not have anything in common with those values; they have the freedom to practice their religion, but use that freedom against the Swedes themselves, they tell the Swedes that they want halal shops and they have it, they say to the Swedes that they want pork meat to be removed from school menus, they have it, I can go on and on about this subject, and the Swedes are not the only ones facing these problems. When you have a population in concentrated areas, where you find people with no means of employment and other possibilities, chances are that their frustrations can turn into riots with the police, however; this does not excuse their behavior because there are also many migrants in Sweden from other backgrounds who struggle to find jobs, but do not use riots as a solution to deal with their problems. When you have a country in that situation, the mainstream population will begin to be frustrated, that is a natural way of reacting,on the other hand when you have the media in the same country and politicians not having the courage to deal with these matters forcefully, and to forbid people from dealing with such issues harshly, then the mainstream population gets even more frustrated. Now the negative response from some frustrated Swedes is to turn to Neo-Nazi groups for solutions, thinking that they those parties solve their problems, which is even way worse because every immigrant who is non-Aryan ends up paying a huge price, even if that immigrant is not a Mohammedan. The solution besides dealing with these Neo-Nazis is to make tough requirements to Muslim immigrants and others who are in Sweden, and if they do not want to abide by those conditions, then they better be deported; if they have the Swedish citizenship, then they should lose it and go back to countries where they have universal values. Another solution is control mosques, to surveil them and to ban hate preaching imams. You can also look at a limit on the amount of people coming in Sweden and do mass deportations of illegal migrants living in Sweden illegally, that is why the Sweden Democrats is the third largest political party in the country, and they are rising in the polls. We're talking about importing a group of men in Europe who view their women as properties and second class citizens, the same group of men views believes in stoning people who have an affair, we're talking about a group of men who believe that fornicators have got to be punished, we're talking about groups of men who think that people who are involved in same-sex relationships must either be beaten or killed, and we're talking about groups of men who view white and other non-Muslim women as natural meat, slags, sluts and you are all shocked about what is happening in your countries when you bring such groups of people. That's why you have racist parties rising across Europe when you have governments that make excuses for Islam and Muslims as a whole. You invite many aggressive Muslim men in your countries, giving them food, shelter, clothes, jobs, money, housing and the response you're getting is more crime, more violence, and more rape. Can you believe that Sweden has the second highest level of rape in the world, after South Africa? Sweden! If anyone told me this many years ago, I would think that that individual is crazy, but it is true that many Swedish women are assaulted, beaten and raped by Muslim immigrant men because of what they are. In Norway, the same thing is happening; most of the rapes that are committed against Norwegian women are done by Muslim immigrants from the Middle East and Africa. In Rotherham, England many ethnic British girls and boys were raped by Pakistani men, the British media did not address that issue until recently, isn't that a hate crime? Let me ask you, the reader who is reading this book, isn't this a hate crime? Isn't this a racist crime? How do you expect the mainstream populations in those countries to react? Do you want them to keep quiet about it? Listen, my humanity stops when you have a group of people who do things like that, justifying it in the name of their religion and the communities belonging that that particular religion fails to admit that there is something in their religion and culture that allows these things to happen and fail to keep their own houses in order by making too many excuses about this stuff not having anything to do with their religion and cultures. The same communities send death threats to people who dare those problems and criticize their religion. My humanity stops when you have groups of Muslim men killing people in Europe and elsewhere because cartoons of their religious leader is drawn or the "religion of peace" is criticized. My humanity stands with those women who are raped by men who view them as easy meats, my humanity stands with people who are believe that all religion and cultures are subject to critique, my humanity stands with people who are called all forms of racial slurs in the name of free speech because they happen to have a different skin color and have another background; my humanity stands with Hungarians and other people who are protecting their national borders; my humanity stands with Armenians who fight very hard to get their awful history recognized worldwide; my humanity stands with people in Darfur who are butchered because of their race and religion; my humanity stands with Yazidis and Christian minorities who face discrimination in Muslim countries; my humanity stands with Jews who suffered in WWII; my humanity stands with Romanies who face rejection everywhere they go; my humanity stands with Israel that tries to fight for its survival as a Jewish State; my humanity stands with Muslim apostates; my humanity stands with men who are victims of domestic violence; my humanity stands with women who are victims of domestic violence; my humanity stands with victims of genocides anywhere; my humanity stands with people who are victims of tribalism anywhere; my humanity stands with Muslims who question their beliefs and values; my humanity stands with Christians who do not impose their religion upon others; my humanity stands people who have the willingness to rebuild their nations; my humanity stands with French people, Congolese peoples, Portuguese people, Angolan people and Egyptians; my humanity stands with people who were victims of Islamic injustices centuries ago; my humanity stands with people who were taken as slaves; my humanity stands with tribes who were forcefully convert to Christianity, and my humanity stands with people who call things by their name and stand up for justice and equal rights for all, i.e their religion has been criticized; my humanity does not stand with those who do not question their beliefs; my humanity does not stand with fundamentalist Christians, fundamentalist Jews and fundamentalists from other religions; my humanity does not stand with people who go to other countries illegally; my humanity does not stand with murders, thieves, gangs, sadists, far right groups, drug dealers and other groups of people. In my birth country, France there is a town known as Calais; it is a town where there is a harbor with ferries that head to the United Kingdom, in Calais there are groups of illegal immigrants stranded on the French border because many of them want to go to the United Kingdom. When their plans do not succeed they stay in Calais illegally and create an area known as the Jungle, there they create their own laws and live as if they are in a Third World country, sometimes they go after trucks where they can penetrate illegally for their ticket to Great Britain. Any ethnic Frenchman who dare to take a stand against illegal immigration and the Jungle is accused of racism by anti-racist organizations, while many people in Calais do not feel safe in their own city, to you the reader who is reading this book, do you think that it is fair for people not to feel safe in their own cities? The French government is not deporting those people, but putting them in other asylum centers, even though most of those people are economic migrants. The French government is "afraid to violating international human rights laws"; you know what? When you go to another country illegally, you violate that country's right to self determination. Why doesn't the United Nations demand the same standards to non-Western countries that treat illegal immigrants like dogs? Why is it only Western and other White majority countries? It seem like non-Western countries are given a free pass because they were once seen or are still seen as subordinates, because that many believe subconsciously, without knowing it that Universal rights are not for them and many non-Western countries that are members of the UN get away with a lot, when it comes to their views on peoples from other tribes, peoples from other races, peoples from other religions, peoples from nationalities, corruption, political instability, bad governance and basic needs. It is always the Western civilization who is to blame for all their misery and those of their citizens, even on things like infrastructure and investments, I am going to raise a debate about this situation on chapter 12. The concept of islamophobia was invented by the Muslim Brotherhood and the Organization of the Islamic Conference to prevent people in Western countries and other parts of the non-Muslim world to come up with critical arguments against Islam, Muslims, the Quran and the Islamic culture; it even surprises me when Liberals from the left and some Conservatives on the Right use the word "islamophobia", when someone makes critical remarks about Muslims; what they do not understand is that the term "islamophobia" is shoved down on their throats, this is how Islamic supremacists manipulate Western politicians, the media, churches, synagogues, trade unions, NGOs and other institutions. They use the term "islamophobia" to silence anyone who is against the Muslim Brotherhood's cause for the Islamic government in the world. I think "islamophobia" is justifiable, when you so much violence committed by Muslims anywhere in the world and the goal they have to destroy non-Muslim countries, then it is natural to have such a phobia, and it is not my responsibility to change it; only Muslims themselves can do something about it. Europe is also facing illegal immigration from Africa; there are many Africans who risk their lives, some even drown on the Mediterranean Sea when they make attempts to come to Europe for a better life. Those who survive the journey make in countries like Italy, Malta and Greece. I am going to go deeper with this topic on chapter 7 when I am going to talk about many issues facing Africa today. When it comes to illegal immigration in the United States from countries like: Mexico, El Salvador, Guatemala and other Latin American countries, I find it unacceptable that Democrats and some Republicans have been feeding on this problem for decades, none of them has come up with solutions on how to deal with illegal migrants living in America. The U.S. has at least 11 million illegal migrants, most of whom are Hispanic, what really strikes me is that many Hispanics in the USA take it personally when someone like Donald Trump or even Ted Cruz talk about deporting illegal immigrants back to their countries, Democrats are encouraging illegal immigration so that they can get more popularity from the Hispanic community. To you who might be a Hispanic or a Left wing activist who gets offended when Donald Trump wants to deport 11 million illegal immigrants from the U.S. to Mexico, let me ask you these questions: How do Mexicans, Salvadorans, Guatemalans and others deal with illegal immigrants from other countries? If I was an illegal immigrant in a Latin American country, how do you think the authorities in one of those countries would deal with me? Why do you think that the United States has the obligation to take in illegal immigrants from Latin American countries? The truth is that there is a lot of crime involved in Mexico and other Latin American countries when it comes to the drug cartels and other types of violence, it is true that many of those illegal immigrants do not have America's best intentions; there are many Native Born Americans who are killed by illegal immigrants, and no Leftwing activist even raises an issue about it, not even President Obama, but when Donald Trump, Ted Cruz, Ben Carson and other debate about illegal immigration, somehow they are bigots and hate mongers. I do not hear you criticizing Mexico and other latin American countries for the way they treat illegal immigrants there, I do not even hear you making requirements to migrants who come to the United States. There are immigrants from all over the world who have waited for years and paid fees before they received their Green Card from the

American authorities; they come to the U.S., with their skills, knowing that they have come to contribute, not to demand welfare benefits. Why is it that illegal immigrants have to have special treatments? You do not even raise the issue of racial conflicts between African Americans and Hispanics, also between African Americans and Asian communities. To be honest with you, even though I am not an American, I still believe that it is not the job of the United States government to take of citizens from other countries that are coming in illegally; whether they're Mexicans, Salvadorans, Guatemalans, Liberians, Nicaraguans, Cubans, Nigerians, Ghanaians, Chinese, Vietnamese etc., it is the job of the governments of those countries to take care of their own citizens, under their own terms. The job of the United States government is to take care of its own people first, especially those who are homeless, those who go to bed hungry, those who are on food stamps and those whose communities are struggling etc, the illegal migrants can wait in line or go home; that goes for any other country, whether it is Denmark, France, Netherlands, Sweden, Germany, Belgium, Japan, Spain, South Korea, Brazil, South Africa, Singapore etc. The job of those governments is to take care of their citizens first, especially those who are vulnerable; the Western world cannot take in the misery of the entire Muslim world and the rest of the Third World, it is an impossible task, why does the Western world have to be required to do that? I know that some people in Canada will remind about how I went there and my intentions; let me tell you that my goal was never to immigrate to Canada illegally, my goal was to stay there for a period of time and find legal ways to contribute to the Canadian society. When I left Denmark 2 years ago, I decided to live because I would not see myself living in a country where I had no chance of making a significant progress as an immigrant of color, I also felt that it was not healthy for me to live in a country where Blacks like me are called Negroes regularly by the Danes. Grumbling was not an option to me, I just felt like I had to leave Denmark; I look forward to my next move, leaving Scandinavia permanently.

CHAPTER 4

WHERE THE LEFT & THE FAR LEFT GO WRONG

The Left prides itself as a political movement that fights for social justice, gender equality, equality for all, rights for sexual minorities, unity, multiculturalism and other bill of rights. The Left was an organization that took a stand against racism, poverty, discrimination, anti-Semitism, Holocaust denial, Apartheid in South Africa, racial segregation in United States, Southern Rhodesia and other universal values. The Far Left wants those values, but uses brutality to try to get their way; many countries that are governed by governments from the Far Left happen to be oppressive regimes that enforce Socialism, Communism and Marxism. That ends up sacrificing human lives for the sense of ideals; we see it in North Korea, Cuba and countries that were once under Communism. Unfortunately, the Left and even the Right for that matter have lost their moral authority when it comes to racism, honor killings, gender discrimination, tribalism, discrimination and oppressive regimes in non-White countries, and the troubles Islam pauses in the West and the rest of the world. The Left has lost its moral authority when it comes to Arab slave trade of Blacks by Middle Eastern Arabs and other similar groups, the Left has lost its moral authority when it comes to the racism on non-Whites in Middle Eastern countries like: Morocco, Turkey, United Arab Emirates, Saudi Arabia, Algeria, Tunisia, Libya, Yemen, Iran, Afghanistan and other Middle Eastern countries. The Left has lost its moral authority when it comes to tribalism in Sub-Saharan African countries. The Left has lost its moral authority when it comes to anti-Semitism in Muslim countries and some other Third World countries. The Left has lost its moral authority when it comes to Muslim immigrants in the West denying the Holocaust. The Liberal left has lost its moral code because it aligns itself with Islam, a religion and a political movement that discriminates against minorities of any race and religion in Muslim majority countries, a religion that views women as lower inteligent animals, a religion that murders anyone who comes up with critical remarks about it and its followers, a religion that wants Jewish blood pushed out to the Mediterranean Sea, and a religion that imposes its will wherever it and whenever it does not like the way people things in non-Muslim country. Both the Liberal Left, the Right and the Far Left have failed to make critical remarks on Muslim and people with other cultures out of the fear of being called intolerant. The anti-racist organizations in the Western world have made it their mission to fight racism, discrimination, homophobia, gender quality and other forms of injustices. Where many anti-racist organizations go wrong is when they call anyone who is critical of Islam, Muslims and the Quran as a racist; first of all, Islam is not a race; it is a political movement masking itself as a religion and a political or a religious movement is an idea, so you cannot be racist for being critical of an idea. Second of all, Muslims are not a single race; you find White Muslims, Middle Eastern Muslims, Turkic Muslims,

Black Muslims, Mixed Race Muslims, Hispanic Muslims, Indian Muslims and other Asian Muslims, however; Islam is a Middle Eastern Arab religion founded by an Middle Eastern Arab man in the 7th century. Third and last of all, the Quran is not a race; it is a political/religious book used by followers of that particular religion, that is why anti-racist groups are send a confusing message when they call anyone who is against Islam a racist, but they do not do the same thing when it comes to Christianity, Judaism, Sikhism, Hinduism etc. Another problem with anti-racist group is their failure to address the issues like honor killings, terrorism, the impact Muslim immigration has on open societies, crime committed by immigrants from non-Western countries, the grooming of white girls and boys by Muslim immigrant men etc. When the police, the media and anti-racist organizations cover up the grooming of white English girls and boys by Muslim immigrants out of the fear of being characterized as racists, bigots and hate mongers; they are covering up a hate crime, they are covering up racist crimes, being an anti-racist is not just standing against racism against peoples of color; it is also racism against Whites, equal rights for all before the law. This is why everyone needs to be held to the same standards, my god; we live in pluralistic societies, we cannot just have one standard for one group and lower expectations for others. When there are injustices in other parts of world, such as human trafficking, slave labor, child labor, Sharia Law etc., it is ok to say that those cultures that practice such unjust things are inferior, when we do not do that we are ignoring the victims of those injustices because of our desire to appease for the sake of not being called an islamophobe and a hate monger. When you have criminal gangs protected because of their ethnicities out of the fear of being characterised as racists, while you have White English, German, French, Italian, Swedish girls/women being groomed by the same people you are encouraging racism from the other side, when those victims are ignored, this leaves the vacuum to the Far Right organizations that will begin to pick the pieces, we all know what happens when the Far Right exploits such situations. When you have a fear of an ideology whose culture and religion is not compatible to yours, that fear is rational and it has nothing to do with racism. People in Germany, Holland, Sweden, Norway, France, Britain, Belgium and other West European countries who were chanting "refugees are welcome here!" had good intentions, believe they had good intentions, but they never asked themselves if those "refugees" whom most of are economic migrants were suited to integrate in their countries. When they oppose organizations like PEGIDA, the Alternative for Germany, Riposte Laïque other similar organizations by calling them hatemongers, they are not doing those migrants and the women from their countries who face assaults, beatings and rape because of them being local women a favor.You cannot respect people's beliefs without knowing what those beliefs are and whether they have your best interests. I have heard this statement before: "You cannot judge an entire community because of the actions of a few," that 's right, it is like saying that you cannot judge an entire rugby team based on its results. Anti-fascists groups often use that analogy as an excuse to protect Muslim immigrants and other kinds of immigrants criticism. If you believe that the Far Right is using those situations as an excuse for their reckless arguments, then defeat them by showing them what kinds of fools they are. If a few members of a community is involved in criminal activities somewhere, then they have to be exposed for what they are, and it is up to their community to keep the house in order. The Liberal Left, especially those on the Far Left have been so naive when it comes to the objectives of Islam, both the Far Left and Islam have an irrational hatred for the Western world, and the Far Left focuses too much on racism in the United States, South Africa, England, Australia, Russia, Germany and other white majority/minority counties, but the Liberal Left does not have the courage to raise questions about racism that minorities of different races and tribes face in majority Muslim countries, especially in Middle Eastern countries like Turkey, Morocco, Libya, Egypt, Tunisia, Algeria, Iran, Iraq, Qatar, the UAE, Kuwait, Saudi Arabia, Mauritania, Oman, Bahrain, Jordan, and Afghanistan, I guess White Liberals on the Left and the Far Left could not care less about societies that are far more racists than their own; communities where minorities of different races and tribes are treated like dogs and slaves, nations where Africans whose kidneys are taken away and being sold in the black market by Mid-Easterners because the same White Liberals have lower expectations on Muslims as a whole and still see Mohammedans as victims, even if they oppress other groups of people. As long as their daughters are not raped by Muslims of different ethnicities, as long as it is not their sons who are groomed by the same groups of people, as long as it is not one of their friends who is killed for criticizing Muslims and Islam, as long as the Scandinavians can keep using the N-word, as long as they do not have Sharia Law in their neighborhoods, then they do not mind at all. Their cowardice is encouraging more hate speech, more honor killings, more racism, more female genital mutilation, more sharia courts, more hate preachers, more Islamic terrorism, more human rights abuses in Third World countries, more killings of apostates, more killings of sexual minorities, etc. In countries that are governed by Sharia Law, male family members see themselves as guardians of their siblings, daughters, female cousins, etc. Those females are treated like cattle, and they can be killed for doing something that the males do not approve, and those males cannot be prosecuted there. White Liberals do not call things by their name out of the fear of being called ethnocentric, racists, imperialists, colonialists and that is why they continue with this lower expectation narrative, which does not encourage Mohammedans and other people from other Third World countries to be held to the same standards as White Liberals themselves. Some of them are so naive to the point where they even encourage the Far Right to use racial slogans out of the fear that if they do not then those Far Right groups will go underground, well, who cares if they do go underground because had they had their way, you and I would not have rights at all; you could kiss goodbye to those bill of rights if you dare to think differently from them, this is a huge problem in Scandinavia as a whole, especially Denmark and Finland. Any Mohammedan who is honest with himself/herself or with his/her deity needs to realize that many of the post Quranic scriptures, the Hadiths and the Sunna are not compatible with this modern age where we are right now; no one following religions like: Hinduism, Christianity, Buddhism, Jainism, Voodoo, Judaism and some other religions is encouraged to behead, burn, groom, rape, kill and cause terrorism because scriptures told them to do it and because their god told them to do it like Muslims do. I even notice in the media and elsewhere that Muslims always say that this has nothing to do with Islam, then what religion are those terrorists following? Muslims always make excuses for the terrorist attacks and other crimes committed by their fellow believers for centuries, including 60 million Christians, 80 million Hindus and 120 million Black Africans; the way Muslims make excuses, especially those from the Middle East is by attacking what someone outside Islam did, whether it is about the Crusades, whether it is about America and Israel, whether it is about Blacks taking each other as slaves before Mid-Easterners did and so on and so forth. This is how Muslims justify their hatred towards non-Muslim, and that is how narcissists behave; they tend to be self-congratulatory, when you raise tough topics about their religion they tend to look the other way and White Liberals on both the Left and the Far Left have encouraged this madness to happen by facilitating Islam's desire for dominance in the Western world. Not just White Liberals by the way; Black Liberals tend to look the other way when many Blacks in Middle Eastern countries suffer racism, and they tend to look the other way when Blacks in Darfur are being killed by Arabs. Liberal Hispanics tend to look the other way when illegal immigrants are treated like animals in majority Hispanic countries, and they also happen to see Muslims as subordinates, even if those Mohammedans are killing Yazidis and Christians in the Middle East. Another thing that gets to me is Liberals Jews who feel offended when Muslims are criticized, comparing the "treatment" of Muslim to the Holocaust, ignoring that many Muslims out there do not recognize the Holocaust, ignoring the fact that the Grand Mufti of Jerusalem, Mohammed Amin Al-Hussein wanted the Jews dead, not because they are Israelis, but because they are Jews. White Liberals are naive when they feel the need to protect Muslims whom they see as victims, while people who are victims of Islam are being ignored in the name of multiculturalism and diversity. Individuals who are dealing with the problems with Muslim immigration are sidelined and called names, people who are against Sharia Law are called racists. Most of non-Muslims, especially Liberal Whites, Liberal Blacks, Liberals Hispanics, Liberals Jews, Liberals non-Muslim Asians are afraid to challenge the Islamic culture out of the fear of being threatened or killed by Muslims or out of the fear of being called intolerant, possibly they believe that all cultures and point of views are equal, which in my opinion is another way of taking poison, hoping that it is the healing medication. When you allow hate preachers with the money from Arab countries to come and build mosques where they can cultivate hatred, polygamy, anti-Semitism, the subjugation of non-Muslims, the killings of Jews and sexual minorities, the subjugation of women and the enforcement of Sharia Law, which advocates slavery, even in a civilized country, you have lost your moral authority. I am not just being critical of the Liberal Left in this situation, but also the Nobel Committee, some weak Conservatives and the rest of the Academia because their cultural relativism is enabling fundamentalists Mohammedans to walk in the streets of London, Luton, Amsterdam, Copenhagen, Paris, Lyon, Berlin, New York, Sydney, Stockholm, Vienna,

Madrid, Toronto etc. to promote killings, anti-Semitic, anti-Western and some other ideas that do not comply with our modern societies. But if a non-Muslim like me or Tommy Robinson, or Pamella Geller or Donald Trump, or even Robert Spencer made protests against Sharia Law and the Islamization of the West, then the media, the academia and many people on both the Liberal Left, the Far Left and many Conservatives on the Right slander us by calling us intolerant, racists, hatemongers, warmongers while fundamentalist Mohammedans get a free pass. People of color who are very critical of Islam and Muslims are called all sorts of names, and racial slurs are even used on them by White Liberals who are against racism. To give you my personal example, I made some very critical remarks about Islam and Muslims on Youtube and there was a Left winged Swede who wrote to me and said, I quote: "You used to eat monkeys, gorillas, dogs, cats, elephants, wild birds and living in huts, now you're joining the racists". I replied to him harshly by calling him a fool for believing that Islam and Muslims are a race, and I even told him Islam and Muslims are not above criticism, then he replied to me by saying, I quote "Hello, King Kong, you use to live in huts, you were eating dogs, you were eating cats and had no clothes, but now you're joining the racists, I know that

Islam and Muslims are not a race, by the way, we Whites are still enslaving you Africans, we are just doing it in many different ways anyway, you are still a slave in our eyes and always will be." I was very shocked at first because I never expected these statements from a Swede! A Swede and a Liberal Swede! I could not have grasped it, to me it did not make any sense that there are Swedes who are like this individual, oh my god, I just could not understand it. It was actually in 2011. Then I got so mad and began to confront him until I reached the point where I had to ignore him at last. Muslims who live in the West should be the first to say, not in our backyard, if you want to impose Sharia Law, if you threaten people who criticize Islam, if you impose halal meat in the continues, if you impose gender segregation in meetings, if you do honor killings while you are still living in a civilized country that has taken you in because you fled the horrors of your country, then you need to pack your bags and buzz off to an Islamic country that is governed by the Sharia, we do not want it in Canada, we do not want it in France, we do not wanted it in Germany, we do not want it in Holland and elsewhere in the civilized world. We believe that religion is a personal matter and what goes on privately between two adults is none of your business, you do not have the right to promote terrorism, you do not have the right to feel like your existence depends on us being victims, you do not have the right to impose your system of values in a country that does not have it, you do not have the right to demand that all supermarkets sell halal meat, you do not have the right to demand more mosques and more madrassas in the West, while you do not even allow Christians, Jews, Yazidis and other religious minorities to practice their religion freely in Islamic countries, you are not going to do this in our name, you are not going to kill fornicators and homosexuals in our name, you are not going to kill apostates in our name, you are going to respect the rules of the countries where you have decided to migrate, you have to accept that we are a minority in a country where we came as guests else you've got to leave. If Muslims did that, I would have more respect for them than I do now. There are so many White, Black, Hispanic, Mixed Race, and Jew Liberals who have convinced themselves and others that you are not allowed to criticize Muslims, Islam, and the Quran. There are many Muslims in Western countries and majority Muslim countries who are critical of the Wahabi version of their religion being imposed on all of us by Saudi Arabia, Qatar, the UAE, Kuwait, Turkey and some other Mohammedan countries by corrupting Western governments and those same Muslims do not understand why White Liberals, Black Liberals, Hispanic Liberals and other groups of Liberals do not join them in that fight. I guess it has something to do with White guilt or the idea that Muslims are subordinates, yet the same groups of people are quick to be critical of Christianity, Judaism, Buddhism, etc. Lower expectation narrative. When was the last time Liberals and Conservatives have ever been critical of rich Arab countries? Money is talking, and it is talking Arabic, money is talking Turkish and the language of the OPEC. Those who have the power to take a stand against evil, no matter where it comes from are those Liberals from Western countries, what I mean by that is mostly White Liberals. If they witness injustices being done by Mid-Easterns on minorities of any race and religion, if they stand aside and watch girls being killed by their male guardians in the name of Islam, if they stand aside and encourage Turkey to deny its crimes against the Armenians, if they stand aside and allow people to be racially bullied in the name of free speech, if they stand aside and allow one tribe hurting another because of hate, if they stand aside and ignore black on black crimes, white on black crimes, black on white crimes, mid-eastern on black crimes, Hispanic on black crime, black on Hispanic crime and so on, then they are equally guilty as those who are involved in those evil deeds. You cannot take a stand against evil without identifying it by its name first; you have got to have the courage to deal with bad harshly. When White Liberals are preventing people who criticize Islam from coming up with all their arguments on why Islamic immigration is a threat to their civilization; they are also increasing the power of the extreme right wing groups across all white majority countries and they are going to be the ones picking the pieces and raise debates about Islam, immigration, diversity and white genocide. The people who are going to suffer from their propaganda are: Blacks, Hispanics, Asians and other groups of non-Whites who live in White majority countries. When White Liberals criticize the Crusaders without realizing that the Crusaders were a solution to the Islamic invasion of Europe by Middle Eastern Muslims who subjugated native populations and imposed their way of life on those people, then White Liberals are also ignoring their own history. The Crusaders did not do anything wrong; in fact if it was not for them, Europe would not be where it is today, may be countries like: United States, Canada, Australia, South Africa, Brazil, Argentina, New Zealand and other similar countries would not have existed. Those countries owe their existence to the Crusaders who have fought, bled and died so that the West can be more civilized and liberated from the Islamic invasion. White Liberals should defend the Crusades, instead of apologizing like headless chickens to the Muslims for what the Crusaders did. Under the dominance of the Islamic Empire, also known as the Islamic Caliphate, the surface of the Earth was more covered than it did under the Roman Empire, during those times 280 million non-Mohammedans were killed by Muslims who were enforcing their beliefs on different populations around the world through a declaration of a holy war against non-Muslims. When you are at war with a third of the population worldwide that wants to destroy your way of life because they view it as immoral, decadent and condescending in the name of their religion, you do not have time to be politically sensitive towards the people who follow that specific religion.

CHAPTER 5

THE TROUBLE WITH THE FAR RIGHT

Before I talk to you about the troubles with the Far Right, I would like to share a few of my personal experience with many people who have racially abused me from the Far Right in Denmark. I am going to go back to 2004 when I was visiting one of my parent's Danish friends; I was wearing African clothes and they began to laugh at me and said I quote: "Look at this Negro wearing some strange clothes and he is weird." They did not just stop there; they kept on laughing, this was happening in Aalbaek, a small town in the Northern part of Jutland. Between 2002 and 2006 I was very critical of the Danish migration policy and their failure to recognize that they have never been good enough at integrating minorities, I even talked about them using a racial slur on Blacks that they keep using until today. I wrote so many articles about integration and assimilation, I spoke about why it is possible to integrate in the Danish society, but not assimilate because the Danish culture is like a homogeneous tribe where it is tough to be accepted, I even talked about my father who was educated in

France and a diplomat in South Africa, but struggled to get a job that matched his qualifications because he is Black and a foreigner, those were times when I wrote an article in the form of a letter to the then integration minister Bertel Haarder in 2002. I have received a letter from a typical Dane who said I quote "Balthazar Nzomono-Balenda, to you who thinks that you are so wise and intelligent, to you who has a father who was a diplomat who told you to come to our country, why don't you go back to France where you come from? It is because of people like you that there is a crime in this country, foreigners commit 80% of the offenses in Denmark, go back where you came from, we do not want you here". I wanted to respond to him harshly, but the individual never gave his address. I decided that I am going to on and raise such debates and I would not allow myself to show the letter written to be by that lousy Dane to a local politician from the Liberal Party, she encouraged me to go on and never stop, even though some people want to do anything to intimidate me. I went on and on to criticize the Danes once again in various newspaper articles and I was not mincing words. I felt the need to get tough and I did in style. I published at least 200 articles during those times. In 2005 I published many other controversial articles where I raised the debates about the use of the N-word in Denmark and I got some positive response, but most of the reaction that I was getting were very derogatory and condescended that in fact contributed to the enormous amounts of prejudice that I began to have towards the Danes and some other groups of Scandinavians. Maybe that's why Denmark is known as the Mississipi of Europe because the huge amount of people using the N-word regularly. I published another article about the utilization of the N-word by the Danes and I sad that many Germans don't use it, many white Americans do not use it, many Swedes do not use it, many white English people do not use it and many French and Norwegians to not use it. Then I got a response from a Danish supporter of the Danish People's Party who said, I quote "Balthazar, do you know how Norwegians call Black people? Do you know how Germans call Black people? Do you know what word a white American man uses on a black woman? Do you know how Swedes call Black people? Did you come to teach us something? You came to tell us what to do, right? We did not invite you here, we are individualists what do you Negroes call us white people in Africa? You are just like a Muslim who makes lots of demands, maybe those are things that you must do in Uganda or Zimbabwe, not here." The individual who wrote this letter to me left his phone number, then I called and confronted the individual by calling him an idiot for suggesting that I am like Muslims, then the individual went on to say that he used Uganda and Zimbabwe as examples because those are places where whites are being persecuted by Africans and no one in the media talked about it. He even told me to raise those debates in those places and leave Denmark, then I replied, I quote "You lousy pig, retarded Dane, bloody Scandinavian piece of garbage, White Trash, Nougat Plow if you want me out of your country, make sure that you tell your fellow Danes who live abroad to come back to Denmark, make sure that you isolate yourselves and your tribe, then I will be more than happy to leave your country." The individual from Horsens kept on telling me that I will always get away with my statements because I am a non-white if it was a white person who did it, then he/she will be prosecuted for racism. I went on to ask the individual from Horsens if could call him a filthy Scandinavian, he said that I will get away with it anyway, then he later apologized for using the N-word on me and for saying that I am like Muslims, then I told him that a stupid Dane like him must not mess around with me like he does with other African immigrants and shame on him for suggesting that I am like Muslims, shame for trying to keep me quiet from that day, he never used the N-word on me ever again! The next episode was about me writing controversial articles again in 2006 Danish newspapers, being critical of both the Danes, Muslim immigrants and other types of immigrants as well; I raised lots of topics about the ignorance of the Danes and the savagery of Muslim immigrants and other immigrants as well. Then on August 2006, I saw a logo from the Danish Front on my mailbox and I did not understand why, there was no warning, no message, just the logo when I was living in Kolding. Then a couple of weeks later, around mid-August there was a group of men from the Danish Front that came to my apartment and began to violently kick my door around 10pm in the night, at least 8 times and when I called the police and explained to them that it was the Danish Front kicking my door, they did not believe me and they just told me to relax, the group of those men went away while I was talking to the police and then they came back again and began to kick my door so hard; they were really determined to come in my apartment and assault me. I called the police in Kolding for the second time, then the police did not want to believe me, I told them that they did not want to believe me because they will always cover up for their fellow Danes and if it was a immigrant, whether from a Western or non-Western country that was doing this it would come on the news and they would make arrests. I also told the police that they probably do not want to believe in me because I am a black man, then the police in Kolding replied around 1 am I quote "France is used to have Black people, here in Denmark we do not have a history of having Blacks in our country." He said it because told him that the Danish police are incompetent and should learn more from the police in France. Then the police from Kolding told me that they would come and they came about 2am, when they came I convinced them that it was the Danish Front that stood behind and they left their logo on my mailbox as a warning, then the police did not believe me and they told me to go home, relax and drink some water. After the police left, the groups of skinheads from the Danish Front came again and began to kick on my door so many times that I just felt like I had to take matters in my own hands and I did around 3am in the morning by screaming inside my apartment and saying I quote " I am fed up with you guys and I am not scared of you anymore, if you are true men come and get me, I would rather die than putting up with bullies like you!" I was so mad that I opened the door while they were still kicking and I was ready to face the skinheads from the Danish Front, I was even ready to fight and die and they ran. I spend days without being able to sleep properly, then I spoke to my neighbors about the incidents that took place in my apartment and the way the police handled this case, I was recommended to ask my fellow neighbors who were Danes and foreigners to sign a petition and most of them did, after that they even were angry with the police and the brutality of the Danish Front. I went on the write another article where I said that the Danish police are incompetent and they should learn from countries such as: United States, Germany, Norway, France, Sweden, Netherlands, Britain, Italy, Belgium, Spain, Canada, Australia, Monaco, Brazil, Portugal and New Zealand. I went on to say that the Danish police would cover up for Danish crimes to protect their fellow Danes and go after people who are only foreigners, I was not politically correct and I did not mince words. I sent the petition to the police and I received a letter from them telling me that they expecting me, after an interview with a journalist. I also told the journalist from Politiken who interviewed me that I do not have any trust to the Danish police and I gave him my deepest reasons about it. When I went with one of my Swedish classmates, John at the police station in Kolding, then I told the policeman who invited me that I do not trust the Danish police anymore, then he replied that I have a problem, then I told him that if I was the one doing this to a Dane I would be quickly arrested and this would be reported on the media. The Danish police in Kolding and the rest of the country read my article at Politiken and they have come to a conclusion that the way they dealt with the situation was wrong and the apologized my former classmate, John from the University of Southern Denmark who is Swedish was very shocked about what happened and could not believe his eyes, he also had some things that he needed to say to the police about what happened to me. The police kept on apologizing to me about the way they handled the situation and the persuaded me that they would do things differently and they told me that they could not do anything about forbidding the Danish Front because it is a legal organization, but they do not approve of what the skinheads did to me, after the police apologized I wrote another article where I warned the members of the Danish Front that if they set their feet in my house again, they would regret the day each one of them was born and I was ready to face them again, just in case. To those of you who do not know anything about the Danish Front, I would like to tell you that it was an extreme right wing nationalist network in Denmark whose goal was to keep Denmark for the Danish people, many of those people use violence to get their points across and they were members of the another far right party in Denmark, the Danish People's Party, a political party, which another one of my classmates supports and his name is Flemming. Flemming is a white-nationalist, an anti-Semite and a supporter of Islamic terrorist groups such as Al-Qaeda and Hamas and he never shied away from showing his true colors. The Danish Front dismantled in 2007 and merged with another extreme right wing group known as Denmark's National Front who have the same agenda as those from the Danish Front. In 2007 my former classmate from the University of Southern Denmark, Fleming began to racially abuse me when I told him that the world does not owe him anything and I would not put up with his stupidity when he said that my patterns were underdeveloped. Fleming began to racially abuse and guess what he called me? We do not have to go there again because the answer is in this chapter, both him and John began to bully me and call me names my back, we are talking about a Swede from the Far Left and a Dane from the Far right working together against me by psychologically hurting me with racial and homophobic slurs, even if I am not a homosexual at all. While John was saving his skin, Fleming went on to use a derogatory name that begins with N, which whites were using on Blacks during the 17th century and you guys know what that word is because I have mentioned it a couple of times in this chapter and other chapters as well. The he began to tell me that I come from a bit and that is how someone shits me out, sorry for my profanity. When I started to call Fleming names and use offensive words towards him on the phone, I could sense that he was starting to dismantle, yet he had nothing to say to me than calling me "Negro" 18 times, then he threatened to get into a fight with me and he told me to go back to Africa where I come from. I said one of the teachers at the University of Southern Denmark that Fleming wanted to fight against me and I was advised, both by the police and by the board of members not to fight against Fleming, I sent them the email that Fleming sent to me where he began to use racial and demeaning slurs on m. When I told Fleming that I reported his stupidity to the study board and the police, the Danish People's Party sympathizer began to dismantle again and that's when I started to make life difficult for him, and then he began to play the victim card by saying that "I can't say anything I want in my own country anymore", then I began to make life harder for him on the phone by using racial slurs on him that have destroyed his life until today, he had nothing to say but kept calling me the N-word. Then he went on to say that he can say what he wants in Denmark, I must just go back to Africa where I come from. When I tried to reach out to John and told him about the story, John was so angry with me and began to talk to me about his problems with his now ex-wife, well he was 45 back then and I was 25,lol. The only thing John was interested in was to convert Windows users to Apple users; he is an Apple fundamentalist. The chairwoman of the study board had some harsh words for Fleming and a day later she called me for a meeting and asked me how we can move on from here and I was ready to listen to her ideas. Most of my fellow students and the University of Southern Denmark knew about the racist email that Fleming sent to me, I would also like to add that Fleming is an advocate for racial segregation and the hatred of the Jews; he even admires Hitler, this man whom I study with at the University of Southern Denmark hates the USA and believed that the 9-11 attacks were justified, but likes white supremacists from America, those are ideas that many members of the Danish People's Party hold. I just knew that I had to make some efforts to leave Denmark and go to another country with a healthy amount of pluralism. In 2011 and 2012, an Neo-Nazi sympathizer from Iceland, Gudmundur because to call me the N-word because I was against the legalization of drugs and I was listening to a music that typical Black man listens to, classic music. When I told him that I did not want to hear his story about drugs and the legalization process, he racially bullied me until he faced a backlash from me when I called him a Scandinavian pest, a vermin from Iceland, a rat and a honky I called him so many awful names to a point where he felt like a small child complaining to others about me being evil. Gudmundur has connections to the Neo-Nazi movements in Iceland, Denmark, Sweden and other Western countries and he proudly supports them, even though he is married to a woman from Thailand. You may wonder where I met this fool, I met him when I we both were students at the Nordic Multimedia Academy in Kolding, back then I did not even know that he had connections with Nazis, but I knew that he was fighting very hard to legalize drugs in any country around the world. But I could see some warning signs and a friend of mine whose name I am not going to mention in this book warned me about him, even before we planned to start our own company in 2011. I began to feel like there was something weird about that man and I made plans to find an exit path, but I made his life very difficult indeed by telling him to walk from his home to my place so that he can get the thing that I wanted from me, also I began to call him a Nordic pest, Scandinavian scumbag, Honky, Cracker, Vermin, Icelandic parasite, White trash and I used slurs that are even worse, which I am not going to include in this book. I even told Gudmundur that he blames Africans for all his failures in life and his addiction to marijuana and alcohol. I told him to start dealing with alcohol addiction and start thinking about saving for his retirement programs. This lead me to a situation where I began to have a negative view of all Libertarians, including people like Ron Paul and Rand Paul. This made my prejudice towards the Nordics way way worse as well because of the negative experiences that I have had with different groups of Scandinavians. I talked about how ignorant the Danes, the Norwegians, the Finns, the Icelanders and some Swedes are about different non-Western cultures, yet they choose to import immigrants from the Islamic world and blame all the problems on all immigrants, whether they're Muslims or not and both the authorities and populations are very lousy at making signalements when it comes to describing the individuals who are involved with crime; in the U.S., the authorities will deliberately describe the perpetrators as either white, black / African-American, Hispanic, Middle Eastern or Asian, whereas the Danes for instance describe the perpetrators as light, dark, foreigners or immigrants. This makes it even more confusing because you wonder what they mean by that. To make matters worse there were a group of Middle Eastern Mohammedans who were using similar racial slurs on me for criticizing Muslims; many of them even admitted that they were the first people to enslave Blacks and they could do it again with me, but I am not someone that allows other people to walk over me, especially when it comes to hate speech from Mid-Easterns towards Blacks and Romanies, then they began to face a backlash from me, and they were met with insults and humiliation from my part, and I was not afraid of their death threats because I told them that if they came to my place there would be war and they would wish that they never faced a black man like me. The bad experience that I have had with many Danes who used racial slurs on me lead to a situation where I said to myself that I would never join the PEGIDA movement in Denmark to avoid people using the N-word one another black person or me, I would even avoid joining the movement in Denmark known as For Freedom. If I want to accede to the PEGIDA movement, I would like to do it in my country of birth, France or I could also do it in Germany, Canada, United States, Sweden or England. I have a friend from Germany whose name I am not going to mention in this book who sympathizes with PEGIDA. The awful things that I experienced in Denmark lead me to a situation where I had to force myself to leave Denmark and go to Canada. In late 2006-07, there were many of my fellow Danish students from the University of Southern Denmark who have recommended me to leave Denmark and go back to my country of birth, France; my countries of origin, the Congo and the Democratic Republic of Congo, and they even recommended me to go to South Africa, Netherlands, Hungary, Portugal, Egypt, United States or some other countries because they believed that it would not be healthy for me to stay in Denmark. 5 years earlier there was a Danish man at the Christian Baptist Convention in Manager, which takes place each single year in the Summer, who asked me where I originally come from, I replied that I originally come from the Congo, then that Danish man asked me when I am going to go back, I did not know what to tell him and when I told many of his other fellow Danes, they were shocked and angry about his remarks. I did not steal his money, I did not commit any crime, I did not go to the Danish parliament and demand religious prayer services, I did not insult him or anyone else there, I did not make plans to turn Danmark to an African majority country in 2070, I did not declare a demographic war on the Danes, I did not rape any Danish girl or woman, I did not behead a Dane in Copenhagen or elsewhere, I did not ask for a French or a Congolese parallel court system, I did not infiltrate the Danish media nor did I infiltrate the Danish politicians, I did not ask for an imposition of French and Congolese foods in all Danish kantines, I did not ask France, the Congo, the Democratic Republic of Congo, Angola and Portugal to finance Catholic and Protestant Churches in Denmark and I did not force Denmark to reject Secularism and enforce Christianity everywhere in this country. Yet he wanted me out his country, yet he never wanted to see my black face in Denmark. I have some good news for him; he is not going to be disappointed because I will leave Denmark permanently and go to another country, I will not discount when it is going to be and, which country it is going to be, but I can guarantee him and the rest of the Far Right and the Far Left in Denmark that I will leave their country and not bother them anymore.

I have learned to live with the reality that i will always be a foreigner in Denmark, no matter what happens; many people have reminded me time after time that I am a foreigner in this country and I have never taken it personally. I know where I am going and I look forward to move on with my life and be a hard working individual. Many of us on the Right believe that the Liberal Left is all about globalization and the destruction of national borders and people's feeling of self belonging, although it is true there is another factor that some of us have been ignoring, nationalism on the Left and the Far Left. When it comes to the nationalism on the Left as a whole that nationalism is based on social equality, popular sovereignty and the rejection of fascism, racism, right wing nationalism and imperialism, parities like: the Indian National Congress, India; the African National Congress, South Africa; the Congolese Worker's Party, Republic of the Congo;the Scottish National Party, Scotland; Plaid Cymru, Wales, and some other Left-wing parties worth mentioning, the problem with the Left-wing parties is their naivety when it comes to the so-called religion of peace and its desire to
dominate the global stage through the use of holy wars against those who do not belong to that particular religion. When the Left ignores this problems it leaves

the vacuum, which is now taken over by the Far right because not even the Right wants to raise serious issues with the so-called religion of peace and its influence on Western societies. The primary reasons why there is a rise of the far right across Western societies it's primarily because of economic uncertainty, the amounts of refugees and migrants rising in many of those rich countries, the failure of the governments to forbid Saudi Arabia, Qatar, Kuwait and other rich Muslim countries to build more mosques in the West, the failure to address the threats that Islam brings in Western societies, the failure of Western governments to raise debates about demographics and where are their nations going to be like in 2 to 5 decades from now, the failure of Western governments to withdraw citizenships from those who are involved in terrorist activities and those who wage Jihad on the West, the hatred of another person because of a different race, the fact that Saudi Arabia is one of the allies of the West and the fear that migrants will take advantage of the welfare protections that are enjoyed by citizens. The problem with the Far Right is that it exploits the opposition of Islam and immigration from Muslim countries to hide behind their racist worldview, far right parties like the Ku Klux Klan, United States; the Danish People's Party,

Denmark; the Progress Party, Norway;the Vlaams Blok, Belgium; the Danish Party, Denmark; the National Front, United Kingdom;the Identity Block, France; the Swedish Party, Sweden; Jobbik, Hungary; the True Finns, Finland; the National Democratic Party of Germany, Germany; Heritage Front, Canada; New Order, United States; the British National Party, United Kingdom; Neo-Confederates, United States; Unity 88, New Zealand; BORN, Russia; Australia First Party, Australia; Freedom Party of Austria, Austria; Nordic Resistance Movement, Sweden; Icelandic National Front, Iceland, and Proud of the Netherlands, Netherlands are using the threat we are all facing from Islam for political gains. Their view is that there is a genocide going on against Whites and Jews are responsible for bringing multiculturalism in white majority countries, they also believe that while Africa happens to be for Africans, Asian countries for Asians, Middle Eastern countries for Mid-Easterns, white countries happen to be for everybody and the anti-racists laws are anti-white. Many of these Far right parties also have something in common with Islam in areas where Islam encourages Muslims to deny the Holocaust, both Islam and the far right believe in the concept of the pure and the impure and are both unapologetic of the evils done by their predecessors, both ideologies believe that not all men are born equal before the law and both believe in the superiority and the inferiority of people. Many White Supremacists praise the nostalgia of Germany in the 1930's and fundamentalist Muslims do the same thing. White supremacists encourage

the nostalgia of racial segregation and the use of racial slurs on non-whites, Muslims promote the separation of Muslims and non-Muslims and they're not allowed to be friends with non-Muslims, Muslims are also invited to use slurs on infidels and Jews. Far-right political parties want to keep all immigrants who are critical of their host countries quiet and want them to shut up, and Islam wants non-Muslims and Muslim reformists to be quiet and stop criticizing Islam. Both the Far Left, the Far Right and the Islamic Political Ideology have the willingness to sacrifice lives for the sake of their ideas, by creating a new world from dead ashes. Both the Far Left, the Far Right and the Islamic Political Ideology want to use the bill of rights to destroy the law of duties; they want to replace it with electric and divisive political systems that benefit only some, not all. Both the Far Left, the Far Right and the Islamic Political Ideology want to persecute sexual minorities whose lifestyle they find abnormal, immoral and undesirable; some of the groups want sexual minorities to die. Both the Far Right and the Islamists are very good at showing the appearance of moderation, while behind the scenes they prepare for evil deeds against ideas that they find decadent and unifying. Both the far right and the Islamists are very good at playing the victim; Muslims play the victim by crying Islamophobia when they are challenged, whereas far right supremacists cry the victim over Whites being under siege, yet they both have the willingness to destroy or kill anyone who does not look like them or share their views. Both the Far Left, the Far Right and the Islamists are used to the idea of keep people ignorant and in control so that they can go on and use them them as puppets for their destructive purposes. A Danish politician from the far-right Danish People's Party was welcomed in New Zealand with open arms in 2013 and she was welcome by the Maoris performing their dance, she was so shocked that she went on to say that the Maori culture is uncivilized and a grotesque mark of multicultural worship. Marie Karup went on to say that she did not like way the Maoris were performing their dance and rituals and she felt like an idiot. Other white supremacists in New Zealand and elsewhere where so happy that Marie Karup spoke her mind and equating that not all cultures should be given the highest honor according to their view of the world and their nations. Some white supremacists were even wondering if it is not the time for the Maoris to move from their cultural evolution. This crazy creature that has her roots to the Vikings that also were uncivilized goes to another country and expresses a controversial view that is welcome by some white supremacists because she is a Caucasian. If it was a non-Western immigrant who was criticizing whites in New Zealand for the way they treat the Mioris, hell would break loose with racial slurs, death threats and the individual would be told to leave New Zealand and if it was someone like me being critical of the Danes in Denmark, nationalist Danes of her kind would be the first to condemn me and tell me to leave the country, not just Danes like her, but white nationalists from other white majority countries would attack me racially and verbally, sometime violently as well. This is how the far right wants to keep non-whites quiet in white majority countries by threatening them with deportation if they dare criticize their host countries and how non-whites are treated there, especially if the non-whites write articles on newspapers, speak to the media or are named for a specific post. The goal for the far right is to make so uncomfortable for the non-whites so that the non-whites can leave or the use of force through hate crimes and possibly a plan for another holocaust. Their goal, just like the islamists is to eradicate those whom they view as impure from the face of the Earth and create a Fourth Reich. Some white supremacists are even willing to work with Asian supremacists as allies to eliminate Africans and other people whom they view as undesirable, and then turn back against the Asians themselves, some white supremacists would want to work with Arab, Persian and Turkic supremacists to eliminate Jews from this world. Muslim fundamentalists also plan to kill anyone who does not want to be a Muslim, especially if you are not among the people of the book(Jews and Christians), you either convert or die and if you are a Jew and a Christian who does not want to convert to Islam, you are going to be treated as a dhimmi, in other words, a second class citizen and you have to pay the Jizya or the protection tax to stay alive. At the same time you are not going to enjoy the same rights that Muslims have in a majority Muslim country, white supremacists like Marie Karup and company also believe in the nosology of treating non-whites as second class citizens in white majority/minority countries with fewer rights or no rights at all. Let me tell the Danish nationalists and other white nationalists who to exotic countries, even those white nationalists who are from my own birth country and call those cultures uncivilized, first of all you were not forced to go there, don't hide behind the arguments of free speech like many hypocrites like you do when you're trying to insult the cultures of the countries that host you because they happen to be non-whites or poor that matter and second of all when I am critical of you, the Norwegians, the Icelanders, the Finns, the Poles and other groups of Europeans you are quick to shut me up and threaten me with deportation and violence, you are quick to tell me that I was not invited in Denmark or Norway and so on and I must go back to my country of origin, you are quick to use racial slurs on me and any other immigrants who speak their minds through articles, the media and so forth. You are quick to play the anti-white victim card when another group of Caucasians stand up for equal rights for all. You are quick to tell me that I am not French or another person of color is not English, Dutch, German, Swedish, Hungarian, Russian, Portuguese and even American forgetting that there are Singaporean Caucasians, there Kenyan Caucasians, there are Namibian Caucasians,there are Japanese Caucasians, Mexican Caucasians, Angolan Caucasians etc. People like you accuse me of being a Liberal, a Leftist and a cultural Marxist, yet you have the nerves why don't you bring the Danes, the Norwegians, the Swedes and other groups of Caucasians who are in non-white countries back to their respective lands and create a segregated world with segregated nations by race? You, Marie Karup, you, the Dane who went to New Zealand by choice if you did not like there why did you go? You knew that the Maoris are indigenous New Zealanders, didn't you? Didn't you know anything about the Maori dances? I am not even a Maori myself, but let me tell you that that's how they do things when they welcome a politician from another country, Danish lady. It has an important play in their history, you ignorant Dane. When I write critical articles about the Danes using the N-word, people like you wish that I leave Denmark, when I write articles about discrimination on the Danish labor market, people like you use the N-word to me and tell me to leave Denmark, people of your kind what all immigrants to keep quiet and behave like small children, people like you want to treat even hard working immigrant as abusive men treat their wives and, tell them they're welcome as long as they remain second class citizens who should go back to their countries. If you were in Australia and you were welcomed by the Aboriginal Australians, you would use the N-word on them and call them uncivilized because they are not like people of your kind. Poor sud, white supremacists like you need to civilize yourselves because you are bunch of savages who are not different from those of the Muslims Brotherhood and Tribalists who divide the world into the pure and the impure. You want to act like you're the masters of teaching others how to be civilized, but you and your Neo-Nazi collaborators come with no solutions to the fears that your nation and other nations face, oh no, you just know how to use racial slurs, hate and encourage discrimination in the workforce. People like you really enjoy the idea of seeing riots in disadvantaged areas so that you can raise debates and gain more points from concerned voters. Your party had a change to govern your country, why didn't you guys want to govern then? Because you guys are really incapable of governing and you know that one mistake can cost you the vote in the next election. Your party has never been suited to govern because you're not a clean party, but a polluted party with polluted ideas. Even the people from the Sweden Democrats are more smarter than you, at least they are able to govern their country. The United Kingdom Independence Party has the ability to govern the UK because they have more common sense than you, even Marine Le Pen from the French National Front has more common sense than you, no one from the Danish People's Party and other similar stupid political parties measure up to Marine Le Pen. Marine Le Pen can win the French elections and become president in 2017, how about you and your political party? Yet you're going to New Zealand and insult people who have not done anything to you, people who haven't used a racial or ethnic slur on you and your people, yet you somehow give yourself the right to go there and insult their way of life because the Maoris are non-whites, we did not see you open your freaking mouth to any White New Zealanders out there, did you? To them you were too busy being politically correct because you knew what the consequences would be if you opened your mouth, I guess your cracker brain did not drive you crazy enough to say rubbish, you and your fellow throwbacks have ideas have no right to be respect, just like ideas of Islam have no right to respected because both of you are two sides of the same coin as I described earlier on this chapter. Although the criticism of Islam and Muslims has nothing to do with racism and hate, far right movements across the Western are doing exactly what the Muslim Brotherhood plans to do because they both want the remove ideas and people whom they view as impure from the face of the planet and create a Caliphate or the Fourth Reich; there is no such thing as a moderate Islam or radical Islam, Islam is Islam in its purest form. There is no such thing as the moderate as a moderate far right or supremacist group, once a supremacist, always a supremacist, once an ultranationalist, always an ultranationalist, once a far leftist, always a far leftist; you shall know them by their fruits. By the way, did you know that far right extremists in white majority countries also happen to have terrorist cells in the West and Russia? They use those cells for plan for hate crime and assassinations against people whose views they do not like or make plans for state coups to overthrow democratically elected governments so that they can continue to enforce fascism, Nazism, White supremacism with means of dictatorships, just like Mussolini and Hitler did in the 1930's. Far right political parties also exist in Turkey, Japan, Thailand, Zimbabwe and some other non-white majority countries in fact, in Japan there are also Japanese Nazis who have some kinds of beliefs about themselves being above everyone else, Japanese Nazis, can you believe it? I find it amusing and I laugh out loud when I hear such people making a fool out of themselves. What motivates far right extremists everywhere to use racial slurs and beat the people that they do not seem fond of? In my view, I think you need to look at it from different nuances and it depends on which country you're looking at, if you take the example of Zimbabwe and the rise of ZANU PF that rise was rooted due to racial segregation in Zimbabwe, a country where Blacks are the majority and whites are a minority, but Blacks did not not have equal rights as whites did in Zimbabwe, which was known as Rhodesia back then. Blacks were treated like second and third class citizens in Rhodesia and they had no rights to own farmlands, these far right policies lead to the rise of another far right political party that was determined to stand up for the dignity of blacks in Rhodesia, that's when Robert Mugabe and the ZANU PF came and fought hard against the Apartheid government in Rhodesia, until it became Zimbabwe in 1980, then 20 years later the current president made plans to give the farming lands that were owned by white zimbabweans to black zimbabweans, this resulted to many white farmers in zimbabwe being thrown out of the country and some were even killed. In this case, discrimination and racism lead to another discrimination and another form of racism. In the Western world the rise of the far right is the result of many local populations feeling like the establishment is not listening to them and they feel like the political establishment does not take them seriously, especially when it comes to the issues of immigration, islamic immigration and asylum seekers. Another reason why the is a rise on the far right and Neo-Nazi groups in Europe and other parts of the white majority societies is because of the killing of white farmers in both Zimbabwe and South Africa by poor black activists. Western countries have been ignoring the rise of radical activists and post-holocaust deniers, profane Hitler and Mussolini worshippers. The refugee crisis has strengthened the rise of far right parties in Europe because the established politicians have not raised serious questions about whether Germany will have Germans in 2055, whether Italy will have Italians in 2040, whether France will have ethnic French people in 2038, whether Britain will have ethnic Britons in 2047 etc. , I guess you get my point, when the establish political parties on the left and the right do not raise serious debates on such issues, which I am going to cover more on chapter 8, they give power the barbarian people who are like dangerous animals with the willingness to kill for sports, just like the indominus rex from Jurassic World. When those savages take over they act like they are on drugs and they kill for passion because they love attacking people who are of a different race than their own. In my opinion, all forms of extremism is bad and destructive for our societies, whether it is the far right, meaning far right parties, white nationalists, white supremacists, Neo-Nazis, supremacist Jews, black nationalists, mixed race supremacy, Asian nationalists, Arab nationalists, Hispanic supremacists, tribalists, religious fundamentalists of any kind because when they are given platforms they use those platforms to attack the very ideas that have given their voices and use it against anyone who does not look or think like them. On the Far Left you also have extremists like the Communists, the Marxists, the Lenninits, the Maoists and other group of Leftists who have committed acts of genocide as the Far right and the Islamists to sacrifice lives for the sake their ideal. Extremism, whether it is political or religious is all about creating new heavens on Earth, even those who do not believe that there is a heaven and a hell want to create new heavens here, but in order for that to happen lives have to be sacrificed to get rid of what they believe to be the impure and leave empty vacuums for people and ideas that they find pure and refreshing, anyone questioning ideas from the Klan is either ostracized, faces death threats, treated as a traitor or in the worst case scenario, those who question ideas from the Klan are killed because they are viewed as enemies from within that need to be slaughtered. Anyone leaving the Klan faces death threats, violence or death for betraying what the ideologies consider as pure. The Far Right and the Islamists hold more extremist views than anyone else, but the Far Left is not far behind; around the world in countries that are governed by elements from the far left, there is more dictatorship, more poverty and corruption. When extremists from the the Left, the Right and the Muslim community are in the minority they demand rights and complain about not given platforms for freedom of expression, but when they grow in numbers and become the majority they deny those bill of rights to anyone that does not share their philosophies or anyone that belongs to another race, tribe, religion, political view, social class, sexual orientation, gender etc., it is all about them wallowing in self-pity so that naive activists can feel sorry for them and tell others about their rights, otherwise those people are going to go underground, like I said before; for all I care if they go underground, they can stay there anyway because they are in charge of their own behaviors and cannot make demands that they do not deserve by trying to manipulate the system so that they can get their way and get by with their stupidity. The idea that somehow that all points of views are equal and who are we to judge leads to a situation where it encourages radical affiliations of any kind to find ways of dismantling the bill of rights that have given them the liberties to be the useful idiots they are. Totalitarian ideologies fight for total control.

CHAPTER 6

WHAT ABOUT THE JEWS?

Many Jews are beginning to leave Europe and going back to their ancestral homeland, Israel; some even choose to immigrate to countries like: United States, Canada, Australia, New Zealand and other parts of the new world because they do not feel safe in Europe anymore. You might wonder why are Jews not feeling safe in Europe anymore? Isn't anti-Semitism over? This is where it gets more interesting; Jews do not feel safe in Europe because of the anti-Semitism that is coming from Muslim immigrants who live in Europe, they sand for most of the violence against the Jews than the far right Europeans do, not to undermine the anti-Semitism on the Far right, but also on the far left. Despite Jews facing persecution, discrimination, racism and anti-Semitism for centuries, and even the Holocaust, Jews have made significant efforts to adapt in their host societies and I can say personally as a non-Jew that they are really resilient and strong minded, but enough about that right now. Muslim immigrants from the Middle East, Africa and South East Asia on the other hand to not integrate as well as the Jews because they are too busy making demands that suit their religious and cultural customs by imposing gender segregations in swimming pools, the imposition of halal meat, the imposition of prayer rooms at work, more mosques and more madrassas funded by rich Muslim countries, gender segregations in political and job meetings and the criminalization of criticizing Muslims and Islam by using hate speech laws, which were well intended by the way against their host societies, you know what? All immigrants are now paying the price for it, even those of us who are not Muslims. Muslims are encouraged to hate Jews because they are Jews, not because they are Israelis, but Jews because in their view, killing one Jew is like killing fifty non-Jewish believers, of course, Muslims are taught to hate all non-Muslims, but mostly the Jews because they never recognized Mohamad as a prophet 14 centuries ago when Islam was more of a religion and less of a political movement. Muslims even teach their small children that Jews are monkeys and apes from a very young age. In the history of Europe there has been a strong amount of hatred towards the Jews for 10 centuries propagandized by the Church and society, Jews were blamed for many sins as well as crime, curses, diseases, Communism, Marxism, Capitalism and the spread of poison. Jews were also blamed for demagoguery, self-righteousness, warmongering behind the scenes and the world's imperfections. During the last centuries Jews did not have the same rights as the majority populations and they were put in ghettos, even in countries like: Denmark, Sweden, Norway, France, Hungary, Germany, Austria, Russia, Poland and some other European countries. Even in countries like: United States, Canada, Turkey, New Zealand, South Africa and few other countries that I could mention, Jews were still facing anti-Semitism and they still do. During the Second World War Hitler and his Nazi counterparts were destroying most of the shops and other properties owned by the Jews. The Grand Mufti of Jerusalem, Mohammad Amin Al-Husseini who was a Palestinian and an Arab nationalist looked for Muslim volunteers in Azerbaijan, Bosnia, Albania and even some non-Muslim volunteers in Croatia and Yugoslavia to join his SS movements and for the genocidal ethnic cleansing of the Jews. While this Arab nationalist knew that Jews were massacred and impressed by the way the Nazis did it, he was the architect of the final solution, of course Arabs and other Muslims will always make excuses for the Grand Mufti because many of them see him as a hero for taking a standing against the Zionists in Palestine, oh my god, I do not know what to say about this and I wonder if I am living in another world. We all know that 6 million Jews were massacred by the Nazis, the Fascists and the Grand Mufti of Jerusalem no matter what Muslims and other Holocaust deniers say about the history of WWII. Liberals, weak Conservatives and Muslims themselves see Muslims as the new Jews whenever Islam, the Quran and Mohammedans are challenged; Liberals and weak Conservatives see Muslims as underdogs who need to protected, even from Jews who are critical of the Islamic belief system, but Muslims are quick to deny the Holocaust and look up to Hitler and Mussolini. Then we all thought it was over, but no, it is not over yet; since the creation of the only civilized country in the Middle East, the State of Israel in 1948, Jews have faced massive opposition from both the Left, the Right and their Muslims neighbors in Middle East and elsewhere. Jews are being blamed for the deaths of Palestinians and other Arabs by the media, Muslims, Libertarians, the far right, the far left and even Africans who fight for the "Palestinian Cause". The question that i ask myself sometimes, before I carry on with this topic is this, what do Black Africans, Pakistanis, Indians,

Indonesians, Bangladeshis, Malaysians, Muslim Chinese, Japanese and other non-Arab Muslims have in common with Arab Muslims? Besides sharing a common religion and common first and last names? What else do they have in common with the Palestinians? Nothing; to Black Africans and Black Americans who convert to Islam, what do you have in common with a Middle Eastern Arab, besides sharing a common religion and adopting Arab first and surnames? Nothing, Arabs have an array of intolerance over non-Arabs whom they see as inferior species, even those who are Muslims; racism in Middle Eastern countries is met with denial from Muslim Middle Easterners as a whole because they have a culture of being in denial of their wrongdoings. Another questions that I have for non-Arab Muslims who also happen to be mostly non-whites, why do you think that rich Arab countries use your peoples as slave labors when it comes to building bridges, stadiums, towers and other infrastructure with no pay and very little food ? Why do you think that Indian, African, Bangladeshi, Pakistani, Indonesian, Filipino, Thai and other non-Arabs/Middle Easterners who work as domestics see their hands being cut and face all other forms of abuse? To a Somali and an Eritrean who does not see himself/herself as an African and who thinks that Bantu Black Africans are slaves, how do you think you are viewed by an Arab Muslim or another Middle Eastern Muslim? I really want to challenge you to ask yourselves these questions and take you and your peoples seriously, that is why you need to think twice before thinking about trying to fight for the "Palestinian Cause" and the "Islamic cause", you are not going to like many of the things that I am going to say to you, and you are even going to be extremely offended by my statements; the questions that I have asked you about about all the unfairness that a non-Middle Eastern Muslim faces in the Middle East is about to let you know that even in some of the most racist white majority countries, you would never face such an injustice, Middle Eastern Muslims are inherently more racists on non-whites than the average European, even at the Mecca where you meet Muslims from different races, non-Arab Muslims who do not have a light skin tone are treated more like dogs than their fellow Caucasian, Arab, Turkic and Persian Muslims whom they claim to be more pure Muslims than Africans, Indians, Indonesians, Malays, Pakistanis, Sri Lankans, Kurds etc., An Arab Muslim sees you as lowlife species who are not pure Muslims, but thinks of you as useful idiots who were defeated when your peoples got conquered by them at least 8 centuries ago, that's how some of your populations converted to the so-called religion of peace. To a Somali, an Eritrean, a Nigerian Muslim other types of African Muslims, especially to a Somali who views other Blacks with thicken African hair as slaves, my message to you is that you are a joke, you are really a joke; to an Arab, any other Middle Eastern Muslims, Bosnians and Albanians you are just Negro slaves who are the lowest of the low and the most impure of Muslims. An Muslim Arab and any other Middle Eastern Muslim view you as servants with no value, yet you are there trying to fight for the same people who do not see you as pure Muslims as them because of the color of your skin. You are seen as people who are of no value and people with lowest IQ on the planet. The racism I have experienced by Middle Easterners is far more worse than the racism I have ever witnessed in any Western country, just look at the way Moroccans, Algerians, Libyans, Tunisians and sometimes even Egyptians treat black Africans who live in their countries, they treat them worse than the way Romanies and Blacks are treated in Hungary. Those Middle Eastern North Africans treat African blacks more worse than the way blacks are treated in Russia, they do not even see themselves as Africans, some would even go so far to think that they are Europeans or Caucasians and their countries are not in Africa. What really shocks me is the ignorance of the majority of Muslims who are not even Arabs, the ignorance that they have about their own religion, Islam; the idea that Islam is a religion that brings unity among races is an illusion, it is a lie and Arab Muslims know it; Islam is a vehicle of Arab supremacism and imperialism which was spread through the use of Jihad and the subjugation of non-Muslims anywhere on Earth. That is why I do not respect the Middle Eastern culture, especially the Arab Muslim culture. Why don't non-Arab Muslims realize that Islam is the only religion on the planet that survive in the Arabic language environment? Every non-Arab who converts to Islam or is a devout practicing Muslim undergoes a complete change of personality, culture, identity, heritage and a sense of belonging, this has an effect in all of his/her life. The individual is required to have Islamic names, which are Arabic names, he/she is also required to learn the Arabic language, dresses and thinks like Arabs. The individual begins to like the things that Muslim Arabs like and hates what Muslim Arabs hate, the individual in this case does not hesitate to hold Arab political views on issues of Palestine, Iraq, Syria, Lebanon and the Arab League. This is how many non-Arab Muslims become prisoners of their own belief system; while they are concerned about the issues of the Arab world, they often ignore their own national interests and allow it to fade away because Islam is both a state, a religion, a legal movement and a political movement. The only groups of Muslims who have withstood domination from the Arabs are the Turks and their Turkic fellowmen; they at least have kept their cultures and ways of life, despite adopting the Arab religion as theirs. The truth is that Islam is an Arab religion founded by an Arabic Middle Eastern prophet for Middle Eastern Arabs and other groups of Middle Easterners its book, the Quran is written in Arabic, which is its language. Non-Arab Muslims need to realize Islam is biased against them because they devote themselves to a religion whose language is foreign and hard for them to grasp, that is why when non-Arab dark skinned Muslims are more concerned about the Palestinian cause, instead of what is going on in their own countries, some Muslim Arabs just laugh at them on the corner, thinking about those dark-skinned individuals and other non-Arab Muslims as their cannon fodders. I know that many non-Arab Muslims are going to be offended by my statements or even make excuses for Islam, but the fact remains that Islam's goal is to bring domination to the world under the Arab rule and all non-Arab Muslims are just slaves and they want to be slaves for the Arab and give their lives for them, especially the dark skinned Muslims who come from many of the world's poorest countries. Those are the same Arab countries that treat those non-Arab Muslims like dirt and they even spit on them, and make them work under conditions that are inhumane, merciless, uncompassionate and unreasonable.This idiotic desert religio-political ideology has given us nothing but terror, enslavements, racism, tribalism, homophobia, anti-Semitism(even though Arabs themselves are Semites), religious discrimination, political discrimination, killings of apostates, prosophobia, gynophobia, epistemophobia, catagelophobia, illuminati phobia, cynophobia, hadephobia, automysophobia, melophobia, potophobia, swinophobia, judeophobia, afro phobia, trypanophobia and all the other phobias that the so-called religion of peace holds. Let me be honest with you: Islamophobia is a lie, phobias are irrational, but the fear of Islam and Muslims is rational; they burn people alive, behead people, spread worldwide terrorism, the killings of those who critique Islam, the amount of death threats the send to those who criticize Muslims and the Quran, they do not want to recognize crimes committed under Islam by their fellow believers, they are racists towards non-whites who speak out against Islam, they want to enforce sharia law, people like Geert Wilders and Lars Viks are living in fear in their own countries because of something that they did that did not please Muslims and I can go on and on about this situation for a very long time, but you can see where I am going with this. I know that countries like Indonesia, Senegal, Mali, Malaysia, the Maldives and Egypt are making serious efforts to accommodate moderation and punish their extremist fellow believers and I really appreciate what they are doing, but the fear of Islam is and still remains rational. There are many Muslims whom I respect a lot because if many of their fellow believers were like them, then the Western world would be safer, even the rest of the world would be safer indeed. The Muslims whom I am talking about are: Tarek Fatah, Zuhdi Jasser, Naser Khader, Dr. Nidal Alsayyed, King Abdullah II, President Abdel Fattah El-Sisi, Irshad Manji, Salah Choudhury, Salim Mansur, Kasim Hafeez, Dr.Tawfik Hamid, Rama Yade, President Abdurrahman Wahid, Nemat Sadat, Abdalla Mwidau, Ed Husain, Mohammad Zahran and other prominent Muslims who have the best interest of mankind. By showing our support to them, instead of caving into the radical ones, we are giving them the power to believe that they can win the battle against the extremists. There are many Muslims in the world who reject the interpretation of the Islamic verses in the Quran that call for violence against non-believers, in other words, those Muslims dismiss the political doctrine of the religion; they reject bigotry against non-Muslims, sexism, homophobia, the killing of apostates, racism, hate speech rhetorics, religious fundamentalism, terrorism and other evil deeds. I do not understand why we are ignoring them and embracing terrorists as our allies, knowing full well that those thugs do not have our best interest all; they want our destruction and they will do anything for it. Is it because of oil in the Middle East that many Western oil companies are bowing down to terrorists out of the fear for their careers? Are these the same groups of people who are lobbying our governments? Are these same individuals who are governing us?

Many Jews are leaving Europe because of a high amount of anti-Semitism from both the far right, but especially Muslim immigrants. When I read the newspapers of any kind, I hear about Muslims leaving France, Sweden, Denmark, Germany, Hungary, Italy, Spain, Russia, Austria, etc. They head to United States, Canada, Australia, New Zealand or their ancient homeland of Israel. Jews do not feel like the politicians in many major EU countries are raising serious concerns about anti-Semitism from Muslim immigrants; they feel that politicians in some European countries are too politically correct and want to avoid the issue out of the fear of being called racists, intolerant and Islamophobes. Especially when it comes to the terrorist attacks in France and other

European countries. Jews do no longer feel safe when they wear the kippah out of the fear of facing violence, racism, anti-Semitism and bullying from Muslim immigrants. Many of them do not trust either the Left or the Right to deal with the issue. That is why they either turn to nationalist political parties or leave for Israel. The irony is that there are some far-right parties that are pro-Jewish, parties like the Danish People's Party and the Freedom Party of Austria. There are even Jews who support the National Front (France), even worse the British National Party and some other racist and anti-Jewish political parties because they feel that those are the parties that have their best interests and raise important concerns about Muslim immigration. The problem is that there are many far right anti-Jewish political parties who blame Jews for non-white immigration in white majority countries; there are conspiracy theories about Jews making plans for genocide against white people. Jews are blamed for multiculturalism and Muslim immigration in Western countries and Hungary Jews are seen as a threat to the national security. White nationalists and segregationists even accuse Jews of enslaving Blacks in the United States, and they blame Jews for slavery as a whole. Jews are blamed for the financial crisis because one of the crooks behind it was a Jew. There are Blacks who believe that Jews are more racists than whites towards them and other non-whites. Jews are even accused of using AIDS as a biological weapon to destroy black populations in Africa, I can go on and on, Jews are blamed for everything wrong with this world in general. The Jewish State is accused of not having enough immigrants but complains when white majority countries take a stand against immigration, those are claims from white nationalists. Muslims have hated Jews for 14 centuries because back then there were many Jews who never recognized Muhammad as their last prophet, even though Muslims deny these facts, just look at the way they talk about Jews in Middle Eastern countries. Just look at the way many Muslim immigrants in the West talk negatively about the Jews.

Many liberal Jews value social justice, equality, human rights and they oppose all forms of bigotry, but the problem with liberal Jews when it comes to Muslims is that they are ignoring the new anti-Semitism, which is flourishing in the corners of Muslim communities across Europe, ignoring the hatred from Muslim communities. When someone comes up with such concerns, the liberal Jews view that individual as a racist, a bigot, and a hatemonger. The liberal Jews will do anything to protect Muslims because, in their worldview, they do not want Muslims to be persecuted like the Jews were in WII, what the liberal Jews forget is that Muslims hate Jews because they are Jews, their so-called scriptures encourage them to hate Jews because they are Jews. Those are the same people who would want to drive them to the sea and kill them there. I can understand that many Jews stood up for Martin Luther King Jr. against racism in the USA, many Jews stood against Apartheid in RSA and other types of injustices, but you cannot feel pity for people who want to destroy you and the existence of your kind. Of course, not all Muslims would want to do that, but the problem lies in the fundamentals of the Islamic religion. There are Jews who tell their fellow men to take off or hide their mezuzah to hide their Jewishness, but some Jews are willing to face the risks and keep their mezuzah and kippahs because they want to be free to be who they are in a free society. There has been violence, theft and murder against Jews in Europe primarily by Muslim immigrants. Every Jew in Europe is seen as a foot soldier for Israel and if you are pro-America and pro-Israel in Europe, then you are an endangered specie and you will be unpopular with people from the far left who also hold anti-Semitic views against Israel because of its policies towards the Palestinians whom Liberals see as subordinates who are persecuted by the Jewish State; you are viewed as a Zionist who is defending the Jewish case and so on. While the Jews have built the most civilized country in the Middle East, Muslims from all over the world are too busy hating them, believing that Jews have too much power, you need to be careful with a Jew and complaints about Jews trying to poison their prophets. Such idiotic reasons are holding many Muslim countries from making serious progress because just look at many Muslims countries today and look at Israel. Muslims live in bandage and and chains because their minds are bounded by stories that took place 14 centuries ago, how on earth is it helping them and how is it making them prosperous. Muslims societies happen to places with the most conflicts. By the way, it is time for Europe to stop blaming itself for everything that happens in the Middle East; it is time for America and other Western societies to do the same thing, Muslim societies create their own problems and they are the only ones who can fix them.I hope that I have not repeated myself again and again; Jews are leaving Europe because they feel like many European politicians are choosing others over them, meaning Muslim immigrants, they feel like European mainstream politicians are not tough enough when it comes to dealing with the sources of the problem, which is Muslim immigration, which in its nature is anti-Semitic, what I mean is that Muslim immigrants bring their anti-Semitism with them to Europe and make Jews feel less safe in the continent, that is why there are many who move to their ancestral homeland, Israel where they will feel better protected and Israel deals with Muslim terrorists in a much harsher fashion than Europe. Those who do not leave try to hide their Jewishness or vote for nationalist political parties that want to put an end to Muslim immigration and other types of Third World immigration. Jews on the Right have the right to be concerned about Islamic immigration because with that comes anti-Semitism from

Muslim immigrants who have been encouraged to hate Jews by their families, neighbors, imams, mullahs, muftis etc. Many Jews are very frustrated over Europe's unwillingness to open its eyes on the possibility of an Islamic overtaking of the continent; the thing that has made the situation even more annoying is the influx of Muslim immigrants and refugees from Syria, Iraq, Somalia, Nigeria, Eritrea, Bangladesh, Iran, Morocco, Algeria, Tunisia, Libya, Mauritania, Pakistan, Senegal, Burkina Faso, Gambia, Egypt, etc. Not all Jews go back to their ancestral homeland; some migrate to countries like the U.S. and

Canada. There are many Jews who rightfully are against Islamic immigration because they believe that Islam is not compatible with Western values and many Muslims are more loyal to their religion than they are to their host countries. Another reason why there are many Jews who are against Islamic immigration it is because of demographics and the amount of Muslims living on welfare. But there are Jews who use this situation to promote their Jewish supremacist agenda, such as Eric Zémmour who is a French Jewish journalist. Although Eric Zémmour is against the Islamic immigration for reasons that are valid, he does not just end there; he also has a strong hatred towards Blacks and other non-whites, Eric Zémmour also happens to be misogynistic, sexist, homophobic and condescending. He even defends the role of Marshal Petain who the leader of Vichy when the Nazis invaded France and many other European countries. He is himself very anti-Semitic and very cold towards other Jews. He feels like France has given him everything since the colonization of his ancestors in Algeria. This is the same man who is seen as a filthy Yid, filthy Ikey, filthy Jew by many people who live in French suburbs, no matter the race and the religion. He is also hated by the very extreme far right groups because to them he is just another Yid who cannot stop talking. Eric Zemmour even advocates that France bombs Molenbeek in Brussel, Belgium.Because of Eric Zémmour's racist views towards Arabs and Africans in France, the Black French Cameroonian Comedian, Dieudonne and Alain Soral believe that Jews like Eric Zemmour whom they see as a Zionist who wants to gain power in France. Dieudonné and other anti-Zionists believe that most of the world's crooks are Jews because in their view, Jews are responsible for the financial crisis. The Madoff Affair has been used viewed as a symbol of Jewish greed because it is believed that Zionists are fighting to dominate the world. Zionists are often accused of running ponzi schemes because Jewish charities are not concerned with helping mankind like Christians do; the vast Jewish charities help their own kind, if you want my honest opinion about it, to tell you the truth, I do not know. Eric Zémmour often says that most of drug dealers in France are Arabs and Blacks and he even points out that Arabs and Blacks represent the highest population of inmates in French jails. Although I agree with Eric Zémmour about those facts and his honesty about the situation, I do not agree about racists remarks that he makes on his own people, and other non-whites because he is "white" and he feels empowered to do that, but unfortunately

Eric Zémmour will never be viewed as a white by a white nationalist because he is a Jew, especially in Russia, Germany, Italy, Austria,Sweden, Portugal, United States, Netherlands, Belgium, Hungary, Poland etc. there are many people in these countries that still view Jews like Zémmour as a Raghead, a Yid, an Ikey, a Kike because to them he is not a Caucasian. Jews like Zémmour are often accused of running the media, screwing people everyday and their greed ruining Europe, and America. Some people wish that a new Holocaust happens because Jews are perceived as vile, warmongers, racists etc. Although some of Eric Zémmour's message are valid, his hostility and hatred of non-whites is like chasing his own tail. He keeps biting his tail over and over again, but his message is not resonating to all non-Muslim French people and that is a huge problem; if you want your message to attract more people, sell it and make it attractive to everyone who is equally concerned about the situation,no matter what race the individuals are. When that does not happen, then you have people like Dieudonne M'bala M'bala and Alain Soral who claim that France is run by Jewish slave drivers and the big crooks of the planet are Jews. France is not the only country in the West dealing with the issue of Jews versus other minorities. Not all the Jews who are against Islamic immigration take things too far like Eric Zémmour and those Jews defend the rights of people who have been victims of Islamic bullying, racism, homophobia etc., those are the kinds of Jews I personally respect because they know that when you do not learn from history you are doomed to repeat it. When it comes to Dieudonne and Alain, well, I do not agree with them on many things also, but the truth is somewhere in the middle.

I am not someone who uses an anti-Semitic slur on a Jew and it is extremely rare, unless that individual uses the N-word on me or other Blacks or bullies others just for the sake of bullying. I think that I have said it a million times already that there are many Jews who have reasons to be concerned about Islamic immigration and rightfully so because of the social and cultural changes it brings with it. There are also many Jews who are equally concerned about not just the Islamic immigration, but illegal immigration from the Third World, especially when uncontrolled immigration comes with a cost for the societies that take them in, but Jews are not the only people who agree with the majority mainstream populations of France, United States, Canada, Australia, Germany, Italy, Sweden, Norway, New Zealand, Belgium, Netherlands, Luxembourg, Poland etc., there are also other well integrated and assimilated minorities who agree with the majority mainstream populations from some of the countries that I have just mentioned because they know that illegal immigration also threaten their opportunities to have jobs. The idea that it is only the mainstream Western populations who are against illegal immigration and uncontrolled immigration from Third World countries is wrong on so many levels because legal immigrants and other well suited minorities want to succeed in the societies that took them in; they believe that they have worked so hard to get where they are and they are frustrated that illegal immigrants are given a free ride and rights that they do not deserve. If I could choose between Israel and Arab countries, I would choose Israel over 99% of Arab and other Middle Eastern countries, but in this situation I am going to use a word that many people are not going to find comfortable, not because I am being anti-Semitic, but because I am standing up to a bully. I told you about one of France's most popular journalists, Eric Zémmour who always attacks anyone who does not share his worldview as a leftist. For instance, I do not agree with Dieudonné M'bala M'bala's views on Jews and his jokes about the Holocaust, nor do I always agree with Alain Soral about Jews being responsible for the social conflicts in

France between different ethnic groups, however; Eric Zémmour has somehow contributed to the problems himself when he said that Dieudonné is the product of the French left's multiculturalism, and that it is the Left that taught the French society since May 1968 that it is prohibited to prohibit that people like him shock the rich Leftists. He also believes that it is the Left that has turn the Holocaust into a supreme religion of the French Republic. This Jews bullies anyone who is not non-white because he happens to despise them so much and looks at them as inferior species. This non-conformist commentator is probably seeking for the approval of the Far Right in France and feels like he is the one who holds the high morals about how people need to behave in the Republic. In my eyes, Eric Zémmour is just another field Kike who is using the Islamization of France, patriotism, French nationalism, Conservatism to walk the fine line with the establishment, he even believe that Africans in France are making plans to Africanize France and fears a civil war in the Republic. He is against the France being a multiracial country, while he himself is not European, nor is he an ethnic Frenchman, but a shady Kike originally from Maghreb. He feels threatened because he sees his people the Jews as a privileged group in France. The problem with some

Jews is that they often pursue their ideological fervor to a point of self-destructiveness and it is not clear that those kinds of Kikes are able to maintain a stable equilibrium, even the ones which were in their favor. Their way of thinking is not that different from those of the Muslim Brotherhood, the world's largest terrorist organization, which was established in 1928 to revive the Islamic Caliphate, which ended less than 100 years ago. Not to forget that organizations like Al Qaeda, ISIS, Al Shabaab, Al Nusra, Khorasan, Hamas, Hezbollah, Islamic Jihad and other Muslim terrorist organizations are all part of the Muslim Brotherhood, which is the flagship of all of these terrorist organizations. The ideas from the Muslim Brotherhood are not different from those of Eric Zémmour and Ron Unzes both have ideas to achieve second tier powers to defend their own interests, in order for them to do that, they have to conquer to divide. Kike Supremacists and Mohammedan reactionists believe in the pure and the impure and they both want to do everything to destroy what they believe to be something untouchable. Do not play the anti-Semitic card with me for raising serious issues about this problem; save your breath if you call me an anti-Semitic because no one is above criticism as far as I am concerned. Save your breath if you want to play the Liberal Leftist card with me because I am not going play the games of the evils of empathy by falling into the your ideas of calling anything that does not suit your far right agenda as emotive because you're not even able to tie my laces. Both Kikes are after the approval of France and the U.S. respectively, but that is not how you find it; they believe that they are defending freedom, while they are killing it by hoping to fly above their limits, but crashing slowing to the ground without even knowing it. What they are trying to do is to destroy themselves so much by seeking for other people's validation, if you are not a better you, you will never be better for your country; the desire to see changes being made in your society starts with you first, if you are a broken man in the inside, no matter how you scream about Leftists being the problem or the Far Right being the problem for everything that is happening in your country, how can you expect to pilot a ship when you are sinking emotionally? Do you want to put others in danger? I guess not, I am myself a French-born of Congolese descent and I have no desire to see my beloved birth country, France being a nation where the ethnic Frenchmen are a minority; that will not be France anymore, but a Third World hellhole. I also happen to love Hungary and Portugal and i do not want to see the ethnic Magyars and the

165

ethnic Portuguese be minorities in their own countries, when you see families disillusioned in many of those countries,when fail to identify morality and virtue as part of a political agenda, when the values of fatherhood and when you encourage the need to depend only on government funds you are letting a vacuum open to ideologies that can end to destroy the societies, which many of our predecessors have fought for, lived for and died for, so that we can continue to make our societies more prosperous for ourselves and for the generations after us, the ideologies that declare on us religiously, culturally and ethnically through the use of demographics will bring our prosperous societies to our knees. We cannot allow that to happen and in this case Eric Zémmour is right, but when you look at the word "think", it can be an acronym for the following: Is it True? Is it Helpful? Is it Inspiring? Is it Necessary? Is it Kind? Your words will plant the seeds of influence of either success or failure in the mind of the other. There are no guarantees that your words will be forgiven or forgotten by some because when you choose the behavior, you choose the consequences. My goal here is not to bow down to the people whose ideology is to destroy our way of life and existence by singing kumbaya my Lord with them, seriously if you thought it was the case, you must be joking; you create your own reputation, you create sticks and stones and you have yourself to blame for it, instead of blaming everything on the media all the time, you are like a man who throws a cat out of the wind and beat your wife for it, even though she had nothing to do with your decision to throw your cat our of the window. Respect is earned, loyalty is returned and trust is gained. People who are used to get hurt in their lives struggle to make reconciliations with their past and when they try to places puzzles to build their futures, they cannot seem to connect the dots, they are used to get hurt and expect to hurt others intentionally to gain popularity from the crowd. On the outside they appear strong, confident with a superiority complex because of what they are, but in the inside they are filled with wounds and scars, which they do not want to bring in the public out of the fear of appearing weak like useless plastics, they make efforts and they have courage,but the purpose of their direction fails to leave credible trails. That is why Jews are their own worst enemy, among their own kind, you have those who deny that the Holocaust ever happened, among their own kind you have people who do not want to recognize Israel's existence, among their own kind you have people who do see non-whites as insignificant subhuman animals and I can go on and on on that. A Jew's worst enemy is primarily another Jew; when you get hurt so much, you finally say that you're used to it.

CHAPTER 7

SOME HARSH WORDS FOR MY BLACK BRETHREN AND AFRICA

When I was 12 years old I began to wonder why many Sub-Saharan African countries and other Black majority countries outside Africa struggle to develop, I had many kinds of questions rotating on my mind. There were many things that I saw in my primary country of origin, the Congo that I did not like; I saw the levels of service declining, there is litter everywhere, the roads have holes, people just throwing things in gutters(open sewers); rivers; streams, roads are dirty and often neglected, many unpaved streets, neglected sinkholes and the number of people living without electricity. Despite the fact that many Sub-

Saharan African countries having rivers, streams, lakes, oceans and creeks there are still many individuals who do not have running water in their own homes and they have to go and fetch water in rivers, lakes, streams and so on. Do not get me wrong; there are many people on the African continent who have electricity, but over 50% of Africans do not have access to electricity and this made me very angry because the Congo that I remembered when I left France was more organized and things were on the verge of being in order. My second country of origin, the Democratic Republic of Congo was the second most industrialized country in Africa after South Africa, both the Republic of the Congo and the Democratic Republic of Congo had potentials of becoming First World countries eternally and they could have been very developed nations where citizens can build their own fates had they been governed by the right people. Those countries had the means of becoming industrialized countries and I have even had debates about it with my elder sister because I did not understand why Black majority countries are so impoverished, disorganized and at that time I was only 12 years old and my elder sister was 13. Another thing that aggravated me when 12 was the idea that the former President of the Democratic Republic of

Congo, Mobutu changed the name of the country and the cities, like for instance when he was the President of the country, he changed the name of Congo-Leopoldville to Zaïre, Leopoldville became Kinshasa, Stanleyville became Kisangani, Elisabethville became Lubumbashi and so on, I heard lots of the name changes from my parents, my parent's friends, my aunts and uncles and I just did not understand why he did it. But at the same time I learned from my elder sister that perhaps it had something to do with King Leopold II's genocide of millions of Congolese people when the Democratic Republic of Congo was known as the Belgian Congo, during that time it was a Belgian colony. My sister and I were even talking about Lumumba's assassination and how it happened, although we were too small to know the entire details. When I looked at Northern African countries whose majority populations are Middle Eastern Arabs I sended that countries like Morocco, Egypt, Algeria, Tunisia and Libya are to a certain extend more developed than the vast majority of Sub-Saharan African countries in areas of infrastructure, governance, job creation, standard of living, agriculture, export etc., and many Middle Eastern Arab North Africans do not want to associate themselves with Africa because they're not Black and Africa is a poor continent. You will meet many Arabs from Northern African countries who do not consider their countries as part of the African continent, some because of their light skin believe that they are Europeans; no wander you usually hear about Morocco trying to seek for the European Union membership because many Moroccans do not see themselves as Africans. Their views of Africans are far more worse and and far more derogatory than the average White man's view of Blacks. Black Africans who live in Northern African countries suffer much more racist abuse and injustices than those who live in Western countries, regardless of their religion and nationality. When I looked at Sub-Saharan African countries it seemed like the level of development is slow, back then I did not know that countries like Botswana, Mauritius, Seychelles, Equatorial Guinea and Namibia have high standards of living. Back then I also did not know anything about dictatorship, human rights, corruption and religious fundamentalism; I just assumed that North African countries have far more less problems and are far more prosperous than Sub-Saharan African countries and I also assumed that they are better more organized until me, my siblings, my mother, my aunts and uncles were watching a movie, which I would not want to watch today, the movie that I am talking about is "THE ROOTS", a film about Kunta Kinte and other Africans who were taken as slaves to the U.S. and other parts of the Americas by white settlers and at the same time I heard my father talking about politics with his friends and neighbors, my father was talking about French and Congolese politics and the debates were passionate and constructive. My siblings and I were talking about Kunta Kinte and how it can be related to slavery in other parts of Africa, especially during the times of King Leopold II and Pierre Savorgnan De Brazza. Many of us were very frustrated about slavery, but at times it was quite difficult for me to get the answers that I was looking for when it comes to Black majority countries being far more less organized than other non-Black majority countries. Three years earlier, when I was 9 years old, I asked my mother the same question; I asked her why African countries are for more less developed than European and Asian countries and why is it that no African countries has ever manufactured its own car brand. My mother replied by saying that it is a very complex situation, on one hand you have African politicians who just love to keep power to themselves and do not take care of their own citizens and on the other hand you have Western governments that keep those African politicians in politicians in power for their own interests, so there are shortcomings on both sides. Then 3 years later I began to ask myself those questions, but another thing came into my mind; I heard my father and his friends talked about the derogatory names many Whites used to call them in France, Belgium and other Western countries, I began to hear more about the devaluation of the CFA Franc from my uncles, something that was blamed on France and other European countries. Many of my father's neighbors and others began to blame the white man for the failure of the the African progress, while we Africans sometimes make things worse for ourselves. But there were still other adults whom I know/knew that still blamed the white man for Africa's misery and when I was in the fifth grade in 1993, I learned more about racism, slavery, racial segregation, colonization, Africanism etc. There was one topic that I was not covered, the Arab Slave Trade in Africa or Slavery from Middle Eastern people, something that took place before European settlers set their feet on the African continent. I learned about slavery from the Middle East from family members and friends when I became a young adult. When the civil war broke out in the Republic of the Congo in 1993 I was ashamed of my Congolese ancestry, I was ashamed to be black and

I was ashamed of Africa, I just wanted to leave and go back to my birth country. I was tired of seeing the shots and watching the news about different sides of the Congolese spectrum killing each other because of tribe and political affiliation. I was tired of seeing many of my Congolese countrymen being unfree in their own country, I was tired of seeing the destruction of infrastructure and poverty. I did not not want to associate myself with the African continent anymore because I hear more about civil wars in other African countries. Of course, I heard about the civil war in the Balkans, but I believed that the people of from different countries in the Balkans are able to rebuild their nations much quicker than us. There are some things that I am not going to disclose in this book because when I think about those things they get more on my nerves. I have had a huge debate with my elder sister who did not understand back then why I was ashamed of what I am and sometimes emotions were running high. But what I learned from her is that many African countries have natural resources like commodities and other precious minerals and countries like "Zaire" and other African countries have gold, silver, diamonds and other resources that France and other Western countries do not have, but there are Western multinational firms that take advantage of those resources, which do not benefit the peoples of those nations. The situation leads to the suffering of local populations. Me too I began to be angry at the white man for it, but mostly on my own people. One of the things that really got to me was the way Patrice Lumumba was killed by Caucasian Americans and Caucasian Belgians who were working for their Secret Services because they saw him as a threat. I saw on TV the way Blacks were treated in the USA and the Apartheid in the RSA, I watched some of the derogatory names written in this book that were and are still used against Blacks today and I am very angered about, not just when I was a child, but also later in my adult life. The poverty in the two Congos and the rest of Africa made me really ashamed of being Black and when I was in a middle school in Brazzaville, I told my father that I want to go to a school where there are many Westerners because I was fed up with the way we were taught and I was fed up with the way other students were making noise and I was so tired of the lack of other students to question ideas and other things. I was also very tired of the amounts of students that were in my class, about 120-180 pupils. There were some of my fellow pupils who did not speak French to me because they were either not good at it or they were speaking Kilari to me. If there was one of the languages that I did not want to speak it was Kilari and other local languages from the northern part of the Congo because many of the people who opposed the former democratically elected president of the Congo, Pascal Lissouba were Kilaris or Laris as they are called, some were Mbochi people and other tribes from the northern Congo, while my father belongs to the Sundi tribe, which is one of the tribes from the former Kongo Kingdom and others who were supporting the president. Another thing that really made me very angry was watching programs where many Congolese were not speaking French in France and that drove me to the red field. At the school where I went when I was in my 5th grade there were many of my fellow pupils who were calling me Mr. Frenchman either because I speak French or because I am a native of France. You might wonder why I isolated myself so much, I guess some of my way of thinking were and still are not aligned with the African philosophies and I was also frustrated because I wanted the Republic of the Congo to look like France and I wanted the Democratic Republic of Congo, which was known as Zaire to look like Belgium, not the other way around. At the age of 15 I questioned the mentality of my brethren, I asked our way of thinking, our norms and our culture, when I moved to the RSA with my family I was euphoric to make progress to a country that shares common values with my birth country, a country that is very organized and more technologically advanced than the vast majority of african nations. Of course I met many Black South Africans who did not want to have anything to do with other Black Africans because many of those Black South Africans did not see the RSA as part of the African continent. They were telling many other Black Africans to go back to their countries because they believed that other Africans were coming to steal their jobs, many South African Blacks and Coloreds I met did not have any problems with Middle Eastern people, Indians, foreign whites, African Americans and other groups that are not Black Africans. When I arrived in Denmark and grew a little older I began to blame Whites for the suffering in Africa just like many other Africans do, especially some of my family members. In 1997, the Republic of the Congo faced another civil war and this time it was much more brutal at first I blame it on my Congolese countrymen at first, then later I blamed on my French countrymen, especially when i faced so much racism and bullying for being a black man by Afrikaners and the Danes, especially when I saw some of the people in the French suburb who were treated like dogs. I ended up blaming the West for all the misery of the non-white world. There were many Danes who were asking me some of the most childish and condescending questions like for instance if I spoke African or how can I translate things from Danish to African. Among some of the Africans whom i know, there were many people who believed that AIDS was created in the USA by Caucasians from the vast majority white countries like France, Russia, Italy, Germany and other countries, include Japan to exterminate Black populations in Africa and elsewhere and to be honest with you,I was also one of people who believed it. I felt like Africans and Blacks from other places are blamed for AIDS by whites and Middle Eastern nationalists they always use it as an excuse to tease Africans, I was also tired of the way Blacks are treated by groups of other races, it is as if they treat us like outcasts or the lowest of the low of races, I was so tired of derogatory names that are used on Blacks to psychologically put us down.There were times when I wept by myself silently and frustration is part of the human experience, but there was something that I ignored...I was thinking destructively, and my way of thinking was not helping Africa or making Africa's situation better, another thing I happened to forget was that Africa consists of numbers of countries with their languages, tribes, customs, routines and so on. I had to realize that the change had to come from myself first, but it took a very long time, if I am not a better me I will never be good enough for my birth country, nor will I be good enough for my countries of origin, nor will I be better for mankind. I can use the resources given to me by life to be a "blessing" to my birth country, my home country, the nations where I have my lineages, the society where I am currently living and the rest of humanity. I repeat that charity start at home and that home is first of all the home where am living the experiences of life, that home is the home where my existence permits me to explore new horizons. Africa is a continent, home to more than 50 countries and the largest economies are Nigeria, South Africa,Egypt, Ethiopia, Morocco, Tunisia, Ghana, Algeria and Kenya. Africa is a continent that is witnessing numbers of people joining the middle class very fast and there are Africans who lived in poverty and who are now living better than some of the people from various Western countries, but the reality is that Africa is still the world's poorest continent, despite the fact that many of the world's fastest-growing economies are in Africa, despite countries like Nigeria, Egypt and South Africa having some of the most advanced banking infrastructure on the planet and despite the natural resources the continent possesses. There are still many Africans who live off less than $1 a day. During the days when many Sub-Saharan African countries got their independence, the standard of living over 40% higher than what it is now, that means that because of state coups,civil wars and other conflicts many of those African countries have not make significant progress. To many of my Black brethren, there is something that you need to know and I cannot guarantee that you are going to like it, I cannot ensure that many of the things that I am going to tell you are going to pleasant, but I feel the need to begin to say it anyway. We, Black people are our own worst enemy; we are tearing ourselves apart on our own and yet we blame whites for all of our problems and failures in life, yes we have experienced slavery and unfair treatments during colonial times, we have been and we are still racially abused by other groups of people who call us Darkies, Niggers, Negroes, monkeys, animals you name it, but we are doing a better job of disrespecting ourselves by calling ourselves all of those derogatory names, black rappers are doing a better job of making us look like more of a laughing stock, especially men. We do not stand up for Blacks who face racism in the Middle East and we allow ourselves to be taken advantage of by Middle Eastern Muslims,especially Black Muslims. While we focus on the Trans-Atlantic Slave Trade, but ignore the slave trade from the Middle East and we have failed to commemorate the 120 million Black Africans who were enslaved and killed by Middle Eastern Muslims. Amongst ourselves we declare war on each other based on tribe, political and religious affiliation. In South Africa Black men are at least 10 times more involved in homicides, robbery, rape and other types crimes, more so than White men, Colored men and Indian men. In the United States Black men are 8 times more likely to be involved in homicides and other types of crimes than Whites men, Hispanic men and Asian men. We talk a lot about how great our civilizations were in Timbuktu, Nubia and Egypt, but we are not acting like it these days,believe me. We have had great innovators like Joseph V. Nicholas, Lewis H. Latimer, Granville T.Woods, Norbert Rilleux, William F.Burr, Albert C.Richardson and others but we are failing to follow in their footsteps. We have heroes like Desmond Tutu, Martin Luther King, Malcolm X, Nelson Mandela, Rosa Parks and others who have fought, faced abused, bullied and died so that we can be treated like human beings and create legacies that are better than the ones they had, but yet again we fall in the same ditches. Despite of the fact that we have many opportunities in front of us we continue to struggle forward. We happen to be stuck in the defensive mindset because of the things that happened to politicians like Lumumba, Thomas Sankara and other politicians that were killed by Western political or secret service entities for reasons of national interests,once again we have faced so much injustices and we still do at times, but we cannot blame all our failures on discrimination and the hatred that emanates from whites, Middle Eastern people, Coloreds, Asians, Jews and other groups of other people. The way many of my African brethren litter streets, markets, streams and gutters is utterly depressive and this attracts diseases like malaria, cholera and other types of deadly illnesses, it seems like we do not care at all. It seems our governments do not even care at all. Of course, world powers are always going to defend their interests and we cannot do anything about it, we can control the opportunities that are given to us and make the most of them. The countries that many of our predecessors for independence were in a much better shape and now many African countries are failed states. To my black African brethren and to black brethren from other parts of the world, I would like to tell you that we are our own Klu Klux Klan; we are our own worst enemy, we do not need white and Middle Eastern supremacists to kill us because we are already doing a good job for them by killing each other and by being tribalistic. During the times of slavery we were concerned about seeing a Muslim Arab come and kill us if we did not convert to Islam, back in the time of European settlers we had to worry about similar kinds of injustices, we had to be concerned about racist Middle Eastern people who have kept us slaves for 14 centuries and racist Caucasians politicians who could come up with policies that could put us down. Now we put ourselves down, we do not respect ourselves, yet we expect people from other races to respect us. We have never in our history commemorated Blacks who were enslaved in the Middle East, we have never paid attention to what Black Christians in Darfur are facing, and we never have the courage to stand up for Blacks who face racism in majority Arab countries and another majority Middle Eastern countries and yet we want to talk about Pan-Africanism, we want to speak of the "United States of Africa", we want to speak to the nation of Africa, dear God, if you actually exist, I just want to tell you honestly that we Blacks are our worst enemy. We are not even thinking about the fact that we make our choices to attack each other, now that we are free, we do not even question anything about our traditions, cultures, tribal norms, parental instincts, educational abilities and so forth; we do not even value the freedom that we have, the freedom that people like Malcolm X, Nelson Mandela, Martin Luther King, Rosa Parks, Lumumba, Desmond Tutu, Mohammad Ali and those before them who fought, bled and died so that we Blacks who were once called "savages", "slaves", "Negroes", "monkeys" "servants" by both Muslim Middle Easterners and Caucasians to be treated like decent human beings. You can mind your own affairs, but where you have a brother, that brother will interfere in your life and trying to tell you how to live and sometimes gossip about you and your family behind your back, especially in different African communities. Because we Blacks have a collectivist culture, we use it as an excuse to tell others what to do and how to live. Our collectivist culture is a blessing, but also a curse because we are not good at using it to our advantage because we do not lift each other's spirit, but destroy one another. I can give you an example of many Congolese people and other Africans who know me and my family, those are the same people who interfere in my family's affairs and tell my father and even my mother sometimes that we are stupid and uneducated, while they, themselves have a lot of crap going on in their families, when are we Black Africans going to mind our own businesses and stop meddling in a brother or a sister's affair? They do not just stop there, but go around and gossiping about lots of things that are so irrelevant,there is a lot of spite, jealousy, gossip and negligence going on amongst ourselves, yet we do not want to recognize it and do something about it. We Blacks are not the only people who have cultures that are collective, we are not the only race that has traditions, norms, authoritative ways of parenting, religious beliefs and so on, the difference between some different groups and us is that other groups have questioned some of the things in their norms, traditions,cultures etc, in order for them to embrace enlightenment,which leads to progress,while many of us refuse to do so because of our stubbornness; when that happens it produces a negative energy, that is why there are many Black Africans like me and others who distance themselves from the African communities as a whole because when we are a negative influence on one another it influences our abilities to carry out our duties and competence at the same level as whites and Asians. Just look at South Africa under Apartheid it was a first world country, not that I am defending Apartheid in any shape or form, but the African National Congress has failed to keep South Africa a developed country, but a developing country with a high crime rate, Jo'burg was a very clean city before many Black South Africans and other Black Africans moved there, but now it is dirty and unrecognizable.Instead of encouraging Blacks to take control of their lives and be self-sufficient, the ANC and other black nationalist groups go for land reforms to take the farming lands that are cultivated by white farmers away and give it to inexperienced black farmers, just because their ancestors lived there. Well, is that how you honor your ancestors? Do you do it by being a laughing stock? The ANC has not taken a stand against the killings of white farmers who are responsible for the farming structure of South Africa by uneducated black men who have the unwillingness to take responsibility for their own lives,those are the same men who kill black farmers who have the willingness to make RSA great . Zimbabwe was once the breadbasket of Africa,but now it is a third world hellhole because the man who is running that country gave the farming land to incompetent black men who are not experienced in running farms, now many of those farms are run by the Chinese. We, Black Africans talk about how African countries like Botswana, Namibia, Mauritius, Cape Verde and Seychelles are making progress, but what are we doing to follow their footsteps? What kind of actions have we been taking recently to make our nations successful? How are things working for us right now? We talk about the idea of being poor and "having one's own dignity" than being rich and a slave, are you kidding me? When you are poor, you are not free, but a slave of your own destructive mind that keeps you in that environment. The person who is responsible for your misery is still worshiped by you because you believe that he is protecting you from the white man. Many of African countries and some black majority countries outside Africa still depend on foreign aid and most of those nations are still among the most corrupt and the most impoverished on the planet. We are not realizing that our societies are reflections of our own incompetence because we have ignored our inner rivalries and our own demons, in many African countries you have populations that live of less $1 a day, yet we are too busy blaming the white man for all our problems and failures in life. Just look at the results, how is it working for us? We are in chains and we are still prisoners of our own mindsets and beliefs;we are prisoners of our own mentality. Those of us who are religious pray to different Gods for peace, prosperity and the well-being of our nations, but we forget that prayer alone does not do the work, our actions have got to speak louder than our own words. What do we expect? Do we expect that God will come down and make our nations prosperous? Do we expect God to come down like he did to the Israelites that were slaves in Egypt? Do we expect miracles to happen so that Africa can be rich and prosperous again? Well, the problem with us Black Africans is that we have an easygoing attitude towards life and we live without thinking about tomorrow; when we live amongst ourselves, we often realize that we are our own worst enemy, I do not know how many times I have said that I am an Atheist, but if you are a black man or black woman who believes in God, you should know that if God exists, he helps those who help themselves. I do not believe that God will come down and make black majority countries prosperous; we are the ones who have to make our nations prosperous, whether God exists nor not. Of course I do not believe in God, however; if you want to see results, then act. You have not because you ask not, you do not experiment because you don't act, you do not act because you expect things to just fall on you from the sky and that is why we as a third world are underdeveloped, poor and dirty because we do not take enough initiatives to create support systems such as clean water,welfare, infrastructure and education. Speaking of education, in many African countries education is basic and minimal. There are many people on the African continent who cannot afford education for their children and without education many do not have chances to have high paid job. Another thing that aggravates me is that there are many families on the continent who have so many children, but they're not able to support them, that's where religion comes in again because according to them God talks about multiplying and creating families, if there is a God, he would not have told those people to have children without them showing that they are able to support the kids financially, so stop using religion as a matter of excuse for your recklessness. Many African parents use God's so-called commandments as an excuse to discipline their children, especially the one that says "Obey your parents so that you can live longer on this Earth" and "Your parents are God's representatives in the world" well, what about the idea of your parents leading by example? What about stop using any religious book as an excuse to make your children obey you? What about stop playing God to your children? Hello, I do not care whether God exists or not, the fact we suppress ideas, creativity and other things that is why we are where we are and we are truly getting what we deserve. We want our children to follow on our footsteps, instead of letting them explore their own uniqueness and develop their own sense of individuality. We think we are impressing God by worrying about what other fellow Africans think of us, but we are creating our psychological barriers because we do not have the willingness to explore new territories, instead we seek for other people's approval. Political system in many African countries are poorly developed and there is a little civic public participation, which raises a widespread of anger at politicians whom we have chosen to worship as Gods because we believe that they are our champions, while they do the opposite once they govern our countries because those politicians line their own pocket. This leads to high levels of widespread corruption and the lack of accountability, always blaming former colonial powers for our own stupidity. We have made the choice to scare foreign investors who are willing to develop infrastructure and other kinds of essential social services because as soon as we organize ourselves as groups of nations,something always goes wrong because we let our problems grow and expect someone else to come and fix them for us. We complain about foreign assistance in Africa, but we allow ourselves to keep receiving it because we do not have the competence to lift ourselves from our misery. No wonder we are perceived as people who were never advanced and had no leaders of any consequence. Instead of using money to progress the independent nations, whose independence many of our predecessors fought and died for,we are busy spending it on killing each other like a bunch of wild apes, while making excuses about things taking time, well for how long? So things are just going to take time just like that, that is why we cannot even progress our civilization. We complain about colonial powers like Sweden, Germany, France, Britain, Italy, Spain, Portugal and Belgium diving Africa, but what have we done about it? Nothing, Africa is not the only place on the planet that has experienced colonialism, how come Asian and South American countries are ahead of African countries? Did they find a magic wand so that they can develop their nations? No, they did not; they developed their nations despite dictatorships and troubles in those places, another thing that I would like to add is that we blacks do put little value on the individual, just look at what is happening to sexual minorities across all of Africa and some other black majority countries outside the black continent. I know that homophobia exists elsewhere besides the Third World, but I do not see sexual minorities from the Western world standing up for sexual minorities in Africa and abroad.To my African brethren who are against same sex relationships and lifestyles, it is not your job to make a homosexual man/woman straight, you might now agree with their lifestyle, something that you are entitled to, but beating them up and bullying them does not make them straight, live your life and let them live theirs.If they feel like they can be straight because of a certain belief, then let them.When you look at countries from the Western world, the Americas and sometimes even a fee Asian countries, you will realize that the root causes of their prestige and power is first of all their abilities to place so much value upon the individual, another factor that lead to their dominance is curiosity and then what we cannot ignore is that many of these advanced societies used technology and science to make lots of major changes across Europe and other advanced continents, those changes came with a price, but they held on to their vision for prosperity, that is how the Western world became free from pariochal system, which many of us Africans are still struggling to deal with, how many of us will admit it? That is why some Europeans believe that if it was not for them, Africa would still be a shithole. People are stealing from each other, especially in many African cities and in some Western countries it is not that different, let us take a country like the United States for example in many black neighborhoods there is a lot of crime and blacks are killing other blacks, there are some black kids who do not want to go to school because school is only for white people, instead they go around and sell drugs and 75% of blacks under 30 who lose their lives in those neighborhoods are killed by fellow African American men. We have no love for ourselves and call each other derogatory names, yet we are infuriated when a non-black calls us derogatory names, if we do not value ourselves and if we do not respect ourselves, how can we expect others to respect us? Whether those groups of people are whites, Hispanics, Jews, Middle Easterners, Asians, Native Americans, Other types of Amerindians and even biracial people. I am well aware and well prepared about the fact that some of my black brethren who are reading this chapter will accuse of of acting white, they will accuse me of being a house-Negro or a field-Nigger for raising this serious topic, some will even go so far to say that I am a self-hating black man, fair enough, at least I do admit that when I was 12 years old I was a self-hating black boy, now that I am a grown man with a sense of awareness about what goes on around the world and in different societies, I am proud to be black and we blacks are very resilient, but I am ashamed of our mentality and I am ashamed of my mindset. Do you want to tell me that progress is only for whites? Do you want to tell me that human rights is only for whites? Do you want to tell me that turning your country from a third world nation to a first world nation is only for whites? Do you want to tell me that investing in the life,which has been given to you by the Universe is only for white people? Do you want to tell me that developing world class infrastructure is only for whites, hispanics and Asians? Everything is now Europe's fault for colonizing Africa, right? It seems like a defensive arrogant attitude we have because we do not want to deal with things that are holding us back from reaching the summit; we do not question some of the horrible things that our ancestors did, nor do we question their unwillingness to embrace change and develop ideas that can contribute to both ourselves and the rest of mankind. We talk about honor and shame, but we are doing a very good job shaming ourselves every day by stuffing our freedom up, we are acting as if we lack any form of intelligence, even if we have it and this freaks me out because those are the signals that we are sending out there, believe me.I am frustrated when I see many of my brethren throwing away opportunities that are around us to make ourselves prosperous, if you're not a better you, how can you even lead your own nation? We blacks are not a better us; we rule over 50 countries on this planet and almost everyone of them is a virtual disaster, no black majority country has ever joined the Organization for Economic Cooperation Development or the OECD because many of our countries are still receiving tons of aid from Western nations and we make decisions that are self-destructive for ourselves. How can we talk about honor and humiliate ourselves at the same time? You cannot have everything both ways; someone once told me that you've got to choose what you win or lose. If you want to stand aside and watch this life pass you by, be my guess because it is your choice after all. Some of our nations that were once prosperous are now disaster zones. Now is it ok for black witch doctors to go and kill black albinos for the use of their skin to practice their stupid superstitious beliefs? In many Sub-Saharan African countries black albinos are facing persecution and killings by ordinary black people who believe that the use of the albino skin can cure lots of diseases, this way of thinking is absolutely pathetic and it shows once again that we are the ones who are ridiculing ourselves by making us look like bunch fools, no wonder our societies are perceived as societies of losers because our way of thinking stinks. We know that things like that are happening and we are ignoring them out of conformism, another problem we have is that many religious black parents kill their children because they were suspected of being witches, dear goodness, what they hell is going on? Are we confronting the problems consistently? I doubt it, we black people love to blame people from other races for our own failures and the conditions, which many of our societies are in; especially when it comes to the issues we have been facing in our societies and lives for decades, the white man may have pushed us down and devalue us, the Middle Eastern man may have done things that are for more worse to us and destroy our psyche and slavery from the Trans-Atlantic Era and the slavery from the East may have caused our destruction and broken our willingness to go forward, and held on to the civilization that we once were, but the black man's own worst enemy is the individual whom he/she sees in the mirror, that the black man himself, that's you and that's me. We are the ones causing our own disasters by choosing to suppress the individual and imposing conformism upon each other. We do not want to recognize our mistakes and we always make excuses for everything. Some of my fellow black brethren, especially those who are Muslims act like they are still slaves subconsciously because they act like a herd of ship that does not have a leader. We are too tolerant of the wrong things and allow ourselves to be taken advantage of, especially black domestic workers who face racism and injustices in the Middle East, when those women come home their own governments do not even stand up for them. Whenever they are problems, we tend to ignore them until they become big problems, when we are told that there are problems by others, we call them imperialists and colonialists because we do not want to listen until it is too late. That is why the problem with us black people is that we do not do anything for ourselves; we wait for something to happen, but that's not how life works, my friends. We are the ones who keep believing in cultures of honor and shame, but violate them by allowing our nations to become failed states and immigrate illegally to the Western world; China, Canada, United States, Australia, New Zealand, Brazil, Chile, Uruguay, Hungary, France, Germany, Sweden, Italy and other industrialized and newly industrialized countries are getting a good share of illegal black African immigrants and many can already see the rise of racism coming. We run away from messes that we have created and in most cases it is our own fault for making ourselves look like the laughing stock of the world. Our cultures are among the least respected and the most ridiculed on the planet,so do our norms, traditions and our way of thinking because we are stuck on being in denial of our own unwillingness to realize that the vast majority of the suffering and disasters that are taking place in many black majority countries are of our own making, yes, there are Western multinational companies and governments that are also responsible, but in most cases, we are until we face up to it and take responsibility for our own problems, we will continue to be the laughing stock of the world. When was the last time we have rebuilt the castles and other elements that were destroyed by colonialists? Zero! There was a Finn who told me that he does not want black people in Finland because our way of thinking is still from the 15th century and we have the unwillingness to change it,well that should bring more questions about us as a people, don't you think?As a black man myself I am sick and tired of us not taking a hard look at our attitudes and values, I am sick and tired of frequenting the African communities where we hear so much about how colonialism destroyed Africa, I am sick and tired of us not questioning our concepts of tribalism, which is demoralizing our willingness to improve and develop. We do not have the willingness to forsake our tribal allegiances, especially when governments run countries they favor their tribes over others. We African blacks are inherently tribalistic and we make excuses about it, it is mostly our fault because we are the ones making those choices, yet we blame the white man for it. For centuries we have belonged to extended families that in turn belong the clan,

African countries are governed by politicians whose power base and ideologies have roots in tribal institutions because those are places where their real causes emanate from and most Africans have their primarily allegiance to their tribes and tribal structures and the central governments are often viewed as an outside force or an irrelevant entity. This freaks me out once again because this is the mentality that keeps holding us back and this is why Africa could disappear tomorrow and no one will even notice because we know that we have these problems, but we do not do anything about them; our results speak for themselves. Another problem that we blacks have, especially in our families, parents often have the unwillingness to recognize their mistakes towards their children because we have an totalitarian mindset, instead of having an authoritative mindset; black children are more likely to face physical abuse from their parents than children from other races, I am not saying that disciplining your child is child abuse, but over disciplining is child abuse,we make excuses for it all the time because we do not want to be Eurocentric; our idea of being Eurocentric is the idea that all white parents are too lenient to their children, let me tell you, my brethren that we cannot blame our culture for everything; by the way, we are not the only culture that discipline our children, black children, especially those from African countries are at least twice as likely to face child abuse from their families than children from other races. If it is really working, how in American jails, South African jails, French jails, Brazilian jails, British jails and jails from other countries with a minority or majority black population have black men who are among the highest representation of inmates in jail? Are we going to keep blaming racism for this? Are we? I am sick and tired of this bogus argument that I am not a parent yet, so I would react differently when I am going to have children, another kind of nonsense. How come most of black majority countries are either failed states or impoverished countries governed by corrupt politicians? The problem is not with white people, the problem is not even with the sleazy sand people, the problem is not with the

Asians–the problem is with us black people, as long as we do not want to admit our own faults, we will stay where we are for generations to come; no one tells you my black brother to impregnate women and fail to support the children, no one tell you to be a gang who sells drugs instead of getting an education and have ambitions; no one tells you not to have a job and live on welfare for a lifetime; no one tells you to beat up homosexuals because you do not agree with their lifestyle; no one tells you to ask your widowed sister in law to leave her home with her children, so that you can take your brother or cousin's belongings, which you believe is rightfully yours; no one tells you to have 18 children with no means to support them; no one tells you to cheat the system for more welfare money; no one tells you to bully another brother, or killing one; no one tells us to kill each each and stay stuck in our way of thinking, and so on, those are choices you make on your own, those are choices we make on our own. In general cases, white men, Asian men and Middle Eastern men who impregnate black women are more likely to be there as fathers and support their wives/girlfriends/fiancées' children financially than black men who do the same to their black female partners, do you think I am making this up? Look at the amount of African American women in the United

States who are single mothers, look at the amount of Black women from other countries who are single mothers because we,black men are not men enough to take our responsibilities, well, I know very well that it is not all, but let us stop playing games here. The African continent has a wonderful wildlife and some animals are already extinct or on the brink of extinction, yet many black African politicians and ordinary black Africans citizens have no concern for the wildlife and the willingness protect the wildlife for generations to come; it is always in most cases whites who are more concerned about the survival of wild animals on the continent than us and I do not understand why Greenpeace, CNN and environmentalists do not raise serious topics about such a topic. 100% of animal poachers in Africa are black men who kill those wild animals, so that they can sell their organs to the Asian, East European and Middle Eastern markets. I do not want to hear that they come from poor sections of society and they do what they do to survive because I do not buy that crap; being poor does not give you an excuse not to educate yourself, being poor is not an excuse to bring creatures like elephants, rhinos, lions, leopards, cheetahs, wild dogs, gorillas, chimpanzees, buffaloes, wildebeests, hippos etc., many of us do not even give a crap about the conservation of our forests, savannahs and bushes. We have rivers, lakes, streams and creeks, yet many of us still go and fetch water there, instead of having water tabs and clean running water. Honestly, I do not think that we have a desire to fix our problems; we pretend to do so, a lot of us become our own worst enemy because we want to be rotten to the core. If we look at the rise of European countries, Asian countries, countries in Oceania and countries in the Americas one of the main things that contributed to it is the accordance to individual accomplishments, curiosity, the willingness to fail forward, the willingness to take risks and the need to explore new territories in life. We are stuck to belief systems that dated centuries ago, just because our ancestors were doing the same things and we are not even questioning anything, nor do we try to make peace between our values and the century in which we are living right now. We are not realizing that life is too short to play it safe; if people like Nelson Mandela, Muhammad Ali, Desmond Tutu, Malcolm X, Lumumba, Robert Kennedy, John.F. Kennedy, Rosa Parks, Mahatma Gandhi, Ronald Reagan, Donald Trump and others played things safe, we would not have heard so much about their achievements today and our world would be a much different place than it is today. In terms of economics we have a lower standard of living than whites, Hispanics and people from other races. The reason why we are in this vicious cycle it is because we are not good at seeing problems and dealing with them at their roots; we simply ignore the problems and hope that they will go away on their own, but in most cases problems do not go away on their own, that is how we black people leave small problems to become big problems. Our idea of not worrying and just being happy is typically our attitude causes tremendous problems in our lives. Today in countries like Zimbabwe, Burundi, Equatorial Guinea, Cameroon, Togo, Republic of the Congo, Democratic Republic of Congo, Central African Republic, Guinea, Guinea-Bissau, Haiti and many other black majority countries politicians and their rival supporters kill other people and do as they please there is a lack of leadership from opposition parties that can lift up those nations from being third world hellwhole to First World countries. That is why whites and Asians in Africa and other places around the world where you find black majority countries think that they have to think for us because they anticipate that if the problems created by us are left to us alone to solve they will become unsolvable because we make too many excuses. Many of those African governments go on and do far more stupid things by giving away farming lands to sleazy crooked sand people from Saudi Arabia, Qatar, the United Arab Emirates, Oman, Kuwait and other rich sand people from the Muslim world. Those people do not just buy farming lands from locals; they trash local populations by treating them like dogs, especially if they are black. The next thing those sand people do is to corrupt incompetent African governments, so that there can be more mosques and that also means more Jihad and hate preaching against the infidels like me. I do not care if you call me islamophobic,by the way, a phobia is an irrational fear,but the fear of Islam and Muslims is rational because most of the terrorist groups who are responsible for the deaths of both Muslims and non-Muslim are Muslim terrorist whose fundamentals are in the Hadiths, the Quran and the Sunnas, do not tell me that there are over 1.6 billion Muslims around the world, as if I do not even know it. Did you ask those Muslims how many percent of them want the Sharia Law, the killing of apostates, the killing of homosexuals, the subjugation of non-Muslims, discrimination against women, discrimination against those whom they do not consider as pure Muslims because they're not sand people etc.? Do not talk to me about a tiny fraction of Muslims supports terrorism because I do not buy your claim; it is estimated that between 15 to 25 % of Mohammedans worldwide are sympathetic of terrorist activities against the Western world and other areas where Islam is not pleased with the way non-Muslims do things. Going back to the problem with us black people and Africa as a whole, the last thing that I want to focus on is trade; many African societies grumble about their products not being imported in EU countries because the European Union and the Western world makes things difficult for African farmers. Well, let us dig in this case; if you want to export your products, make sure that you comply with the rules and learn to sell your product to those you expect to buy and import it. If that market does not want to import your product, ask yourself what you can do differently and find other markets that are interested in your product. The problem with African countries is that we are not very good at trading with each other, and we fail to understand that the European Union and the rest of the Western world need to protect its markets, its farmers and they are always going to be a priority, something that we will never change, nor can we do anything about it. No one is preventing us from developing and becoming first world nations; we are the ones who are standing in our own way, and we are the ones who creating our own barriers. You might be a black American or even a black African reading this book and wonder what is wrong with me and why am I being a sellout or you might think that I am trying to act white because I am ashamed of being black, let us just call it like it is; I am not trying to act white and I am proud to be black, but I am not proud of our destructive way of thinking, I am not proud of our unwillingness to face our problems boldly and take accountability for them; I am ashamed of us throwing opportunities away because of corruption and megalomania; I am ashamed we talk about Africa being a cradle for human life, yet we are not rising to our highest potentials, instead we think that everyone owes something to Africa and to us black people. Those of us who are religious can pray to the God that we want, but thoughts become things and we must take inspired actions to make our desires become our human experience. Whether you are religious or not when ideas come to you, you must act no matter how irrelevant some of them might seem at first. You will not notice an opportunity until it passes you by, that is why many black majority countries are in such an awful shape.Ok, during colonial times we were humiliated, looked down on,bullied, called derogatory names, treated as inferior species, some of us were even put in zoos like apes, we were treated like things that have no value by whites and sandmen; to my black brethren, I want to tell you that I am deeply sorry for the injustices that we faced back then; I am deeply sorry that the sandman does not even want to recognize his horrible treatment of us, but always blames the West for it. I am deeply sorry for the Apartheid and other types of racial segregations in places where we were treated like second class citizens and so on; we had no control over the injustices that we were facing back then, but we have control over what we can do about those things now and lift ourselves up from deep holes. Our predecessors who went through those horrible time did not face them so that we can ridicule ourselves and live in poverty. It is our job to build ourselves up, both for ourselves and the generations to come. We are going to face all sorts of struggles like racism, tribal hatred, jealousy and so on,but if we want to be great we have to overcome the greatest struggles, which is within ourselves. Let me make something clear to you, as a black man you will face struggles no matter where you are, even in many African countries you will face struggles, but as long as we keep standing there and blame former colonial powers for our own failures in life, we will continue to remain stuck. We cannot afford to wait for something to happen; we have got to do things for ourselves and for the rest of mankind. We are responsible for the conditions we create and the conditions, in which we find ourselves,no doubt that the white man and also the sandman have put us in situations where we are down and do not feel good about ourselves, situations that lead to self-hatred, but we are have got to remember that it is only us who can change our mindset and way of thinking. We have allowed ourselves to be disrespected, now we have the choice to show what we are made, but it is up to you and me to take accountability and stop blaming others for our problems.

CHAPTER 8

THE VALUE OF DEMOGRAPHY

When you live in a society where the level of unemployment is high among everyone, especially the youth, people who are in that situation are demoralized because they feel like they have no options in their lives anymore either for just themselves or their loved ones; a society that has a high amount of unemployment is not sustainable in the long run because when people are unemployed they are frustrated, angry and this can lead to social, political, cultural and ethnic conflicts.If you are not able to provide for your family and yourself, how can you contribute to the well-being of your country? The problem with welfare states is that instead of encouraging people to create more jobs that can last for decades, governments are wasting all of those resources on welfare benefits, which steals your dreams and potentials. Another problem with the concept of a welfare state is the failure of realizing that the Western world as a whole is ageing and there isn't enough hand to sustain the survival of the rich European and other Western economies. European countries like France, Portugal, Belgium,Denmark, Sweden, Germany and other have economies in the Western world are struggling with demographics because there are many couples who have less and less children among the native populations, this makes it difficult to keep the economies going because there isn't enough people to the jobs and pay to ensure the survival of welfare states and help the elderly populations. Europe's crisis is the failure of social democratic policies that has little prospects of recovery because its economy is stagnated by a bloated public sector. Whether we like it or not, every economy is divided in two parts, the private and the public sector; if the larger part of the economy is taken by the public sector, then you've got to expect that there will be fewer jobs in the private sector and that means that the standard of living will dwindle. There are couples who want to have more children, but fear that it is too expensive and they are not given so many options necessary so that they can make things easier for themselves and their children. Despite the fact that there are more people living in poverty in United States than Europe, despite the fact that the American healthcare system is extremely complicated for me to understand the U.S. economy still grows faster than the European economy because the government in America is relatively smaller than those in many European countries. Governments in many EU countries overspend taxpayers' money on Job Centers,which in return do not offer any form of jobs to the unemployed, but seeing them just being rotten from within. When you are on welfare, your destiny is in someone else's hands, instead of it being in your own hands; it also depends on the country where you live, but you have lots of restrictions; you cannot go to another country and shop, you have to ask for permission to go on holiday; you are checked time after on whether you are looking for a job or not, and you are told a million things that you can and cannot do. You are often treated like a child by Job Center services where some view you as a do nothing, but a moocher, even though you are the one who is paying them through your taxes. There are many reasons why the public sector is often viewed as an overspender and corrupt system done by the European Union, but the EU is not in this alone; Scandinavian countries are champions of welfare states. The problem with the creation of our welfare states is that people are encouraged to be in an age of entitlement, what I mean by that is those of us who are depending too much on welfare develop a culture of dependency, which suggests that the State owes us a living. We live in moments where unemployment rises and the amount of people living on social security is increasing, especially with the migrant crisis from third world countries. When Europe and the United States take in millions of migrants from third world countries, they also have to be prepared to give them jobs and if they do not do it, then more and more people are going to live on social security; that is really a burden to many local taxpayers. Statistics from Breitbart indicate that 90 percent of Muslim immigrants from the Middle East and Africa live on food stamps and nearly 70% of those refugees and migrants receive some form of governmental assistance. When I talk about Middle Eastern migrants, I talk about those who come from Turkey, Egypt, Lebanon, Afghanistan, Iran, Iraq, Yemen, Oman, Syria, Morocco, Tunisia, Algeria, Libya, Western Sahara etc. The question that I would like to ask to many governments from Western countries is that what is it they are trying to achieve by taking people in without offering them jobs so that they can take charge of their own destinies? Another question that I would like to ask them is that why are they allowing too many people, both locals and migrants to live on welfare for such a long time? In my opinion, welfare dependency is an addiction if you have lived of the system for years. You cannot expect your economy to grow so fast if you have too many people living on social security; consumer spending coincides with the overall consumer confidence in a nation's economy. A higher level of consumer confidence relates to a strong amount of growth in businesses and gives the confidence to many firms, both in the private and public sectors to hire more people and it adds up with demography, because when people have jobs that are meaning to them, then they also have the readiness to establish their own families and invest in both their own and their children's futures. If you are not a better you, you cannot establish a family and be there for someone else, whether you are a local citizen or an immigrant. Welfare dependency is one of the gravest problems in the West.

Now I am going to talk about something that is going to bring some people on a red field; I will be talking about something that has an influence on the way a society will look like in decades to come and the impacts, what I am talking about is the arrival of Muslim illegal immigrants and refugees in Europe, something that draws attention, especially when we are dealing with terrorist attacks in various Western countries and elsewhere. In many Western countries, including France, Germany, United States, Canada, Australia, Belgium, Netherlands, Spain, Sweden, Norway, New Zealand, United Kingdom, Italy, Portugal, Luxembourg, Switzerland, Liechtenstein and Austria there are concerns about the amount of Muslim immigration and the citizens of those countries are demanding restrictions on Muslim immigration and unsuited third world immigration. One of the reasons why there is such concern it is because the amount of Muslim immigrants in Europe and elsewhere in the Western world and the impact it will have on those societies in decades to come. Countries like Germany and France have some of the highest Muslim population in the Western world and the Muslim population in this part of the world is increasing very fast and this makes many local populations uneasy; in order to maintain a culture for at least 25 years there must be a fertility rate of 2.11 children per couple, anything lesser than that number will influence the existence of that culture negatively, in other words, the culture will decline. According to many cultural experts, no culture has ever reversed a 1.9 fertility rate and a rate of 1.3 is impossible to reverse; it will take between 80 to 100 years to correct itself, no economic model can sustain that particular culture in that moment and that is why many French,

Germans, Dutch, Italians, Americans, Canadians, Swedes, Norwegians, Icelanders, Austrian, Australians, Brits, Poles and Hungarians are worried about the survival of their nations in the long run; they wonder what kind of nations are they going to leave behind to their children, grandchildren, and even great grandchildren. They ask themselves whether their children and grandchildren are going to grow up in a Germany, a Hungary, a France, a Holland, a Sweden, an America, a Canada, a Britain or even a Serbia that they can recognize. I am not talking about far right extremists; I am talking about genuine people who have a good heart and who are just concerned about the high amount of uncontrolled immigration happening in Europe and other parts of the rich world. Let me just make something clear; we cannot ignore the fact that the fertility rate in countries like Germany, France, Hungary, Italy, Spain, Great Britain, Russia, Greece, United States, Canada, Australia and Sweden is declining among local populations. If the West continues on this path, it will cease to exist in a matter of decades, 90 % of the immigration in Europe is from Muslim countries. There are many Muslim leaders and terrorist groups who are using demography as a weapon of war against the West and they have the willingness to destroy it with its own hands. You might think that the statements that I am making are very dangerous, but you are ignoring the fact that people like Muammar Gaddafi once said, I quote "There are signs that Allah will grant Islam victory in Europe without guns, without conquests and without swords. We don't need terrorists, we don't need homicide bombers. The 50+ million Muslims in Europe will turn it to a Muslim continent within a few decades." This is not me who is making these statements and this is not me who is waging a demographic war against the West. There are many Muslims who believe that their duty is to declare war on non-Muslims, especially those who are in Europe because they want to bring the Islamic State or the Islamic Empire, which ended in 1923, that is less than 100 years ago. The questions I ask myself very often are that why we are allowing this to happen? Why don't we have the courage to raise some serious debates about this topic? Why are we burying our heads in the sand, while expecting this problem to go away on its own? These problems are not going to go away on their own, believe me, and if we keep ignoring this problem, we will see far right extremists governing not just European countries, but the rest of the Western world because the West has weak leaders who bow down to the Saudis, the Qataris, the Emiratis etc. If we ignore this problem, many immigrants from non-Western countries living in Europe will pay a huge price because when far right political parties are going to govern, they are not going to see the difference between those groups of people anymore and we are going to witness social unrests and possibly a civil war among different ethnic groups. One of the worst thing that can happen could be the segregation of people of different races living in their own neighborhoods. The Western world is inviting groups of people who are responsible for the destruction of their own countries and impose their religious and cultural beliefs upon the local populations that took them in the first place. In Middle Eastern countries wars take place for a long time, and we think that it is our fault, so out of guilt we bring those so-called refugees in and expect them to adapt to our way of life, but we forget that we do not know who many of those people are and how they can be vetted, we do not know if those people have our best interests and we do not know if they are willing to respect our laws. It might be true that the Iraq war in 2003 destabilized the Middle East, but we are not responsible for the rebuilding of Afghanistan, Iraq, Lebanon, Syria, Palestine, Yemen, etc.; they are responsible for the reconstruction of their nations, including schools,

217

hospitals, infrastructure, public sector, police, etc., they have their governments and if they do not, then they are the ones who have to establish their governments. It is not our job to bring human rights and other things that we cherish in those places; they have to learn to earn it on their own if they take themselves seriously. If Colonialism is the responsible for all the awful things that are happening to the Muslim world, then what are Muslims doing themselves to fix their own problems, on the other hand Muslims were also colonizers; just think of the times when Hungary, Serbia, Croatia, Bosnia, Albania, Greece, Bulgaria, Romania and FYR of Macedonia were invaded by the Muslim Ottoman Empire and imposed the Islamic religion on the local populations there 5 centuries ago. Remember the times when Middle Eastern Muslims invaded Spain, Portugal, parts of France, parts of Italy and they were even close to invading Austria had the Poles not stopped them. Remember the times when Middle Eastern Muslims invaded parts of China, parts of the Indian Subcontinent and parts of the rest of Southeast Asia etc. The Islamic Empire ended less than 100 years ago, during the time when it existed there were 270 million people worldwide who were killed by Muslims in the name of Islam, including 80 million Hindus, 60 million Christians and 120 million

Africans who were enslaved by Middle Eastern Muslims, trying to whitewash the evil deeds that the Islamic world has done to others is not helping maintaining peace in the world, nor does it help Muslims themselves. The idea that the Muslim world keeps blaming Western nations for its failures engages in further irrational thinking and confuses the deeds with the doers. Muslim Jihadists have made a choice to declare wars on non-Muslims for 14 centuries, we can try to ignore the problems as long we like, but at the end of the day, they are not going to away on their own. The Muslim world is malcontent because it is its worst enemy, in other words they have the unwillingness to take personal responsibility, that is why the Muslim world is a prisoner of its beliefs, due to the fact that it fails to take personal responsibility by recognizing that the problem with Islamic Jihad is the fundamentals of their religion as a whole and saying so does not make one an "Islamophobe", sorry. Muslims have to face up to their failures and come up with following ways to learn from those failures by resolving them. It is not about trying to take back what they believe was rightfully theirs because Spain, France, Italy, Netherlands, Great Britain, Hungary, United States, Sweden, Canada and the rest of the non-Muslim world was never rightfully theirs; instead

BALTHAZAR RODRIGUE NZOMONO-BALENDA

of declaring wars on what many of them call infidels, they should probably concentrate on fixing their countries and keep their religion to themselves. Before any Leftist begins to say that I am blaming the entire religion, please save your breath; it is baloney to believe that only a small percentage of Muslims wants the destruction of the Western world, let me come up with some statistics from Jihadwatch: 51% of U.S. Muslims want to live under the Sharia in America and 60 % of young Muslims from the USA are more loyal to Islam than the U.S. Muslimstatistics.wordpress.com reveals that most European Muslims want to live under the Sharia, not European Laws and over three-quarters of Muslims in the Middle East, Africa, and Southeast Asia want the Sharia courts to decide family rules and the majority of the people who follow that religion support death penalty for leaving Islam and homosexuality, of course, Muslims differ on different aspects of the Sharia Law and some reject harsher sentences from this law, especially when it comes to non-Muslims. Those of you who do not know the Sharia Law, I would tell you that it is an Islamic law that expresses the highest and the best goals of societies, it is the will of Allah according to Muslims. Things that are included in the Sharia Law are: Beheadings, stoning, hanging, crucifixions, honor killings, genocide, the burning of non-Muslims, supremacy/global domination, welfare/conquest, beatings, torture, limb amputation, genital mutilation, forced conversions, death to apostates, slavery, sex slavery and rape, misogyny, child marriage, wife-beating, censorship, dictatorship, women enslavement, brutality against homosexuals, robbery and pillage, animal cruelty, persecution or death for blasphemy and atheism, bigotry, hatred, racism, prohibition of music and the destruction of pre-Islamic antiques. This Islamic law is not compatible with Western values; it is inferior to Western values and if anyone is infuriated about I have just said, then tough luck; just in case you want to me to say it, I will say it again; the Sharia Law is inferior to Western values, it is also lower than any other value from any non-Muslim country because it violates the principles of human dignity, I do not care if you believe that this law of yours comes from your deity. By the way, what kind of God would want to wipe non-Muslims from the face of the Earth, brutalize women, forced conversions, the killing of blasphemers, etc.? If such a god exists, I would want to associate myself with him. I am sick and tired of hearing Muslims talking about Christians who did the same things; that is just another excuse for them to run away from their personal responsibility and I do not have time for such people who do not accept their infallibility because they believe that their religion and their deity tell them to do so. If you have destroyed your countries and caused your disasters, why would you want to destroy other nations where you decided to immigrate and transform those non-Muslims nations that have taken you in with open arms to Sharia states? Why don't you just stay in your countries and apply the Sharia there, instead of imposing it on those of us who do not have anything to do with your religion and the system of values, which it promotes? I am not an advocate of any religion, and I think that religion is destroying mankind because each religion assumes that its doctrines are part of the absolute truth. Religion also keeps peopled bonded to beliefs and dogmas that may hinder man's progress, instead of preceding our need to move in this journey we all call life. When it comes to Muslims, they demand rights when they are in the minority, such as religious freedom, tolerance, multiculturalism, diversity, interfaith relations, more building of mosques, etc. But as the Muslim population grows in any non-Muslim country, the society changes, unfortunately for the worst. According to Dr.Peter Hammond who wrote

"Slavery, Terrorism, and Islam: The Historical Roots and Contemporary Threat,"and has explored the topic on the impact, which the increasing Muslim population in that particular society. According to his book as long as the Muslim population remains around or under 2% in any given non-Muslim country, Muslims will be regarded as peaceful, loving and not a threat to the majority citizens, in this case, we are talking about the following countries:

- Hungary - Muslim 0.056 %
- United States - Muslim 0.6 %
- Australia - Muslim 1.5 %
- Canada - Muslim 1.9 %
- China - Muslim 1.8%
- Italy - Muslim 1.5 %
- Norway - Muslim 1.8

At 2 to 5% Muslims begin to proselytize from other ethnic minorities and disaffected groups with often recruiting from jails or street gangs.

- Denmark - Muslim 2%

- Germany- Muslim 3.7%
- United Kingdom - Muslim 2.7%
- Spain - Muslim 4%
- Thailand - Muslim 4.6%
- Republic of the Congo - Muslim 2%

From 5% and above Muslims exercise an inordinate influence in proportion to their percentage of the population. For example, they will push for the introduction of halal (clean by Islamic standards) food, thereby securing food preparation jobs for Muslims. They will increase pressure on supermarket chains to feature halal on their shelves -- along with threats for failure to comply. This is happening in:

- France - Muslim 8%
- Democratic Republic of Congo - Muslim 10%
- Philippines-Muslim 5%
- Sweden - Muslim 5%
- Holland - Muslim 5.5%
- Trinidad & Tobago - Muslim 5.6%

At this point, Muslims will work to get the ruling

government to allow them to rule themselves (within ghettos/poor suburbs creating no-go areas for non-Muslims), under the Islamic law by creating a state within a state and the ultimate goals for the Islamic violent mob are to establish an Islamic government worldwide. When the Muslim population approaches 10 %, they purposely increase lawlessness and tend to complain more about their conditions, in cities like Paris, Amsterdam, Stockholm, London, Berlin and the other main cities across the Western world we see people burning cars and other types of violence. Any non-Muslim who takes actions that are offensive to Islam risks facing death threats, physical violence, psychological violence and in the worst case scenario you can even be killed for being critical of Islam, such as in Amsterdam where a Moroccan Islamist murdered Theo Van Gogh, the same man threatened to kill Ayaan Hirsi Ali. In Copenhagen, the controversies about the Mohammad Cartoons lead to many Danish cartoonists from the Jylland Posten hide for their lives because they face death threats from the Muslim world, in Paris journalists from Charlie Hebdo were gunned down by Muslim terrorists for offending Islam, and France went on to witness three more terrorist attacks. Tensions are seen daily in:

- Guyana - Muslim 10 %
- India - Muslim 13.4%
- Israel - Muslim 16 %
- Kenya - Muslim 10%
- Russia - Muslim 15%

When the Muslim population reaches 20% nations must expect higher triggerings of riots, jihad militia formations, the burning of Christian churches, Jewish synagogues and Buddhist temples - this is happening in countries such as:

- Montenegro - Muslim 19.11%
- Ethiopia - Muslim 32 %
- FYR of Macedonia - Muslim 33%

At 40 % nations experience massacre, prominent terror attacks, ongoing militia warfare like for instance in:

- Bosnia & Herzegovina - Muslim 40%

- Chad - Muslim 53%
- Lebanon - Muslim 59.7%

At 60 % nations must be prepared to experience persecutions of non-believers of all other religions, including non-conforming Muslims, sporadic ethnic cleansing through the use of the Sharia as a weapon and demand both Christians and Jews to pay the protection tax if they do not want to convert to the Islamic religion, for anyone else who is not a person of the book, in other words, a Jew or a Christian, it is either convert or die. This is happening in countries such as:

- Albania - Muslim 70%
- Malaysia - Muslim 60.4 %
- Qatar - Muslim 77.5 %
- Sudan - Muslim 70%

At 80 % and above, expect violent intimidations, violent jihad, State-run ethnic cleansing, genocides and the willingness to drive the infidels out of what they perceive as Muslim lands. Such barbarity is experienced in countries like:

- Bangladesh - Muslim 83%
- Egypt - Muslim 90%
- Gaza - Muslim 98.7 %
- Indonesia - Muslim 86.1%
- Iran - Muslim 98%
- Iraq- Muslim 97 %
- Jordan - Muslim 92 %
- Morocco - Muslim 98.7%
- Pakistan - Muslim 97%
- Palestine - Muslim 99%
- Syria - Muslim 90%
- Tajikistan - Muslim 90%
- Turkey - Muslim 99.8%
- United Arab Emirates - Muslim 96%
- Tunisia - Muslim 97 %
- Algeria - Muslim 99%
- Libya - Muslim 96,6%

When the Muslim population reaches 100% that will usher in the peace of Dar-es- Salaam, meaning the Islamic House of Peace and in that moment there will be peace because everyone is now a Muslim and

Madrassas are the only schools and learning more about the Quran is the only education one can get in countries such as:

- Somalia - Muslim 100%
- Afghanistan - Muslim 100%
- Saudi Arabia - Muslim 100%
- Yemen - Muslim 100%

The question I ask myself is this, why is it that peace is never achieved in countries where you have a 100% Muslim population, the reason why peace is never achieved in those countries it is because radical Muslims intimidate, spew hatred and satisfy their bloodlust by killing Muslims who do not think and act like them. This has nothing to do with America's foreign policy; this has nothing to do with us offending Muslims; it has a lot to do with the fundamentals of Islam itself. What Liberals do not understand is that being critical of Islam and Muslims is not racism, nor is it bigotry and Liberals are willing to do anything to protect Muslims and Islam from criticism, while playing the fear mongering card. Of course, not all Muslims are interested in the Sharia

Law; not all Muslims want to establish to Islamic government on Earth, but those who do have to be taken seriously and it is up to Muslims themselves to question the doctrines of their religion. The Western world has to focus on ensuring its own existence and survival because if it does not, then the next generations will never forgive us for defending such a great civilization. That is why demography is very important and that is why you've got to know who are inviting in your societies and who has your best interests. If Liberals continue to equate the criticism of Islam and Muslims as racism, bigotry etc., then they are the ones who will have blood in their hands because they are destroying their own civilization with the help from Muslim Jihadists.

CHAPTER 9

ENERGY INDEPENDENCE SETS US FREE FROM EVIL

The Western world has messes with electricity, it trembles on its own without knowing how to get out, the simple explanation for this is oil from the Middle East, which is the largest producer of the black gold. The Western world is the world's top importer of oil from the Middle East, especially Saudi Arabia. Those Middle Eastern countries are positioned to determine the price of oil through the OPEC, and they can make the world market go around. I have never understood that Western governments can be so stupid on the level where they put the survival of their nations at risk because they do not want to offend Saudi Arabia and other Middle Eastern oil producing countries. Western leaders do not dare to confront Saudi Arabia when it comes to women's rights, gay rights, minority rights because the Saudis and others have bought their silence. We are talking about a country that does not allow women to drive, we are talking about a country whose population lives by a very strict Sharia Law, we are talking about a country where religious minorities are denied rights to practice their faiths, and we are talking about a country that practiced slavery until 1961. Another way many wealthy Middle Eastern countries are buying the silence of Western leaders, football clubs, tennis tournaments, funds, etc. is to control football clubs, news agencies, and other activities. Some of us do not even question their objectives we allow ourselves to receive blood money. What objectives do countries that are the heart of Islam is have? Those are countries where you are not even authorized to criticize Islam, those are also countries where people who hold Israeli passports are not allowed to enter and in Saudi Arabia, non-Muslims are not allowed to set their feet on the Mecca because we are viewed as filthy. Yet this is one of those rich Middle Eastern countries to which we bow down because we have made a choice to give them power because they have most of the black gold. The Islamic Empire ended less than 100 years ago in 1923, what happened 5 years later was the creation of the Muslim Brotherhood. The Muslim Brotherhood's goal is to destroy the Western world and create an Islamic government worldwide because they believe that the Western world has subjugated Islam and Muslim; they want they believe was rightfully theirs. The Muslim Brotherhood plans a civilization jihad against Europe, America and the rest of the non-Muslim world. The two events that have strengthened the position of the Muslim Brotherhood are the oil from the Middle East, which the Western discovered but was too naive to trust Middle Eastern countries to nationalize their oil, and the rise of Ayatollah Khomeini in Iran who was exiled in France. They seek to impose their Islamic Sharia Law on everyone, whether those people are

Muslims or not. Where Sharia is dominant it also dictates the way non-Muslim must act, think and behave. In cases where Muslims defend the Islamic cause are encouraged to lie to non-Muslims to carry on their goals of creating the Islamic Empire on earth. Many people in the Western media who hoped that the Arab Spring would bring democracy in the Middle East ended up being disappointed because in most of those countries the Sharia has become the way of life and it governs all aspects of society, law, social order, behavior, conduct etc. some Westerners naively view the Muslim Brotherhood as a secular movement that wants to bring democracy to Egypt and the rest of the Middle East, but what many of those naive Westerners do not know is that the Muslim Brotherhood is the world's oldest terrorist organization; the Muslim Brotherhood was founded in 1928, in Egypt by Hassan Al-Banna who was disappointed with the fall and the destruction of the Islamic Empire, which was lead by the Ottomans after the First World War and was ended by Kamal Attürk, Hassan Al-Banna declared that Islam must dominate, it must not be dominated, he also believed that Islam must dominate all nations of the world and subjugate all non-Muslims under the Sharia. The Brotherhood is a very disciplined organization, they are very organized, they are very ruthless, and their set of values are rooted in a Salafi form of Islam, which they want to enforce to everyone on the planet. The goals of the Muslim Brotherhood are clear: Promote the Sharia Law worldwide and secure its triumph, reconstitute the

Islamic Empire and the goals are identical those groups who splinter the Brotherhood, groups such as ISIS, Khorasan, Boko Haram, The Taliban, Al Qaeda, Al Shabaab, Hezbollah, Hamas, and other Islamic terrorist groups. Those terrorist groups are derived from the Sharia, and their goal is to declare violent Jihad against Jews, Christians, and other non-Muslims, and the Muslim Brotherhood's slogan is: "Allah is our objective, the Prophet is our Leader, the Quran is our Law and Dying in the way of Allah is our highest hope". You can already tell that this organization is not interested in promoting democracy and human rights in Egypt and around the world; their objective is to declare a holy war against non-Muslims because they want to advance the Islamic cause worldwide by forcing non-Muslims to convert or die. This organization has values that are inferior to those of the Western world, and its set of beliefs are not compatible with Western values. In my opinion, the Muslim Brotherhood is a corrupt and decadent organization because of its primitive and uncivilized values, which its wants to impose on the rest of the world through violence, murder, beheadings, rape, sexual slavery, imprisonment, bullying, racism, homophobia and the hatred of non-Muslims. Such an organization is funded by Saudi Arabia, Qatar, Kuwait, the United Arab Emirates, Bahrain, Brunei, Turkey and other Islamic countries. Until now the Muslim Brotherhood uses first the civilization jihad against our civilized societies by making us the infidel feel subdued by Islam through the commandments of the

Quran, the Hadiths, and the Sunna. The Muslim Brotherhood's activity or stealth jihad is known as the Project, whose plan they have written for the destruction of Europe and the rest of the Western world through infiltrating governments, infiltrating the media, infiltrating political parties, promoting a face of moderation, information dominance, keeping non-Muslims ignorant; discourage blasphemy against Islam, Muhammad, the Quran, Allah and the Sharia; encouraging Muslims to be part of the government and organizations, making it illegal for non-Muslim to be critical of Islam, calling anyone who hates Islam an Islamophobe , fundraising for terrorist organizations etc. The Muslim Brotherhood has phases of the underground plans is to create front groups fight for the Islamic cause worldwide, especially in the West. The organization that is helping the Muslim Brotherhood's cause by imposing the Sharia Law worldwide is known as the OIC, which is the acronym of the Organization of the Islamic Conference, an organization that holds 57 Muslim countries and it is the world's number 2 organization after the United Nations. It is a very powerful international entity, which many of you have not heard of, thanks to the oil enjoyed by its members it is the most powerful multinational organization in the world. Like the Muslim Brotherhood, the OIC's goals is to promote and enforce the Islamic Law in the world, through their campaigns, it even supplanted the UN's Human Rights Universal Declarations by subordinating all bill of rights under the Sharia Code and respects none of them, for many years , the OIC has pushed for laws that must make it punishable in any country to define religion in the United Nations, typically , only Islam. The OIC's goal is to pass international laws by getting members of the UN to criminalize and prohibit expression that offends Muslims. In many Western countries, those who are critical of Islam, the Quran, Muhammad,Muslims, the Sharia and the Hadith face legal prosecution, death threats, violence, murder and bullying for giving offense to Muslims in the Netherlands, Sweden, Canada, United States, France, Germany, Austria,Denmark and Britain. People who have faced legal persecution by Islamists are Geert Wilders, Lars Hedegaard, Mark Steyn, Ezra Levant, Elizabeth Sabaditsch Wolff and Pamela Geller. They have been prosecuted in their own countries for being critical of a religion by Muslims who cannot stand critical thinking. There are even people like Ayaan Hirsi Ali and Molly Norris who are subjected to the fatwa by Muslim terrorists whose culture is nothing but barbaric and savage from Europe to Southeast Asia. There are situations where people who criticize Islam public fall in the risks of losing their jobs, expelled from schools, called names for criticizing and hating a religion. This leads many of those who are critical of Islam to go hiding and change their names, change their appearances. This sends signals to journalists on their obligation to censor themselves if they want to keep their jobs and live safe lives. The question some of you might ask is that why Western governments are giving in to this kind of blatant manipulation? I can understand those in the Western world who believe that Western governments and many other non-Muslim governments around the world are giving up their own citizens freedoms to pacify those who do not have the willingness to seriously take a look at their own religion and its values, which are responsible for the deaths of millions of people worldwide, whether those victims are Muslims or not. We do not hear many moderate Muslims speak up against terrorism and Jihad because some of them sympathize with the Jihadists and some are afraid to be called apostates. Another group of minorities in the West who are giving in to this manipulation is homosexual communities and Atheists who think that Christians are evil and Muslims are underdogs, yet in Orlando, Florida there has been a terrorist attack in a gay bar where 50 people were killed, and 53 people were injured because a Muslim terrorist decided to kill because his religion is not pleased with the way people do things anywhere. We do not know who we are declaring war against because many of us do not want to call a spade for a spade; our governments are cowards because they do not call things by their name, some of us do not even know what kind of elements are seeking to destroy us and which countries are financing them. We are at risk of losing our nations unless we do not allow ourselves to submit to the Islamic doctrines and conform to its information dominance if we do not take this battle seriously; Muslim Jihadists have made a choice to declare war on non-Muslims worldwide, they have also made the decision to declare war on Muslims who do not think like them for 14 centuries. While we are pumping gasoline in our vehicles, they are putting poison in our universities, football clubs, political parties, NGO's, primary schools, news agencies, journalists, governments, other sport clubs, International sport federations etc.; they are buying their way to our silence and do not have the interest in being our allies, allies do not make plans to destroy their partners. The reality is that many of those Muslim countries do not have our best interests, yet we choose to blame ourselves for their problems and disasters. To be honest with you we are not helping ourselves, nor are we helping Muslims by treating them as underdogs. Instead, we must hold them accountable for failing to question doctrines of their religion that encourage violence; that is why we must be energy independent and find other places to import oil or invest in the discovery of oil in our shores. We do not need those Middle Eastern countries, and they do not need us; they are using their oil revenues as weapons of wars against us. Many of those oil-rich states buy their way to silence us because they do not want us to question anything about the way they treat women, sexual minorities, non-white minorities, other Middle Eastern tribes and religious minorities; just look at what is happening in Qatar, the country that corrupted its way to get the candidacy for the soccer world cup in 2022. The shameful treatment, which many non-white workers who are treated like slaves in that country and other Middle Eastern countries; in

Qatar alone are packed in 8 or 10 in a room squalid, to make matters worse those workers are placed in unsanitary labor camps for years without any form of legal protection. Their passports are taken away from them by their Middle Eastern Muslim employers who force them to work to death with little amounts of necessities needed. Those are the same stupid Ragheads who claim that those non-white workers from Southeast Asia, Africa, and Central Asia die in the worked from natural causes. Migrants who live in Qatar are forced to live in squalor, while the FIFA, UEFA, CONMEBOL, CONCACAF and the AFC are looking the other way because they do not want to say things that are unpleasing to the Qataris and other wealthy Middle Eastern Ragheads; they do not want to make those precious Middle Eastern minds angry because those people can threaten to take away their sponsorship in various FIFA organizations, football clubs, and other entities. You might ask yourself what does this have to do with the Muslim Brotherhood, I can tell you that it has a lot to do with it because that is the way the Brotherhood wants to cultivate Islamic intellectual communities and advocacy groups worldwide to legitimize their Islamic laws because under Islam all men and women are not treated equally under the law. Now, the Brotherhood's plan to destroy Europe and turn it to an Islamic continent is a manifesto titled "The Project" and this plan has been penned by Said Ramadan who is the in law of the founder of the Muslim Brotherhood, this manifesto was written by the man in 1982 and those savages have a 100 year plan to destroy Europe from within, guess how they are doing it? They are Networking and coordinating actions between like minded Islamic organizations´.

They are Avoiding open alliances with known terrorist organizations and individuals to maintain the appearance of moderation. They are infiltrating and taking over existing Mohammedan organizations to realign them towards their goals. They are using deception to mask the intended goals of Islamist actions, which are not conflicting the Sharia Law. They are planning to avoid social conflicts with Westerners locally and globally that might damage their long-term ability to strengthen the Islamic power bases in Europe and the rest of the non-Muslim world. They are putting watchdog systems for monitoring the Western media to warn Mohammedans of international plots against them.They are instituting alliances Western Progressives to create organizations that share similar goals. They create autonomous security forces to protect Muslims in the West.They are taking control of existing Western institutions until they can be converted to Islam or put into service for Islamic causes.They impose their will through encouraging committed Muslims in democratic institutions on all levels in the Western world, including governments, NGOs, political parties, private organizations, trade unions, churches, synagogues, etc. They use their oil revenues to build social networks of schools, hospitals, charitable organizations so that they can dedicate those who receive their help to Islamist ideas, and they create Middle Eastern study departments in universities and community colleges so that they be in contact with Muslims in the West and the rest of the non-Muslim world constantly. They collect sufficient funds to perpetuate and support Jihad worldwide indefinitely.

They make the Palestinian issue a global wedge cause for Muslims. They demand more building of mosques and madrassas across all the non-Muslim world and fund hate preachers. They create constant campaigns that incite hatred against the Jews and reject any form of coexistence with them. They actively fund Jihadists in Palestine and across the rest of the non-Muslim world. They make alliances with Leftist groups, folks, and organizations that keep themselves in a blind spot when it comes to Islam. They take advantage of the so-called Palestinian cause by using Palestinians as human shields to gain sympathy from Liberals and other activists to get the whole international community to condemn Israel for all the evils of the Muslim world. They inflame violence by encouraging Muslims to kill those who are blasphemers, critiques and freethinkers to keep non-Muslims and peaceful Muslims from criticizing Islam in the Western world, that is how they keep Muslims living in the Western world in Jihadist frame of minds. They say one thing to the non-Muslims and another amongst themselves; that is how the Brotherhood supports Islamic terrorist movement across the whole Muslim world through hate preaching, personnel, funding and operational support. The creation of the Islamic Caliphate is their plan to dominate the world, one of the tactics that they are using is the fight for the Liberation of Palestine from Israel, and another is to lie to non-Muslims about what Jihad means, something the Brotherhood is using to make non-Muslims believe that they are fighting oppression and injustice for Muslims. Another memorandum that the Muslim Brotherhood created reveals their strategic goals to destroy North America and it is a plan, which they wrote in 1991. Their goals are to present Islam as a civilization alternative and support the establishment of the global Islamic State wherever it is, and this plan was submitted as evidence in the Holy Land Financial Trial, which is the largest terrorism trial in the history of the United States and it happened in Dallas, Texas. During that time, the American government handed 108 guilty verdicts to Muslim Americans and Muslim American organizations across the U.S. The reason why that trial occurred it was because the Holy Land Foundation and other Muslim organizations were raising money to support terrorist activities in the Middle East and Elsewhere to the tens of millions of US Dollars. The Muslim Brotherhood's initial plan for the Americas is to adopt the concept of settlement and understanding through its possible meanings, in other words, they want to sabotage the rest of the Western civilization from within with its hands by making their religion victorious over all other religions worldwide. The Muslim Brotherhood holds 29 Islamic organizations in North America with a particular goal of sabotaging the U.S., Canada and the rest of the Americas from within. If you are not familiar with these organizations, I do not blame you; I am even going to name a few for you, here they are:

- ISNA (Islamic Society of North America), an organization that is even advising the 44th President of the United States on foreign policy in the Middle East.
- MSA (Muslim Student Association), the

Muslim Student Association, has more members from the university and college communities across the U.S. than Democrats and Republicans combined. It is problematic because if you are a person who is critical of Islam, if you're pro-America etc., you have to have security protection before you even speak in universities and colleges.

- NAIT (North American Islamic Trust), this is an organization that owns almost 90% of mosques in the U.S., something they do to use deception for masking the intended goals of Islamist actions against Americans and the rest of the Western civilization with their miserable hands.

- MAP (Muslim Association for Palestine), which later became CAIR (Council on American-Islamic Relations) and this organization is a front group for Hamas in North America. Another thing that concerning is that CAIR are the ones talking on TV about Middle Eastern affairs and they are invited to the White House for dinner by the 44th President of the United States, to make matters worse, they even speak in the State Department and the Pentagon. This is not a military war because the military war is taken care of by radical Islamic terrorist group worldwide; this is what I call stealth Jihad, the way to use the Constitution of the United States against the United States, its people and the rest of the Western civilization; this is how they are planning to destroy America and its allies from within, while our enemies have been planning for our destruction for years, we have made decisions to bury our heads in the sand because we want to be sensitive towards Muslims. This is so dangerous, not just for our countries, but for the generations to whom we are going to leave our nations. These retarded maniacs are not just attacking militarily; they are also waging wars of civilization and pushing for more racism and prejudices, and the thing that is empowering them to do those kinds of evil things are the oil revenues and the Islamic conservative regime in Iran. They are infiltrating every part of our societies to destroy us from within and encourage us to hate our countries by making us feel like we are the oppressors and the Muslim world is the victim., they do this by holding media departments, education departments, political agencies, sports departments, music departments, business departments and so much more, while they are working so hard to destroy us we are busy fighting each other to score more points for the gesture of goodwill. The Muslim Brotherhood is using our laws and rights against you and me, while we pump gasoline in our vehicles, they put poison in the minds of our societies. The Fascists and the Nazis took children and changed society for ten years that is how they got so powerful and began WW II, which is responsible for 60 million lives being lost. Our enemies talking points are now being taught to our children and young adults across the Western world; this is why you are seeing many Westerners converting to Islam, and then later they join Islamic terrorist groups. Our enemies are doing all of those things because these children and young adults are going to be news anchors, opinion shapers and so much more, they are being manipulated against their will.

CHAPTER 10

LABOR MARKET'S EFFECTS ON TRADE & IMMIGRATION

On this chapter, I am taking a look at a critical topic that has an influence on how the world works, digging deeper into this conversation I will be focusing on trade because it has shaped our nations, cultures, and way of thinking for centuries since the early times of our existence. Business benefits countries that fully committed to it and those that are ready to join the competition and be mentally prepared to face the fact that there is hurt in every trade patterns; no pain, no gain. I have been digging in the challenges that developing countries face when it comes to the policies of the World Trade Organization and I am trying to analyze if the WTO has failed developing countries when it comes to delivering pro-development changes for farmers in poor countries by giving them access to export their materials to the rich world, or is there something else that is holding many developing countries back from gaining access to the rich global market; the truth is somewhere in the middle, my goal is to make further research on this topic and come up with my conclusions. The WTO

was established in 1995, and the purpose of this
organization is to provide framework for negotiations
when it comes to trade agreements between developed
and developing countries, one of the roots of the
problems between developed and developing
countries is that developed countries want to protect
their domestic agricultural sector, while developing
countries want the substantiation of fair trade on their
agricultural products and it seems like no one is willing
to find a compromise about this situation. I am also
going to talk about the impact it might have on poor
countries if they feel like the WTO has sidelined them
and how far will it go when it comes to the influence it
can have in the rich world. According to the WTO,
developing countries comprise the majority of its
membership; those nations are classified as either
developed, least developed or developing according to
their standard of living, life expectancy, infrastructure,
levels of corruption, the level of governance, etc.
According to the WTO, the advantage that many
developing countries have is i.e. special and differential
treatment provisions, in other words, developing
countries in the organization have special rights that
give them options to be treated more favorably than
other members. If I can add a couple of examples in
this case about this case, I can include for instance
longer trading agreements and commitments that
serve the increasing in trade opportunities for
developing countries. Another example that I can give
about this case is the WTO's goal to support
developing countries to handle disputes, implement

technical standards and special provisions related to many of the least developed countries worldwide. Now that I have discovered the WTO's goal to help developing countries have a thriving trade, I would also like to find out about why other economists, bloggers and influential people believe that the WTO is failing developing countries. I am also going to take a look at things from their perspective, and once I find a balance on both sides, then I will come up with my take on what is up and own about this situation. Some influential people from different areas of the media, academia, sociology and various other sectors believe that the WTO has failed to live up to its promise when it comes to helping developing countries, an agenda that was adopted by the Doha Development Round of trade negotiations in 2001; this plan came as a response to the anti-globalization protests in the 1990's. The argument is based on the WTO's failed pro-development policies for developing countries, which are sidelined by economic and political interests of global powers. I have looked at some of the examples where some influential economists, bloggers, journalists, politicians, religious leaders and actors believe that the WTO has failed developing nations, I am going to focus on trade agreements, commodities and legal costs. Let us talk about one of those products that have created lots barriers for many farmers in some of the world's poorest countries, the product, which I am speaking about is cotton, according to the Fairtrade Foundation there were US $ 47 billion in subsidies paid to rich countries for the past decade that has created barriers for farmers in many West African countries, and those farmers believed that their lifeline was their only way to trade out of poverty. In many other parts of the world, there are similarities when it comes to other commodities besides cotton, and this results in millions and millions of people forced out of their businesses and deeper into misery, the case does not end there; when it comes to other agricultural means or products, the Fairtrade Foundation believes that the WTO has failed to reduce subsidies paid to rich world farmers, whose production continue to threaten the livelihoods of those in developing countries. The Fairtrade Foundation has also found out that the WTO has failed to clarify to developing countries by making rules that are complicated and ambiguous when it comes to concluding trade agreements that allow the world's poorest countries to be manipulated by wealthy nations, like for instance many African countries and some other poor countries have been forced to eliminate tariffs that are up to 90% of their trade because the rules that should exist to offer them protection are not there. When it comes to the decision-making, many poor countries find themselves in situations when they do not have a voice in trade negotiations. The WTO has failed to improve its pricey legal system; no African country has ever been successful at acting as a complainant when it comes to how it is treated unfairly. When it comes to medicine, many poor countries do not have access to affordable medications because of failed agreements between members of the organization, the failure to clarify the need for governments to protect public health and the property rights of pharmaceutical firms. Now that I have looked at the case from both sides, and I am going to say what I think about this problem, on the other hand, I am not going to hide from the fact that there are faults on both sides, and I am going to give my reasons based on the research that I have been making. I do not claim to be an expert on the subject of the WTO and the problems that many developing countries from Africa, Latin America and Asia/Pacific, but I believe that the WTO has to make it clear to the skeptics that it can treat all of its members equally and promote fair trade between nations because right now, the WTO has a reputation of protecting only multinational companies and wealthy countries and it is up to them to work on their credibility. When farmers in the developing world do not have access to the market from the rich countries it results in more and more people leaving their businesses and falling in a vicious cycle of poverty; when that happens, this leads to mass migration from the Third World to the First World because they believe that they have no other option left and the First World cannot handle the misery of the entire Third World population. I do agree that the WTO has failed to raise concerns about child labor, the migrant crisis and the trouble with human trafficking; you might think that all of these topics do not have anything in common, but they do; in countries where you have massive populations living in poverty you will often find a higher amount of child labor, human trafficking, other forms of slavery because in those parts of the world your only focus is to your survival. My opinion is that free trade will be a critical step for developing countries because it relaxes the agreements on tariffs and trade within Third World countries and the abilities of governments from those countries to strengthen the private sector and lift millions and millions of people out of misery. When the developed world gives loans to many developing countries, loans that they cannot afford to repay it contributes to impossible trade restrictions and to make matters worse, they keep witnessing broken promises. Developing countries do not need aid; they need to be given opportunities to export their products to the developed world, if it is not the case, then other doors should be open, doors where developing countries can trade with each other. Many in the far right complain about immigration, but many of the people who immigrate would rather stay in their countries if conditions there good enough for them; I am not in any way making excuses for illegal immigration, what I am trying to explain is that multinational businesses often contribute to the destruction of the livelihoods of farmers from developing countries and them are the same ones who are encouraging illegal immigration by hiring the illegals and violating the laws of their nations. The World Trade Organization policies are poor results from multinational firms and governments from the developed world, but governments from developing countries also have an ownership to this situation

because in most cases they are the ones who prevent
the progress of their people by keeping them ignorant
and laying all the blame game of their incompetence
on global powers. If you look at the world's most
corrupt countries, over 90 % of the world's most
corrupt societies are developing countries and
unfortunately corruption has become a way of life
inflicted in the psyche of many populations from
developing countries because even if the same
governments in power are responsible for their misery,
the same people continue to worship those
governments out of the idea of standing up to the
West, but you are still poor and miserable, and your
situation has not changed. Not all developing
countries struggle with the WTO's trading rules and
principles, not all developing countries fail to gain
access to the market of the EU, the U.S., Canada,
Australia, Japan, Singapore, Hong Kong, Brunei, New
Zealand and other parts of the developed world;
Newly Industrialized Countries like Brazil, Turkey,
Thailand, South Africa, Indonesia, Malaysia, China,
Mexico India and the Philippines export many of their
goods to developed countries, yes, there are
restrictions and many other kinds of rules, but that's
how trade works. Developed countries will always
protect their farmer's livelihoods, whether many
governments from poorer countries like it or not, that
policy is here to stay. The question is what have
governments from many of the world's poorest
countries done for the last decades to help their
farmers? What have governments from real Third

World countries done to lift many of their citizens out of poverty, especial those in the African continent? Do governments from poor countries expect global powers to defend the interest of their poor citizens at the expense of their citizens from the rich world? Dream on, if the meetings taking place in the WTO are not bearing fruits, perhaps take a look from within and ask yourselves why many of the things you have done are not working. I know that what I am going to say now will bring many people on a red field; governments from many of the world's poorest countries and the populations of those nations are primarily responsible for the messes that they have created, we allow, (I say we because I have roots in both the Republic of the Congo, the DRC, and Angola), we allow corruption to reflect our societies and embrace ignorance on the same levels as our politicians, our governments and ourselves included lack the capacity or capacities to cooperate with Western countries on specific development projects. We do not even work well on specific development projects with countries like China, India, and Brazil, yet we wonder why we are where we are. Our way of thinking matches the levels where our societies are right now, and it is up to us to change it; no global power is going to clean our messes for us. Every time someone has a project in an African country that can benefit the population of that particular state, politicians from there want to be bribed first so that they can use the money for being party animals, women, impressing others etc., while the majority of the population could benefit from that project development and increase their hopes of staying in their country. By the way, did I forget to mention that Singapore was a Third World country and it later became a First World country within amounts of short decades? A state that does not have any form of natural resources, how do you think it happened? Croatia was one of those countries that were a victim of the Balkan Wars in the early 90's; it is a member of the European Union, how do you think they achieved it? I know that every nation is different, and every culture is different, but please do not use it as an excuse for your failure. I am sick and tired of the irrational tribal mentality, which many populations from Third World countries have, instead of recognizing that to some degree we Africans are in charge of the nations we run and how they are, our governments are in charge of our countries and the way they are governed; our countries have now been independent for more or less than 50 years, and we have been unstable for the majority of those times because we did not want to invest in resources and the commitment to be successful societies. We have often ignored that communities that have higher unchecked amounts of birthrates also happen to those with highest infant mortality rates, those are also the same countries that receive more foreign aid and numbers keep increasing. Why are we choosing to depend on other people when it comes to foreign aid? Why? Don't we have any form of dignity? We have got to recognize that the reason why we are where it is because we are not well-organized, we lack a lot of discipline, or we do not use our control to our best advantage; we whine a lot about poverty, but do not want to do something about it. Instead of begging other people for food, learn to grow your food. We complain about the First World being responsible for our misfortunes and believe that it is the reason why we are not making the progress that we should, although it is one of those factors our success and failure is in our hands. We talk about how the socio-economic and political divide between the North and the South and the impact it has on how advanced the North is and how less advanced the South is, I do not ignore that those divides exist, but the main problem of the South is its failure to deal with a dysfunctional education systems, dysfunctional political systems, the lack of food, water, and shelter, etc. and progress is not being made quickly and as long as no one takes the initiatives to recognize that the South is its worst critique and it is only the South that can change if things will improve in that part of the world.

CHAPTER 11

A LETTER TO WESTERN LEADERS &

WESTERN ORGANIZATIONS

When it comes to the threat that the Western world is facing from jihadi threats, we are often only fixated on what terrorists do by killing many people in different countries around the world where those primitive insects believe that Islam is not pleased with the way people live their lives and the values many of us cherish. But you and the mainstream media downplay what I call stealth jihad from different Muslim Brotherhood front groups in the Western world, anyone who expresses concerns about such threats is referred to as an "Islamophobe" and an anti-Muslim bigot. You have given countries like Saudi Arabia, Qatar, the United Arab Emirates and other similar countries since they nationalize the oil, which your scientists discovered, by giving them too much power, you have allowed them to build more mosques in the Western world and those mosques there are lots of hate preachers who preach hatred against our way of life and us as peoples. Many of you have foundations that receive money from those oil-rich states and with that comes to their power to buy your silence. You all know that in those countries minorities of different races, religions, and tribe do not enjoy the rights of the majority populations like those of us who live in the Western world, yet you have unwillingly ignored to challenge them on that issue, you also know that in one of those countries women are not allowed to drive, and those are the same countries where women are treated as second-class citizens, yet you have not had the courage to hold those states accountable out of the fear of the impact, which it might have on your careers and our nations' economies. It looks like you have sold your souls to the devil, and sometimes I wonder if you are serving the interest of your peoples or if you are serving the interest of a part of the world whose values are barbaric, sadistic and brutal. You all know that those maniacs have made a decision for 14 centuries to declare war on those of us who do not share or practice their system of beliefs, yet you are walking on eggshells out of the fear of being treated as hateful, bigots, imperialists, colonialists and so on; those people did not have power over you, you and your predecessors have allowed them to have power over you and play you like violins. They have played you like a game when they are using the "Palestinian Cause" as a way to manipulate your emotions, while they are using your humanity and your willingness to care for you. It is not just those countries, but the rest of the Arab League and the OIC. We are at war against an enemy who does not wear uniforms; we are at war with an enemy who is being on our destruction; we are at war against people who believe that their duty is to take back what they believe is rightfully theirs, and this is nothing new because they did it in the past when they conquered Spain, Portugal, parts of France, parts of Italy; they defeated Hungary, Serbia, Croatia, Bulgaria and they even conquered parts of Russia and they have enslaved many Africans. The Islamic State or the Islamic Empire ended less than 100 years ago by Atatürk and fundamentalist Mohammedans want to restore the Islamic Empire through terrorist acts, this idea happened before the United States had an open foreign policy, this happened before Israel ever existed; we are talking about the late 1920's and the early 1930's. Every time we discussed the issues of the Islamization of European nations and the rest of the other non-Muslim nations around the world, every time we have addressed the issues with mass migration, fake refugees, open borders, illegal immigration, frauds and so on it seems to come together as one unit, yet we are still walking on eggshells. We are making a decision to walk on eggshells by not wanting to recognize radical Islamic terrorism as the threat of our time, since Communism, Fascism, Nazism, etc., radical Islam is back on the rise because it goal is to establish the Islamic Empire, which ended less than a century ago; in order for them to carry on with their objectives, non-Muslim lives have to be sacrificed for the sake of the ideals in the name of the deity they worship, I do agree with Speaker Gingrich about testing every

person with a Muslim background and those who
want to be governed by the Sharia have got to be
deported, repatriated or leave United States, France,
Canada, Sweden, Germany, South Africa, Australia,
New Zealand, Hungary, Angola, the Congo, the
Netherlands, The Democratic Republic of Congo,
Italy, Brazil, Paraguay, Peru, Serbia, Croatia, ,Belgium,
Argentina, Uruguay, Chile, Cameroon, Thailand, the
Philippines, China, Japan, Mauritius, Seychelles, Cape
Verde, Spain, Portugal, Czech Republic and other
non-Muslim countries. Like or not Sharia Law is
incompatible with Western values and it is even
inconsistent with the values of any non-Muslim
country; Muslims who do reject Sharia Law should be
treated fairly, just like anyone else with respect and
dignity. This is the time for the Western world to be
relentless for the sake of the survival of its values and
its civilization, it has to be constant against medieval
barbarians who make decisions to behead those they
do not agree with, it has to be harsh against the same
savages who kill women for not wanting to have sex
with them, those are the same people who throw
homosexuals down from buildings and I can go on
and on about other sick ideas they are involved in, but
you get my point, I hope. Anyone who works on
websites where they favor the Muslim Brotherhood,
Al Qaeda, ISIS, Al Nusra and all those Islamic Jihadi
groups has got to lose his citizenship, whether it is an
American citizenship, whether it is the French
citizenship and so on, the next thing that needs to
happen is that the individual has to face deportation

back to his country of origin. Any organization that is engaged with such a felony should face legal charges and shame publicly. Any organization that funds terrorist organizations must be held to account and those who are involved in such activities should be deported, forget about the jails because jails are already filled up with Muslim fundamentalist inmates who radicalize non-Muslim prisoners and those who refuse to convert to Islam are often beaten or killed. Any Muslim inmate who threatens to beat or kill any other patient who does not want to convert to Islam has got to be flown to Guantanamo for waterboarding and hard labor. We can also engage with North Korea when it comes to using those dangerous Muslim inmates in North Korean labor camps for at least 5 decades, I can tell you that the North Koreans authorities will teach them how to behave. I am fed up hearing about the world's most wealthiest non-Muslim nations whose values are far more better and superior to those with Islamic values, those nations that are among the most powerful countries in the history of our world is helpless in the face of medieval Islamic savages who are funded by barbaric Islamic governments in Saudi Arabia, Qatar, the United Arab Emirates, Turkey, Bahrain, Iran, Brunei and other nations from the Organization of the Islamic Conference. There are 44 conflicts around the world between Muslims and non-Muslims, regardless of the race of those non-Muslims, regardless of their tribes and regardless of their religions, and their political affiliations and those wars are costing lives, especially

in places where we do not report much of it, like in
the Philippines, Thailand, Indonesia, Lebanon, Iraq,
Egypt, Algeria, Djibouti, Eritrea and so on because we
do not want to make Muslims angry. Cry me a river; I
am sick and tired of being told to be reasonable to
people who do not want to be reasonable to me, I am
sick and tired of being told to be sensitive to the
people who want to kill me because I am criticizing a
religion, I am sick and tired of being told to be told
not to judge because doing that makes me intolerant, I
am sick and tired of being told to be tolerant to those
who are intolerant to me; I am sick and tired of
hearing President Obama and Hillary Clinton not
calling thing by their names; I am sick and tired of the
FBI not calling the threat from Islamic terrorism for
what it is; I am sick and tired of Muslims demanding
special treatment in the name of their religion, while
they do not stand up for religious minorities who are
treated poorly in majority Muslim countries, and I am
sick and tired of Muslims blaming the Crusades for
their misfortunes, while they, themselves were
colonizing non-Muslims in non-Muslim lands before
the Crusaders made the decision to stand for the
people of their nations. These incidents are happening
because we have weak leaders who do not have the
courage to confront the problems out of their sources.
Those on the Left and the rest of the political elite can
say...Do you want us to kill all 1.6 Muslims? Hello! We
are at war against an ideology whose fundamental
values are part of the Islamic religion, and those who
are responsible for that political ideology are

fundamentalist Muslims who are the ones with the loudest voices and they also happen to be the ones with the money; where there is money, there is power, that is just the way life goes. In case you did not know out of 1.6 billion Muslims there is a group of Muslims who want to destroy us and they do not care about your goodness, they do not care about your generosity, they do not care about the time when you once helped them or fought for their rights, they do not care about who governs your country and they do not care about you as a human being; they want you dead, unless you decide to convert to Islam. Don't tell me that it is just a tiny few because there are 100s of millions of Muslims out there who want to be governed by a strict form of Sharia and those will do anything to kill in the name of their religion and their deity. Just in case you do not get it out of your nativity, Muslims have been reading same religious texts for 14 centuries, whether those texts are in the Quran, the Hadiths, and the Sunnah and they have been using the same books to declare wars on non-Muslims since their Prophet became a military warrior. To you who is reading this book, all of those things we are witnessing in many non-Muslim countries are the faults of Western political elites from both the Left and the Right, it is also the fault of many leaders from the rest of the non-Muslim world who are corrupt and allow their peoples to suffer and pay the price because they get money from Oil rich states from the Gulf who buy their silence. They do not have the guts to confront this problem of our time when it comes to doing what is right and necessary to protect their countries and their peoples. Those are the same leaders who do not have the guts to tell us the truth, and this starts with the 44th President of the United States and many other leaders of the free world, as well as leaders from the developing non-Muslim world. The mainstream media in the Western world is also to blame for failing, to tell the truth about the problems with radical Islam and how countries like Saudi Arabia are financing terrorist groups by using their oil resources as a weapon of war against us, by the way have we forgotten that we are infidels in the eyes of those who are determined to kill us? How can countries like France, Britain, Germany, Sweden and others allow the Sharia Law to run parallel to their constitutions, while it is hostile to our constitutions because it is man made? It does not make sense that we have given too much power to those Gulf state nations for reasons that I just cannot understand, why on Earth are we bowing to them? Why? Anyone who tells me the contrary is lying because if those barbaric nations did not have oil, we would not have allowed the Sharia in many of our societies. I also believe that you need to monitor mosques and madrassas because they are the sources of the radicalization that many of our societies are dealing with. Like it or not mosques are the primary sources of recruitment for Muslim Jihadists. Madrassas that teach children only to follow the Quran have to be closed, and those who are infiltrating our media, our governments, our organizations and political parties have got to have a one-way ticket back to their countries. There have to be consequences when it comes to dealing with such a threat of our times because we are right now is very different from where we were 18 years ago, 20 years ago, 30 years ago, 35 years ago and so on. We are not following the policies of telling the truth because we are willing to cover up and protect the corrupt who buy our silence by investing in our soccer clubs, universities, owning shares in our firms; indoctrination our primary schools, high schools, colleges and other sports clubs; we are acting as if we are ship of fools who wonder why wolves and coyotes are keeping on killing us. We are making excuses for people who are opposed to our way of life, we are making excuses for individuals who are opposed to our system of values; we are making excuses for people who make it clear to us that they want to kill us, and they do not mince words; we are making excuses for individuals who impose their way of life in our societies by making demands on halal meat in continues, schools, restaurants and supermarkets; we are making excuses for people who demand more mosques and pray in our streets, while Jews and Christians are not allowed to practice their religions freely in Muslims countries, while they are treated like second and third class citizens; we are making excuses for countries that are funding those terrorist activities and we make a choice to view them as our allies, while at the back of their minds they want to use every opportunity they have to destroy us. We are getting exactly what we deserve, I am sorry for being so blunt and outspoken; we are getting what we deserve because we do not want to confront the problems as they are and Europe in on a verge of a civil war. Those savages are opposed to everything that makes us who we are and they are the ones who have chosen to do it for 14 centuries, they are very honest about it and they are determined to destroy us with all means. There are many intelligence communities who are saying that Europe is on the verge of the civil war. The entire elite media and the whole political class from the Western world and the rest of the non-Muslim world have been desperately trying to keep us ignorant of the truth about where we are, instead of speaking out badly about the problems. I do not understand the idea that civilized countries should tolerate a religiously imposed court system that does not respect the values of those countries in the first place, and ideas that make those civilized societies what they are, what I mean is that Sharia Law must be made illegal in any country that has a human conscious. Muslims who are against Sharia Law are the ones that need to bring change to Islam. If non-Muslims try to do it, it will only radicalize the one's that would have been on our side. They will need our help, but we can not do it alone, but it is primarily their responsibility to take a serious look at the fundamentals of their religion and ask themselves tough questions; the idea of blaming everything on colonization, the crusades, America, Britain, etc. is a distraction and a waste of energy; it is up to Muslims themselves to fix the rotten issues about Islam, and they need to be very honest about the morals of their

Prophet and his character. I am also sick and tired of hearing ridiculous phrases like Man caused disasters, overseas contingencies, workplace violence, etc.; call it as it is by its name, and if you don't, you do not deserve to govern a civilized country. We have made a choice to welcome Turkey in NATO, we have made a decision to elect leaders who only focus on their careers and the interests of those who have the willingness to put an end to our existence. Is Obama going to ban trucks for the terrorist attacks in Nice? Even if terrorist organizations like Al Qaeda, ISIS, Hezbollah whose activities could go down, there are still waves of Jihadists and Jihadist sympathizers in Europe, the United States, Canada, Australia, New Zealand and elsewhere. Europe has a problem with a large demography of Jihadists who control no-go areas where the police are afraid to enter. Those savages are determined to destroy the vibrant economies that have given them the opportunities, which their first countries could never give them and they do not give a flying potato on how good and reasonable you and I can be to them. We have the political elite and the media elite in the fantasyland and people like you and me who watch Fox News and other similar news living in the real world, which fundamentalist Mohammedans want to turn into an Islamic planet, that is how they expect peace to rule in the world once it becomes a Muslim world. They are not going to give up until lots of lives and bloods are sacrificed in the name of their system of beliefs and their god. The fact that we choose to have Saudi Arabia, Qatar, Kuwait,

Kosovo, Albania, Pakistan and others as our allies and it is coming back to bite us very hard because many of those people do not have our best interests. The enemy has a plan to steal from us, the enemy has a plan to destroy us and the enemy has a plan to behead us. The enemy wants to advance his theocracy in the societies that have welcomed its followers with open arms. To win a war you have to identify your enemy and you must have the willingness to crush and defeat your enemy. The Liberal Left and the rest of the political elite are defending the backward values of Islam Muslims and LIBERALS. liberals are pro-bad-parenting basically. somehow it's worse when an American or a Frenchman is feeding too many hamburgers to their kid, but when hundreds of millions are practicing teaching backward values to children, then it's like whatever. 'it's their culture.'□ When honor killings occur, well it is like whatever. "It is their culture." When the imposition of halal meat occurs, well it is like whatever. "It is their culture." When people have to hide for their lives because they are critical of Islam and some other Third World barbarity, the Liberal Left will take the side of those who do the wild stuff. The thing is that lots of liberals love terrorism because conservatives hate terrorists, and liberals often have the notion that "An enemy of yours is a friend of mine." Just look at BLM. A group of homosexuals formed BLM to incite ethnic insurgency against law-and-order and conservatives. Sure, a few cops die now and then, but liberals see that as collateral damage that is necessary to get their "equality." When we finally deal with terrorism, we should take this into consideration. We cannot gamble with the lives of the French people and other citizens from the non-Muslim world when you can't tell who is coming in our countries and the fact that some terrorists infiltrate migrants. Why should we take care of refugees who do not have the interests of our societies? Why should we take those who lie and manipulate so that they can live on our shores? We can create safe zones where we can help them where they are, or we can be selective on who should and should not be allowed to come into our countries. There are many religious minorities in the Middle East who face discrimination and persecution because of what they are and because of what they believe, those are the ones whom I call real refugees, and we can do everything in our power to integrate them into our societies; I am confident that those people have the will to integrate in the communities that have welcomed them with open arms. Across Europe we are seeing the second generation Muslims immigrants committing acts of jihad because of Islam. Stop Islam!, Islam is an enemy of a free America. Stop treating Islam as a religion and recognize it as an enemy that wants to conquer. Raze the Mosques, Deport all Imams, stop Islam or it will continue the jihad against us. In many Western countries most mosques are teaching the idea of overthrowing democracy in democratic societies, the hatred of Christians, Jews, Atheists and others and the establishment of the Islamic Caliphate worldwide. Many people from the political class, especially those in the Western world, many, NGO's, Trade Unions, Churches, Synagogues, Buddhist and Hindu temples claim that all cultures are equal, in other words they practice what I call cultural relativism, yet they are the same people who complain about Islamic terrorism and some even question Turkey's presence in NATO and how this madness came about; at the same time many political elite groups from Western countries do not have the courage to confront Turkey by holding it accountable for the genocides against the Armenians and the Assyrians, they do not have the courage to defend people who share common values with them because they do not want to upset Turkey; it seems like Turkey has more power than the rest of the Western world, that is why it is bowing down to Turkey, it seems like the United States is not a superpower anymore who is able to stand up for the Armenians who have more shared values with the ,majority American population than Turkey, which is a Muslim country. Haven't you noticed that members of the Organization of the Islamic Conference stand up for each other no matter what? Haven't you noticed that members of the Arab League stand up for each other no matter what? Yet non-Muslim countries do not that, no wonder we are such easy targets for Islamic savages and their brutal activities. The same political elite who made a decision not to make a trade embargo against Turkey, Saudi Arabia and other Muslim countries that pause a threat to us, yet they have the courage to make trade embargoes against nations like Cuba and other similar countries. Not that I am defending Cuba, which is a Communist dictatorship, but so is China, so is North Korea, so is Vietnam etc., why these double standards? If I have not made anything clear to you about hundreds of millions of Muslims who want the Sharia Law, let me tell you that those are same people who have the willingness to wage war against us until the whole world is an Islamic planet; they are doing it in the name of their religion and their God, yet the political class from Europe, United States, Canada and the rest of the Western world want Turkey in the already fragile European Union, adding more and more the destruction of Europe and the rest of the Western world by allowing it to commit suicide. This will have an adverse influence on the remainder of the non-Muslim world because of the objectives of those savages. The OIC's goal is to make Islam a dominant political movement worldwide, and they do it by bullying their way out of it, yet we are allowing them to get away with their dumb goals. The Western political elite have not learned the lessons of history and they haven't found out that the best predictor of a future behavior is the past; if Muslims from Turkey and the rest of the Middle East invaded Europe at the time of the Islamic Inquisition of Spain, parts of Italy, parts of France etc. ; if the same part of the world invaded the Indian Subcontinent, killing 80 million Hindus and if the same people were responsible for the deaths of 120 million Africans, whom they enslaved and murdered in the name of Arab Nationalism, Ottoman Nationalism and Islamic

Supremacism, do you think that they are not going to
do it again? The United States and the rest of the
Western world have made a choice to have airbases in
Middle Eastern countries, and they wonder why they
are contributing to their destruction, as well as ours by
creating its death. How on Earth do we defend a
country or countries that go rogue against us? Those
are countries that are governed by some form of the
Islamic Sharia Law, yet we are surrendering to those
thugs, we surrender to savages and idiots who want to
impose their New World Order on us, and we just
have to see it as a new regular in the same of
Globalization and Globalism, right? I am sick and
tired of this being a new normal, I am sick and tired of
my fellow countrymen and women putting up with
being governed by Islamic Fascists; Every time
someone says Allahu Ackbar when they commit
terrorist acts against Western and other non-Muslim
interests, we need, to be honest and forthcoming
about who is doing it, and I can tell you that those
people are not from Austria, nor are they Catholics,
nor are they Methodists and they are not Buddhists.
They are Muslim fundies who are acting upon the
violent verses of the Quran, the Hadith, and the Sunna
and they have been reading the same books for 14
centuries; they have declared war upon non-Muslims
for 14 centuries. They are determined to kill people
whose lifestyle they do not approve, they are
committed to killing individuals who belong to
different religions, they even kill their own fellow
Muslims who do not believe and worship the way they

do, they make it clear to us that they do not want us alive, unless we convert to their religion and the want to restore the Islamic Caliphate worldwide. We call them all sorts of names, but those terrorist groups have a common objective, and they are willing to die for their god, their prophet and for the declaration of Jihad against those of us whom they view as unclean, filthy, unworthy and decadent. We are partially brought this insanity upon ourselves for importing millions of Muslim immigrants in our Judeo-Christian countries without even knowing who they are, what they believe and if they have our best interests; we have decided to bring unskilled immigrants from Third World countries and gave false hopes, when they look for jobs, they are placed at the back of the bus, and we all know where those people find their source of pride when there is nothing left to live for. That is why in Europe there is a rebellion against the assent of Islam, and things will get worse before they get better. Since the early 1950's there have been trading agreements between Western and Middle Eastern governments, which have resulted in more Islamic immigration in Europe and the Western world; this meant that Muslim immigrants were not required to integrate and respect the law of the lands where they have their new homes, another thing that contributes to the plan for the Islamists to take over the Western world is demography because Muslims have much higher birthrates than Westerners combined, no matter what country where those Muslim migrants live, to make matters worse, the

substantial of Muslims who arrive in Western
countries as refugees from Syria, Iraq and the higher
amounts of migrants from other Muslim countries
whose goal is not to search for a better life, but invade
Europe and the rest of the civilized world. When you
look at suburbs in many European countries, the
populations that are represented there are Muslim
migrants and migrants from other parts of the Third
World and those suburbs are of poor shape many of
the people in those areas depend on some government
handouts, countries like Morocco, Algeria, Tunisia,
Egypt and even Libya could turn out tens of millions
of the so-called refugees in Europe, and this will mean
more and more people living in social challenging
areas, a white flights, more violence, more mosques
and more welfare dependence. The people who will be
paying for it are both hardworking Frenchmen,
hardworking Germans, hardworking Italians,
hardworking Swedes, hardworking Spaniards, hard
working Russians, hardworking Hungarians,
hardworking Britons, hard working Dutch people,
hardworking Belgians, hard working Poles,
hardworking Australians, hard-working Canadians,
hard working Luxembourgians, hardworking Serbs,
hardworking Croatians, hard working Americans, hard
working Portuguese, hard working Slovaks, hard
working Slovaks and so on.; that is why I believe that
Europeans, Americans, Canadians, Australians and
others will say no; and they will say enough of this
rubbish, those groups of peoples represent between 70
to 95 % of their respective populations and this

resistance is building up across those societies. Those nationalist parties are on the rise in countries like: France, Holland, Sweden, Denmark, Norway, Finland, Belgium, Britain, Germany, Austria, Spain, Portugal and even Switzerland. In countries that do not have significant populations like Poland, Slovakia, Hungary, Croatia, Romania, Bulgaria, Czech Republic and other East European countries we are also seeing many nationalistic anti-Islamic and anti-immigrant parties rising in the polls and in some countries they are even part of their respective governments. It is more likely that for much of those countries there are going to be many anti-immigrant and anti-Islamic political parties that are going to take power and govern their nations. It will happen because there is so much anger, distrust, and resentment towards the political elite, the multinationals, the Socialists, the mainstream media, mainstream political parties, etc. I also believe that it is not going to be pretty; those nationalistic political parties are rogue, they are in many areas very extreme, they are rigid and this will cause racial tensions, ethnic tensions and it could even lead to a civil war in some countries. I would also like to warn that there are going to be many lives that are going to be lost and blood will flow in many streets of Europe, possibly also other Western countries. I am warning you that if you allow these transformations of your societies, there will be strife that could lead to wars and violence. Please reassert your values, reassert your immigration and foreign policy, reassert the control of your borders, reaffirm the existence of your civilization before the far right savages do it for you, get your priorities straight. I feel like I am repeating myself with many different words about this topic; I feel like am I am recycling my message time after time in this book. Please think about your existence for the generations to come; they will never forgive you if you allow your Judeo-Christian nations whose values have been based on humanism, liberty, reason and enlightenment out of the fear of being politically sensitive towards Muslims and appease to their demands. Save your existence from the immaturity of the Muslim world, please. Another political ideology that makes some people stupid besides Political Islam is Libertarianism; They believe that disrespect for individual rights is the essential precondition for a free and prosperous world, that force and fraud are good things in human relationships, and that only through slavery can peace and prosperity be realized. Another stupid thing about Libertarianism is the legalization of drugs, Libertarians are very tolerant of wrong things under the umbrella of freedom, that is why Libertarians do not have any ability to govern a country because their policies are decadent, egocentric and inconsistent; we can criticize China for so many things, but one of the things that I like about countries like: China, Singapore and Japan is that those societies isolate people who refuse to be responsible and the Western world doesn't under the umbrella of Human Rights; well, let me tell you something: When you make a decision to sell drugs, when you make a decision to traffick drugs, when you make decisions to kill each other to control the narcotic market, you are contributing to millions of people being addicted to all forms of drugs, and you are contributing to the deaths of those who take illegal subsidies, and you are destroying many lives; you do not have the right to do that, I do not care about your financial situation, nor do I care about your life situation - no matter what, you do not have the right to do that; it is not the fault of your governments that you decide to sell drugs and get into such a dangerous business because you are looking for "easy money", people like you must be shamed, judged and look down on buying your communities, no matter what country you come from. I do have to agree with Bill O'Reilly from Fox News that while China isolates people who are irresponsible from communities, the Western world keeps growing so permissive, and it is blind solving the problems with poverty in its stores - it seems impossible now for the Western world to lift working class communities and minorities up from poverty and give them a sense of purpose in their lives. We are now living in a time where we have a culture that glorifies crude and criminal behavior; I am not blaming this on Hollywood because if you do not know the difference between a movie and a reality, then something is wrong with you. Libertarians glorify the narcotic industry, which is based on weak areas in the name of freedom and Liberty; that is not freedom to me, it is stupid and irresponsible. In many of those soft communities, there has been a failure to lead on the culture and family issues, something that leads to bad behavior and crime - this is excuses by Libertarians and sometimes even accepted. Anyone like me, any person like Sean Hannity, any person like Bill O'Reilly and others who sometimes questions anything that glorifies such bad behaviors is called old-fashioned, out of touch with the real world, not calm, dull and so on. Anyone who questions cohabitation, having children out of wedlock, etc., whether that individual is religious or not is criticized for not catching up with time. While there is so much money poured in public schools, nothing gets better; the system refuses to provide discipline, authority, the rule of law, this gives students with no other options, but not wanting to listen to their teachers, swearing at their teachers, swearing at their parents, swearing at the police, stealing, smoking marijuana and selling other drugs, etc. While this is happening, there are many people, both young and old, Blacks, Whites, Asians, Hispanics, Jews and others who are getting up in the morning - starting their own businesses, going to school for their education, working one or two jobs, writing books, looking for a job, taking action for the future of their nations and so on, not taking the immoral lazy way out of committing crime, smoking marijuana and taking other drugs. Those who want the legalization of all drugs are enabling such decadent behaviors and they have blood in their hands; Singapore has shown us the way to handle idiots who are involved in drug activities by executing them, please do not tell me about Human Rights and personal freedoms, those imbeciles are violating the lives of those who are dealing with drug

addiction and the impact it has on their loved ones -
not just that, but the impact that it has on us,
taxpayers. We do not want to learn and apply the
principles that China, Japan, and Singapore have, and
that is why the war on drugs has failed in the Western
world. The solution is not to surrender to something
that destroys your lives; the solution is to be forceful
and learn from those nations in the Far East that have
death penalty for drug traffickers, another solution
that I propose is to send drug dealers to labor camps
in North Korea, Russia, China and other places where
they can reap the benefits of their stupidity. We as
customers have a responsibility to stop buying illegal
subsidies from those who traffick drugs. I am sick and
tired of hearing about the excuses about alcohol being
a drug, that's why drugs must be legal, hello; Coffee is
a drug, nicotine is a drug, and medical prescriptions
are drugs, but it is not stopping drug dealers from
killing those who criticize their activities, it is not
lifting people who are addicted up to the mountains
and nor is it helping them taking their lives and power
back. Do we have control over drugs or do drugs have
power over us? You decide.

CHAPTER 12

IS THE U.N. FAILING ITS OBJECTIVES?

The United Nations is an organization whose policies struggle to deal with a divided world; in other words, the UN has difficulties dealing with profound challenges in a world that is changing very fast, for better or worse. During the Cold War, the UN was suffering greatly from its marginalization during the time when there were political battles over the International Economic Order and from the abuse heaped on its wealthiest member states, on the other hand, the challenge of sovereignty has grown significantly from the end of the Cold War. During the

last decades, governments have made it their mission
to preserve and protect their prerogatives and defend
their national sovereignty. The UN's policies might be
looked at as a sequel of the early beginnings of its
existence, but the regard that I have about the UN
today is troublesome, let me explain to you why I
think this way; the state where the United Nations is
today is problematic and its role in the world today is
often questionable, especially when it tells Western
countries to make it illegal and punishable to criticize
religion, in this case it is always about Islam. The role
of the United Nation is also questionable when comes
to dealing with the Darfur Genocide, the Eastern
Congo Genocide, corruption in many Third World
countries etc.; it seems like there is a double standard
here, it seems like the UN demands more to the
Western world and other majority European countries
than it does to Middle Eastern, African and Asian
countries. The United Nation's multilateral system
struggles to respond to high amounts of global
problems in the 21st century: Despite the UN's
Charter that persists the sovereignty of nations, the
organization faces obstacles to find consensus and
exercising leadership in a world, which is deeply
divided by relative wealth, cultural practices, religious
ideologies, political beliefs, system of values, psyche,
democracy, theocracy, unequal power, contending
ideas, poorly communicating cultures and forms of
rigid governments. In order for us to wonder why the
UN is in the state it is today, let us look at its roots
first; the United Nations' idea was part vision and part

ideology, whose goal is to bring peace and stability on
the planet since its birth, after the Second Word War;
what frustrates the United Nations is the evolving of
deadlines and the costliness of wars, not just
monetarily, but also the amount of people who have
to pay time after time for those wars by being killed or
by being left with psychological scars. This influences
a large measure of its response to the world affairs of
today and the structure of international relations. The
UN that existed between its birth and the times of the
Cold War is not the same organization anymore; you
might think that I am an alarmist or someone who is
reactionary when I talk about this situation, but the
truth is that the United Nation struggles to cope with
nations that have contending ideologies and they
represent most of the world's populations, especially
the Islamic ones. The United Nations of today has a
system that represents firm convictions of the New
World Order and this system is not compatible with
the desire of the political, moral and economics
foundations of liberalism, conservatism and other
civilized values, which are necessary and essential to
building, maintaining - and promoting world peace
and stability because the UN appeases to contradictory
globalizing paradigms: The Arab and Islamic
diplomatic, legal order and those who are helping it
achieve its vicious objective that is different to the
unity of humankind. A system like the UN, which is
intergovernmental because of its structure as an
organization that has different charters worldwide
various member states should never compromise its

Westphalian sovereignty based rules, ethics, norms and principles by bowing down to nations that have weak communicating cultures; this organization has to make it clear that not all cultures are equal: Nations that want to be members of the UN have to abide by those Westphalian norms, and those norms are not a threat to their national sovereignty; it could be an opportunity for the populations of the nations to begin questioning their own system of values and do the things that are constructive for the nations, so that they can be civilized and be counted as members of the international community, instead of allowing members of the OIC (Organization of the Islamic Conference) to modify their Human Rights Charter, so that those sets of values do not conflict with the Sharia Law. I find it deplorable that the UN is allowing this to happen, and when it does, it has blood on its hands. I have stated in this book many time that the values of the OIC are inferior to the values that the civilized world holds because all of those Mohammedan countries embrace the Sharia Law of some forms. Nations that are governed by politicians who starve their own populations and suppress their own citizens are inferior because they are choosing to not want to evolve from such system of values that are destroying their mindsets, their way of thinking and their abilities to prosper. The problem with the UN is that it fails to name the cause and treat both the symptoms and the roots of the problem by identifying things as they are : Call it like it is, say it like it is and come up with solutions that improve the conditions. If all member nations in the UN were determined to promote, build and maintain peace and stability in the world, this goal would be universally endorsed by the nations and there would be codes of appropriate international behavior that would be emerged from shared values and continued dialogue with people who are able to reason, not those who act like crazy wild animals with very high levels of testosterones. Let us get real here: These ideas have their origins in the Western hegemonic order, which grows and becomes universal. On the human rights charter itself, this proves to be very tricky because it struggles to little capacity when it has an open door to door policy for the development machinery of human rights and the consideration of human rights issues at the General Assembly and the Security Council. For decades after decades member nations have availed themselves by creating new body of commissions. If there is an area where the UN for action has successfully been realized it was in the field of the self-determination and the decolonization of Third World nations, the goal is to present self-determination as an opportunity for the international community to further develop the Charter and build the ability to realize collective action. The problem is that it has not been successful because the General Assembly, the Economic and Security Council do not reflect the values of most of the member states, I am not saying that there is anything wrong with the General Assembly or the Security Council for that matter - I am trying to point out that the UN did not anticipate religious tensions, tribal tensions, political tensions, civil wars, failed states and activities of Islamic terrorist organizations, also other forms of terrorism. During a particular time, the UN is called to respond to different types of conflicts, and the results have been less satisfactory. Despite attempting to learn from learning from its failures to resolve clashes in the 1990s and the peacekeeping capacities that the UN has made, the reforms have remained constrained on the ground by political interests and governments from countries with weak communicating cultures. I am not optimistic on how the UN deals with matters of the 21st century because it caves too much into the OIC and the failure to hold Third World accountable to the same standards it does for First World Nations. Whether the UN has to be reformed from within or not, it is a subject that is open to debate, but the way I am observing this organization it has been weak when it comes to dealing with Islamic terrorism and countries like: Saudi Arabia, Turkey, Qatar, Oman, Brunei, Sudan and other Muslim countries that sponsor Islamic terrorism. The UN has also been weak in dealing with Turkey's denial of the Armenian, Greek and Assyrian Genocides and the other genocides, which Islamic empires have been responsible for, for the last 14 centuries. The UN has also been weak in dealing with Third World governments that suppress their own citizens and those maniacs go with impunity or without sanctions. The greatest threat we are facing on Earth is not Global Warming; the biggest threat, which we are facing is Islamic terrorism and the failure to confront political Islam, which is responsible for most of the terrorist activities around the world. Another threat, which the world is facing is a very fast growing population in Third World countries; many people in that part of the world have too many or even extremely too many children, but they cannot even support them morally, financially and they cannot even offer them an education. This results in many children working so that they are the ones supporting their families, instead of parents helping them. Child labor is troublesome in many Third World countries whose governments are not competent enough to deal with such a deplorable issue. The world's population is 7, 5 billion today, in 2050 the world's population will be 9 billion people and in 2100, the world's population will reach 11,2 billion people. Let me make something clear for you; when you have such an increasing population, the impact on resources like water and other kinds of resources is enormous; you cannot avoid being in situation where this might result in another world war because as the population grows people are going to fight for resources, and there are always going to be some who are going to be left behind. Those who feel left behind will respond to violence to make their cases heard, those that have the resources will fight hard with all means to protect them. In my opinion, it is troublesome that the world's population is growing fast and my question to you, the reader is, do you believe that we have enough resources to sustain a rapidly growing population?

Whether Global Warming is real or not, I am not going to get into that debate; I just wonder if we are focusing on the right priorities. The United Nations has not been effective when it comes to illegal immigration and the migration crisis we are witnessing these days; it is asking Western countries to take more "refugees", but the UN is not asking Saudi Arabia, Qatar, the UAE, Malaysia, Brunei, India, Indonesia, Ethiopia to take in more "refugees", the question is why these double standards? What about Western countries that do not have the experience of integrating migrants of color, will they be able to cope with such a challenge? What kind of jobs will those nations give to the migrants? How are they going to encourage migrants to feels good about themselves, so that they can contribute to their "new societies"? What about illegal immigrants, what answers does the UN have for those people? Are countries like France, Netherlands, United States, Canada, Sweden, Germany, Spain, Italy, New Zealand obligated to keep those illegal migrants in their territories? What about their right to sovereignty? Is it a right for an illegal immigrant to violate laws of a country where he/she enters illegally? Do Muslim immigrants have the right to impose their cultural and religious customs in societies that have taken them in and do not share the same values? What does the UN do about mosques that preach hatred and the killings of those who do not believe in Allah? The UN cannot react quickly to threats to international peace and security, and it is not the UN's job to develop the economies of Third

World nations or, even other countries for that matter -the UN has not been able to produce consensus and norms in the international community over universal values , and these types of conditions are unfortunately not likely to change in the foreseeable future because the UN has lost its moral authority. On this chapter, I am looking forward to talking about why the United Nations is facing huge problems and the impact they have on its credibility when this organization does not reflect the century where we are right now. I am not saying that the United Nations has only failed and there are no successful stories, since its existence in 1945; that will be an understatement, because this organization has also had lots of successes; like for instance the prosecution of the former Liberian dictator, Charles Taylor, protecting the Galapagos Islands and one of the things that are open to debate is the fact that South Africa and Kazakhstan gave up on the Nuclear weapons. That is why I am saying that this is not about the UN just having failures. The organization is not alone to blame for everything wrong with many less developed countries, their governments and populations are primarily responsible for their fates, I know it sounds intense, but it is a fact. The reality is that most of the countries in the United Nations are both Third World and Newly Industrialized nations. I have raised parts of this topic in my book, let me explain; I have talked about many majority Black societies being their worst enemy because the way those nations look reflects a lot of us and the way we think, let me go further into the details; creating is an interesting thing, our way of thinking and our psyche is not helping us, but hurting us, especially when we do not feel good enough about ourselves. The UN has failed to dress this problem poorly out of the fear of not making Third World Nations unhappy. Another good thing that the United Nations has done successfully is the adoption of its peace operations to address problems in many failed states around the world by making improvements on its civilian administration. The United Nations has also proven itself to be in opening space for international civil society, something that gives different people from all over the world opportunities to address global challenges, such as poverty, famine, female genital mutilation, honor killings, human rights, religious fundamentalism, sexism, domestic violence, sexual slavery, child abuse, racism, homophobia, xenophobia, modern day slavery etc., but in my personal view many Western countries that are members of the UN should continue to impose upon nations that have weak communicating cultures a form of Westphalian state system from, which the populations of much of those developing countries can get some inspiration and make plans to rebuild their nations and enjoy the benefits of being in their lands; it will also be in the best interest of many of those Western countries that might be attractive places for illegal immigrants who go to those nations for seeking a better life. The UN has to defend its Westphalian values without making any form of apology for it; make it part of the charter.

CHAPTER 13

THE CURSE OF HUMAN TRAFFICKING

On this chapter, I am looking forward to raising very significant concerns about human trafficking and the impact it has on the victims, their families and society in general. I am going to write about something that is really deplorable, degrading and unpleasant; it is critical that there are robust debates about this uncomfortable topic, which imprisons the life of many women, men and especially children who are trapped because they are used as merchandises by groups of criminals who do not have any form of consciousness in their heads. We also need to discover the reasons why many of those people are still seduced by the false promises of those cold criminals who are just using them to make illegal money. Human trafficking is the world's second most lucrative crime, surpassed only by the traffic of narcotics. Human trafficking is not an illusion; it is real and we need to stop being politically correct about and call it like it is. We need to ask ourselves, how do the traffickers get the money to traffic innocent people? Who is helping them? Who is profiting from human trafficking? Who is profiting from the misery of the victims of human trafficking? We need to come up with honest answers and begin to deal with those who are running this rigid business from the above; I have a feeling that someone up there somewhere is hiding something, there are people on the above who know fully well how that vicious business is operating and they are keeping things in the dark. It can be politicians, corrupt governments, some of the super wealthy, some contractors from different secret services, some businessmen and businesswomen and the list goes on. Some of you might wonder if I have any form of evidence in my claims; I do not pretend to be an expert in human trafficking, but I do not believe that those traffickers are not managed from the above; believe me or not, they get orders from someone or a group of people who have access to governments, police, banks, firms, secret services and others, just like those who are involved in the traffics of narcotics; the formula is similar and this time traffickers are trading their fellow man, just as they traffic drugs. I do not believe that those traffickers are alone and I do not believe that they are the only ones running this vicious business, which impacts many families around the world. Those who are controlling the traffickers and the criminals who are running can be people who are close to us without you and I even knowing it; they can be your local bankers, your local teachers, your local police officers, contractors from different intelligent services, local governments and we won't even know that they're among us. Human trafficking is a serious crime and a grave violation of human rights, unfortunately each single year there are thousands of men, women and children who are trafficked; I would even go so far to say that over 2 million humans are trafficked every year; it happens in their own countries as well as overseas - this has an influence one way or the other in almost any country, the victims are trafficked through the abuse of power, forced exploitations and some people are given false promises when they are lied to, about life in the rich world. The profits from human trafficking reaches more than $30 billion every single year and it is estimated that the problem is much bigger than we could anticipate. Human traffickers do not see their fellow men as decent people; they see them as commodities, which they have to use to make some profits and most of the people who are behind human trafficking are men, but women are also represented in other areas of traffic. Some researchers believe that it is worse in Europe where you have over 140.000 people trapped in situations where they are victims of violence, degradation, and sexual exploitation. Not that I am undermining this research because these are not just numbers; these are real people with real emotions who are being taken advantage of by those who ought to know better, however, I would say that Human trafficking is far worse in many developing countries where traffickers face far worse forms of abuse, some even go unreported and unchecked, and in many cases many dealers in Third World and Newly Industrialized nations walk with impunity; the reason why those bandits get away with a lot of crap, it is because corruption and human trafficking are closely linked together. The lack of attention on this matter destabilizes the efforts to educate local citizens, implementing traffic policies and measures. It also makes it challenging and complicated to combat the trafficking of persons when there is a sense of powerlessness towards the perpetrators, and then the victims end up paying an enormous price; the scars of trafficking lasts for a lifetime because their lives have been stolen from them by those whom I do not even have enough words to describe in this book. Some of you might wonder what proof do I have to come up with such a statement, well; I do not blame you - however- I am going to say this for the second time in this chapter again, that I am not and I have never claimed to be an expert on human trafficking, but I can tell you that if you do not believe that corruption and human trafficking are intertwined, whether it is happening in a developed country, whether it is going on in a Newly Industrialized Country or whether it is even going on in a developing world, then you probably live in an isolated cave somewhere or perhaps you live under a rock; corruption and the trafficking of persons occur for instance when there are investigations about cases that human trafficking, through accounts of victims and perpetrators, that is where it indicates the corrupt behavior of law enforcers who do lots of favors to traffickers by helping them opening back doors, so that they can carry on with their dirty businesses by recruiting, transporting and exploiting their victims; on the one hand they passing laws, on the other they have back up doors for those beasts. What many corrupt criminal justices do, especially in many developing nations is that they obstruct investigations and prosecutions of cases, which involve human trafficking and this happens both in public and private sectors, such as municipalities, travel agencies, hotels, academia, NGO's, civil society, governments, places of worship, banks and others that may contribute to the trafficking of people. This pattern facilitates trafficking through money laundering, longstanding relationships, mutual relationships, briberies, threats and the abuse of

power. In many Third World countries, corruption has
become the norm, and it has also become a way of life,
a mindset and part of the psyche of the populations
living in the developing world. Those who live in
many Second and Third World countries live in places
where levels of corruption are very high; many citizens
in those countries, whether being men, women and
children face risks of being exploited in so many
critical ways through trafficking. This may involve
kidnapping, manipulation, the falsification of
passports and visas, illegal immigration, sexual slavery,
forced labor and so on. Corruption is a very powerful
tool, which many traffickers use, other devices include
blackmail and guilt by association; for instance,
governments are afraid to deal with dealers, knowing
full well that they are part of the problem; the
traffickers might threaten migrants to return to their
countries if they do not like the conditions offered to
them; they might talk about the police being racists
towards a particular group of people and there are
many more ways, which traffickers use to play their
preys like games of chess, this often leads to situations
where victims are silent about the sufferings that they
have dealt with out of the fear of reprisals from the
traffickers; in the worst case scenario victims do not
even have any form of expectations from their
governments, they even fear being ignored by those
who lead their countries. Either because the victims do
not know the laws in their own countries that protect
them, or they are afraid of the consequences that
might influence them and their loved ones negatively.

The implications of these types of neglects lead to
situations where the victims of human trafficking from
countries that exposed to corruption face the feeling
of guilt and shame, in the worst case many end up
taking their lives. This is not the way things have to be
in a functioning society; victims of human trafficking
have to be protected by their governments, regardless
of their age, gender, race, tribe, religion, political
affiliation, social class, job situation and so on - in
other words, equality under the law. In places where
the rule of law is not guaranteed for the locals who live
there, you cannot expect to be guaranteed protection
if human traffickers have exploited you - you've got to
question the character of those societies, and you've
got to examine the populations who are acting like a
herd of ships without any form of navigation and
path; even ships have a shepherd that protects them
from wolves and thieves. It is a big problem if you are
an ordinary citizen from a country that does not give
you a voice to take a stand against this evil business;
your testimony can save thousands and even millions
of lives, reach out to those you can trust and those
who have your best interest. You don't deserve to be
trafficked, you don't deserve to be exploited nor do
you deserve to be a commodity for others; those who
are doing these criminal activities are idiots who have
lost their own sense of empathy. I don't care what race
you are, I don't care what gender you are, I don't care
what religion you are, I don't care about your social
class or the country from which you come; I care
about you not being trafficked and I care about your

ability to stand up to the bullies who have stolen your life away from you. You deserve to be with people who have the willingness to defend your rights and your dignity. Human traffickers don't care about you; they give you false promises and stab you in the back later; the only thing they care about is your money - in other words, they only care about making money from you. Whether you're alive or dead, it is not their problem; they just look for the next victim to catch prey. To tell you the truth, human traffickers are super predators, and they belong to the basket of deplorable, governments and other organizations whose existence depend on human traffickers belong to the basket of disgraceful, whether they govern First World countries or Third World countries. My message to victims of human trafficking is that those who are involved in it, from top to bottom know that in order for their deplorable business to function, they have to depend on people who do not know anything about their rights and privileges, that is how the traffickers prey on those whom they perceive as easy targets - it is often said that people perish because of the lack of knowledge. Migrant smugglers take advantage of the impunity from a variety of governments, organizations, special interest groups, multinationals and others; they also benefit from weak and ineffective immigration policies in many Western countries, especially the European Union borderless control system, which involves the freedom of movement for citizens and residents of the organization. Migrants smugglers are also experts in Western laws, and they are using those laws against Western society and governments themselves; they know that when illegal immigrants from Third World countries going to arrive in Western countries, those migrants are going to have some forms of protection, food, shelter, clothes, etc., and they are going to have associations that are going to defend them and their rights, something that does not happen in many non-Western countries that have a zero tolerance for illegal immigrants. The smugglers are using the West's system of generosity, humanity, compassion and kindness against itself by empowering more Third World populations to go through illegal means - people who do not meet immigration conditions of the destination countries, most of which are First world nations or NIC countries. When illegal immigrants find themselves in countries that are wealthier than those they left behind, they often face arrests, deportation or if they're not caught, they are involved in illegal jobs, which makes it difficult for the working class locals because the illegals receive much lower wages from firms that hire them illegally. Many of the illegal immigrants are often involved in criminal activities, for them, those are means to survive - they cannot have jobs in nations where they came illegally because they do not have the permission to work and stay in those countries. Not all illegal immigrants are trafficked, some overstay their visas and go missing for months, years and even decades. Another strategy that migrant smugglers use is bribing border officials, governments, companies, etc., to enable the illegals from Third World countries to cross the borders legally by all means, whether by boat, by train, by plane or even by foot. The question that I always ask myself and those who do these kinds of dirty works is it a human right to violate another nation's sovereignty? Another issue that I wonder is...do majority European looking countries have an obligation to take in illegal immigrants from Third World countries, vet them, and even legalizing their status? How long can this policy be sustainable? Is it racism when a European like majority country takes a stand against illegal immigration and is willing to send those illegal immigrants back to their countries? To be honest with you, the answer is no to all of these questions and no First World or NIC state can take in the misery of the entire Third World. Humanitarian associations that fight to legalize the status of illegal immigrants are not doing themselves or even the migrants a favor; they are doing the works of the human traffickers who prey on the misery of these different peoples whose goals is to bring more illegal immigrants to the developed world and create chaos and social unrests. I understand that not all illegal immigrants are criminals and many of them just want to create a better life for their children and themselves, I also know that some of those migrants can be victims of persecution because of political, racial, tribal and religious reasons; but I do not believe that the solution is to enable them to immigrate illegally to another country; the solution is to have an extreme vetting policy, which selects the kinds of migrants who

can benefit the nations of their destination legally and
those who can't need to be helped in neighboring
countries. Another area where human traffickers
involved in dirty works is the brothel industry where
pimps facilitate their successes of their industry by
importing women from Eastern Europe, the Middle
East, Africa, Asia and Latin America to sell their
bodies on the streets of the developed world, and I
will not be surprised if the drug cartel and the gangs
are also involved in this dirty business in one way or
the other. The women who are involved in
prostitution should not be treated as criminals; they
are the ones who are being taken advantage of by men
who treat them like sexual commodities, those women
need help, if they're willing to cooperate with the
authorities; if not, then they have to face the
consequences of their actions and be deported for
good; and the criminals who are involved in smuggling
them to First World countries for sexual slavery.
Women and men who are willing to testify before the
authorities about the brothel business need protection
from the pimps and those who are the primary drivers
of the brothel business, no matter what their
backgrounds are. Sexual exploitation accounts for the
most common form of human trafficking because
most of the victims of sexual exploitation are girls and
women who are given false promises of education,
marriage, employment and material wealth, when they
are trapped into the hands of traffickers, they are
raped, beaten, verbally abused, emotionally abused,
psychologically abused, singled out, rejected

imprisoned and they face a variety of threats from their male and sometimes even female employees. Much of the trafficked women are treated like slaves, especially if they are Black or Asian; they are treated like slaves by their Middle Eastern employers in the countries where those women were promised better jobs and fair treatment. Their Middle Eastern employers confiscate their passports from them so that they can be prevented from leaving the countries where they went to look for work. It also occurs in other places where dirty labor and human trafficking are involved. Commercial sexual exploitation also includes pornography; sex traffickers operate in many different locations such as spas and strip clubs. Like I said before, many of those women from some of the most unstable countries in the world that are also governed by unstable people; they come from countries where there is an extreme level of poverty, those are also societies with some of the highest unemployment rates in the world. Women who come from those unstable nations have no aspects for jobs, even if some of them are highly educated, and their patriarchal cultures have already determined their destinies. I do not mince words when I say that those are societies that are governed by some of the most incompetent people in the world, maybe those so-called rulers of the unstable nations, which they and their partisans have created need an IQ test, this kind of stupidity really gets to me and I take these sort of thing personally. Stupid people govern Those countries, saying so does not make me rude, sorry. If they were able to use their common sense and create millions of jobs for their citizens and had a goal to reduce poverty drastically, those women would not have left their nations to ridicule themselves in the streets of the developed world. By the way, unemployment leaves those women vulnerable to human traffickers who view them as sexual commodities now this is how they traffic desperate people to the developed world to do their dirty work. On the other hand, those women need to take responsibility for their decisions by falling blind to some losers out there, instead of using their common sense, this has nothing to do with the idea of being judgemental -protect your personal space, then the enemy from outside cannot invade you. Despite the global number of children used for forced labor declining, one out of 5 victims of human trafficking are children who are exploited for terrorist activities, child pornography, sex begging on streets and laborers. In many unstable regions such as Africa, the Middle East, South East Asia, especially in the Greater Mekong surroundings; children are among the most trafficked people in those areas, like for instance in many Sub-Saharan African countries children are used as soldiers, untangling fishing nets and as slaves in cocoa farms. It is a shame that Sub-Saharan Africa continues to be the region with the highest incident of child labor and agriculture is one of the segments where children can be found working as slaves. Children who are used and trafficked are enslaved after they are removed from their families, and some families sell their children to traffickers; they are left to fend for themselves on streets in the major cities or rural areas in the countryside. Most of the children who are taken advantage of by brain dead adults whose mindsets are rotten to the core of their internal organs work in agricultural fields and the industry. In my opinion, Human trafficking should carry the death penalty, and human traffickers have to be sent to laborers in North Korea, Myanmar, and other rigid states. We cannot wait or watch human traffickers and those who pay them do their dirty work with any form of impunity; you and I can also be the voice of those who are voiceless, we can be their ears and eyes because human beings are not commodities. Another solution that I propose will sound very controversial, but I want to bring it in the open anyway; human traffickers should be treated the same way as sex offenders, to make things worse for them, put them in camps where they can be shot and killed for taking destroying other people's life for their unworthy gains. You don't traffick people to make a living: I don't buy such excuses.

CHAPTER 14

THE PRICE FOR AN IDENTITY CRISIS

Social alienation is manifested in many forms and situations, whether it is because of looks, weight, illness, gender, race, color, tribe, nationality, sexual orientation, social status, religion, political affiliation and so on. I am looking forward to investigate the impact it has one someone by presenting elements on both sides of the same coin, on this chapter I am going to talk about the consequences of social alienation, which may result in isolation and some cases it could lead to violence, anger, bitterness, the need to seek other people's approval and the need for anything, just to feel accepted. No matter what names you call all of those forms of social alienation, they all feel the same and lead to the same kinds of pain one way or the other; those who are singled out for various reasons often struggle to find their identity, when some do, they hold on to that identity for a long time, while others end up lacking any sense of personality; this leads into situations where they create characters of their own through different means in many different ways. It is all about the ways to find the means to survive in this thing, which we call life; there are some research that reveals that the weak, the overweight, the skinny, the ugly, the intelligent one and others suffer any form of bullying, rejection and frequently experience social exclusion and isolation, alienation, discrimination and unequal treatment. The rich can also suffer any bullying from the poor, especially if the unfortunate happens to resent the wealthy; the overweight can suffer discrimination from someone who has much better looks, but the person who has better may also experience bullying from those others who are jealous and envious of him/her; Whites pupils who go to predominantly Black schools may also be at a high risk of social alienation by Black students who are in that school, and this often goes the other way around. I would like to go deeper with this by saying that they all suffer from any forms of bullying, rejection, isolation, discrimination and unequal treatment. The feeling of being looked down often arises from combinations of many different scenarios: Economics, looks, physical appearance, race, tribe, religion, social class, gender, ability, disability, sexual orientation, marital status and so on. This is not just an issue of rich and poor or a lack of resources - it may also arise from competition, the way you feel about yourself, the need to access information, political situations, social fabric, cultural patterns and so much more. Social alienation also goes on in some families where you have parents who abuse their children physically, emotionally, psychologically, mentally and even sexually. This also includes siblings who reject one of their own because the other looks different from them, has less intelligence than them or some other reasons that vary from family to family, and from individuals of all sorts. These kinds of abuse also occur in schools and religious institutions when it comes to children being abused, bullied and taken advantage. Kids who are bullied find themselves in situations where they feel like something is wrong with them, some do indeed; they have a hard time standing up for themselves and they sometimes believe that those who bully them are stronger than them. I know first hand how it is like; when I was 5 years old I was not able to talk, and many of my father's cousins called me a mutant spastic person because I could talk, and they even told my dad that it would be better if a car ran over me and get killed, so that I can be buried in a cemetery in Brazzaville, Congo; it was happening in my country of origin. I was in a situation where other kids also learned from their parents that something was wrong with me and they started to use the same connotations on me. Many of them thought that I was a disabled person with special needs, so I was attacked from there. The woman who gave birth to me also did not want me; she was also involved in the bullying and wanted me to be a street child in a country that was not mine, even though it is my home countries. The point that I am trying to bring across is that kids who are bullied at school do not have the tendency to speak often about their pain with their family members, especially of those family members mistreat them at home; they have problems coping with school and often get low grades or even fail the exams because their self-esteem is not aligned with desire to do help, the thing that even makes it worse is when adults are involved in the bullying with other kids -

and the bullied kids get no forms of help.Around the world 200 million children and youth are being bullied by their peers, parents, teachers, siblings, friends and even some other members of their own families, what the Kandersteg Declaration Against Bullying Children and Youth has discovered is that kids and youth who are bullied because the way they look, their race, their religion, their social class, their form of intelligence, their surname their tribe and other reasons are three times more likely to show depressive symptoms and they are up to 9 times more likely to either have suicidal thoughts or take their lives. According to their studies and other research from Canada, the United Kingdom, and Australia; girls who are victims of bullying in their early beginnings at primary schools were are more likely to remain, victims, as they get older; girls suffer more than boys on cyberspace, and that's where they are more bullied than boys. As adults you would think that we shall know better, right? No! Adult bullying is something that many of us do not hear that much about, but it is a serious problem, which should not go unnoticed or ignored. I even suggest legal action against adult bullying, regardless of the kinds of the bullying we're talking about; you call them different names, they all feel the same, they feel awful; when you choose the behavior, you choose the consequences, and it is a level of immaturity, but the reality is that adults can be bullies just as children, teenagers, and the youth. According to the studies from bully statistics.org, their several ways to know how adults operate when they intimidate their victims:

Narcissistic adult bullying: this is the type of adult who lacks empathy with others. On the surface, narcissistic people feel good about themselves, but below the horizon, they use their insecurities and personal dissatisfactions as a powerful tool to put others down. Impulsive adult bullying: these kinds of adult bullies are more spontaneous and plan out their bullying tactics out less. Their form of bullying may be sarcastic, unintentional or when they feel upset at the victim or someone else.

Physical adult bullying: There are adult bullies who use their physical abilities to intimidate or harm their victims, the way those bullies do it is through the use of threats, demands, forced submission, verbal bullying, emotional bullying and physical domination through violence. Some bullies go as far as murdering their victims, especially if they believe in their causes, which can be personal, national, social, cultural, tribal, ethnocentric, political, religious and professional. Verbal adult bullying: Words are powerful - life and death are in your tongue, adults who are involved in verbal bullying use this tactic to start rumors about their victims, some even go so far as gossiping, use sarcastic and derogatory languages to humiliate their victims. The consequences of verbal bullying results to destructive patterns, low self-esteem, depression, suicidal thoughts, huge fatigues, procrastination and in the worst case scenario, it can even lead to suicide. Those who suffer from verbal bullying often deal with emotions of disconnect and isolation. Secondary Adult bullying: This form of bullying happens when those do not initiate the scenario join the bullies so that they can avoid being victims of bullying, impress their peers, seeking for attention and acceptance or they just do not like the bullied. Despite some secondary bullies feeling sorry about what they do, they are more concerned about saving their skin then caring about the bullied. Workplace Adult bullying: Life can be quite miserable and painful at a workplace when you face bullies whose objective is to destroy you and make you uncomfortable for a variety of reasons. No matter what they are it is inexcusable from those who ought to know better; those who bully at a workplace, a faculty, and other similar places disrupt productivity and create a very hostile environment for that particular work environment. When productivity is disrupted, the impact is very huge on a corporation's earnings and reputation. No decent investor wants to invest in a company whose atmosphere is destructive; that is just another waste of money going out of smoke. Many adults in many universities, workplace and even pubs use the same destructive tactics when they bully other adults because of their weight, race, religion, sexual orientation, tribe, surname, ethnicity, gender, etc., where do we think children pick up those signs? From us, adults - monkey see, and monkey does; humans are not far behind. The adults who are often involved in bullying others believe that it is free speech and they can do as they please, they believe that they are entitled to use it as they see fit, and they do not care about the impacts their behavior has on those they bully or themselves for that matter. When you make a decision to intimidate another because you believe that you have the right to do it, that does not give you a free person; it makes you a tyrant. You are imprisoned in your mind, and you have some serious problems that you do not want to deal with, but you are "fighting for freedom with blind eyes and chained hands," that does not make sense to me at all, cry me a river. I do not have a definite answer on how you can deal with bullies because different people react to these kinds of situation differently; some people try to avoid or even ignore them for that matter, while others may report to their bosses, authorities, press legal charges or even take matters into their hands. The only thing that I can say to you is that do not put up with a bully nor should you let anyone else walk over you. It saddens me that grown men and grown women who bully their peers lack any form of interest in working things out or even trying to find a compromise, what matters to them is the power to bring others down. If you are looking forward to dealing with bullies through legal means, the right news is that there are civil remedies for harassment, abuse and other forms of intimidation; on the other hand, it is your responsibility to document the case. I do not buy this notion that adults who bully was bullied when they were children, let me tell you something - this is another excuse that I just cannot grasp, it could be true that some of them began to bully as children or were bullied as children, but at the end of the day when you're an adult you make a decision on how you deal with those matters and adult bullies need to get some help for their personal struggles and grow up. I am going to go further about this issue on the rest of this chapter, but what I am looking forward to concentrating on is the relationship between discrimination or a perceived discrimination, social exclusion and much more, one of the most important topics of this chapter is my focus on children of newcomers and their families who arrive in countries like Denmark, Finland, Norway, Sweden,

Iceland, Canada, Germany, Italy, France, Russia, Hungary, Britain, Australia, United States and some other similar countries. I am going to talk about the challenge that those children face, especially those who were born and raised in some of these countries or others. This is not just an issue with immigrants of color; this is also a problem with East Europeans and Romanies. At the beginning of the lives of the children whose parents are immigrants to one of those countries or just minorities are often non-Western minorities, children who were born and raised in the country where they grow up know nothing, but that particular country. At the early stages of those children's lives they have friends who are European looking or Caucasians from one of those countries, and they feel Danish, they feel Finnish, they feel Hungarian, they feel German, Swedish, they feel British, they feel American, they feel Icelandic, they feel Canadian, they feel Japanese(Japanese are Asians), they feel Norwegian and so on and so forth, they grow up believing that that's what they are, and those are the only country they know to be theirs. But as they get a little older, their circle of friends and peers notice that those minority children and children of immigrant background are different from them, they begin to ask them where they come from and what are the names of their countries. There are situations where some of their peers go to their parents and ask where their minority friends come from because they now discover that the physiology, the color of their skin and their hair are very different from the average original citizen from their countries. There are situations where the minority children are treated poorly by their local peers, when those kids say that they are Danes, they are Norwegians, they are Hungarians, they are Poles, they are Spaniards, they are Finns, they are Icelandic, they are Belgians etc., their peers often remind them that they are not Danes, they are not Norwegians, they are not Hungarians, they are not Poles, they are not Spaniards, they are not Finns, they are not Icelandic, they are not Belgians etc., those children of newcomers are now confused; they ask themselves why do many of their peers view them differently, what are they, who are they and some even go and cry to their parents and other family members because they are made to feel like outsiders. Now the situation depends on families; some minority families tell their children that they are not from the countries where they were born and begin to teach them about their origins, their cultures, their ancestors and lineages and some immigrant families persist and tell their children that they are from the country where they were born, but they also need to remember that they have a culture from back home, which they need to hold on to. Many of those minority children who once believe that they are Danes, Finns, Norwegians, Icelanders, British, Americans, Canadians, Dutch, Germans and so on now a face moments in their lives where something kicks in them because they are reminded by their peers and some segments of the societies where they were born that they do not belong to those countries; some even tell them to go back where they come from; when they are racially bullied, they are called Ragheads, Camel Jockeys, Chinks, Kikes, Yids, Wetbacks, Negroes, Darky, animals, monkeys and other nasty things. They are even told that the nations where they come from are shitholes and they need to go back and never return. Some of their peers and the segment of society remind them that they are not from White majority countries because they are not Caucasians and they are impure. This puts many from these minority communities in situations where they begin to build enclaves, and those pockets develop to parallel societies. It is not just immigrants and minorities of color who go through this experience; many East Europeans and other Caucasians from other Western countries face similar forms of exclusions in countries like Finland,

Denmark, Norway, Switzerland, and Austria because of who they are and how they look. I am just going to take Denmark's example; earlier in 2016 there was a debate this year about what Danishness means and what does it mean to be Danish; it was the Danish People's Party that began a campaign by putting posters all over the country about the way they see their Denmark - in other words, the way they view Denmark on the signs they put across the country is a nation which is very homogeneous; in other words, there was a picture of an ethnic Danish family with a dog and there were many Danes who actually agree with it and other statements from the DPP. The one thing that surprised me was that some other Danes took it personally began to make counterproductive posters where they have their views on how they see their Denmark-on their posters there were people of different ethnicities, there were Middle Eastern People, Asians, Blacks, Biracial people, ethnic Danes, Greenlanders, East Europeans and other groups of individuals. The Danish People's Party did not see a problem with their campaign, but those that view Denmark as a multicultural society were furious with the DPP for what they view as an exclusive campaign, some Muslim immigrants said that it looks like the Danish People's Party does not consider them as members of the Danish society. The DPP insisted in their opinion of the way they believe Denmark is and debates about this campaign went on for days, then a politician from the Danish People's Party, Soeren Espersen went on to say the following, after he was challenged by the DPP's campaign on Denmark and multiculturalism, Soeren Espersen went on to say this, I quote"I not see a problem with the campaign we are promoting on our posters,across the country and I am colorblind; we could have placed a Negro there it would not have made a difference". What came out of Soeren Espersen's stupidity is that he used the word Negro on Black people, just like millions and millions of his countrymen/women still do today and there was even a debate about across Denmark and the rest of the Danish media. Soeren Espersen went on to say that he could give an example, for instance Obama is the first Negro president of the United States. A member of the Social Democrats wrote to the White House and reported that Soeren Espersen said that Obama is the first Nigger President of the United States. The debate about this stupidity goes on to a very stupid level because many Danes, Norwegians, Finns, Icelanders, Faroese and even Austrians still use the word Negro on Blacks until today, even though they know that it is a derogatory name. Many people in the Danish Liberal Party suggested that it is ok to use the word Negro on Blacks because it is not the same as Nigger, which I find very idiotic and retarded; trying to teach a Dane, a Norwegian, a Finn, an Austrian, an Icelander and a Faroese to host and integrate non-whites in their societies is like showing a snake how to walk; snakes can never walk. I wrote articles where I began to use racial and ethnic slurs on Soeren Espersen, members of the DPP and the Danes who keep using the N-word on Blacks and I was extremely outspoken because I just did not want to put up with this garbage anymore. The more racist comments I received from offended Danish nationalists, the more worse it got from my side and the more racial and ethnic slurs I kept using on all the Danes who use such a derogatory name on Africans or people who have their roots on the African continent. One day, a Danish nationalist began to use a derogatory name on me and told me to leave Denmark, then I wrote the article that Danes who want me to leave Denmark should come and get me in my home and move me from there; at the same time, they have to make sure that the Danes who are abroad should return to their country, all the Danes who are abroad and I ended up calling all the Danish members of the DPP, some members of the Social Democrats and the Liberal Democrats, as well as the other ordinary Danes "Viking Parasites", "Vermins", "Northerners", "Nougat Plow", "Spirit Swines", "Filthy Norsemen" "Scandinavian rats" and other names on the book on various newspaper articles and I made no apology for it. If I was given the opportunity to do it, I will do it again without any regret because I do not take crap from anyone. No Dane was interested in replying to me, even those who are nationalists did not want to write to me because when they do, they do not put their address on the envelopes because of their cowardice. All the Danes who attack me fear to put their address on their envelopes because they know that I am going to tear them to pieces. Personally, I do not care about the way both sides view Denmark; I personally have nothing to gain from such an issue, but what I do not understand is that how on Earth the Danes, the Finns, the Norwegians, the Icelanders and the Austrians keep using the N-word in 2016? We're not in the times where Africans were taken as slaves; we're not in the 1900s, 1940s and so on and so forth, how can they be so stupid on this level? This is an invasion of someone else's personal space, this is bullying and the mean to do harm. How can the Alternative Right be such idiots by thinking that they are doing their race, which is the

Caucasian race a favor by being bullies against non-whites? Where has that mentality come from? Whites from any country who use the N-word on Blacks are bullies, whether they are Danes, Norwegians, Icelanders, Finns, Austrians, Hungarians, Croats, Poles, Australians, South Africans, just as much as others who just attack them for no reason other than being Caucasians. The idiots from the DPP and other similar parties who use racial slurs on others for the fun of it think that everything is just fun, but it is slander that could be interested in the hate crime division. People on both the Far Left and Far Right just cannot think, they can not sit and reason because they are like wild animals, which do not know any directions where they're going. Those imbeciles from the Alternative Right and the Far Left think that they can sit on their couches at peace without any form of consequences, but they have created records that will never go away and those records are their regular trademarks. Politicians like Soeren Espersen others are paving a way for Danes who encourage themselves to call Africans the N-word regularly, thinking that they are doing minorities a favor by being derogatory to them. According to the research from the NCBI Resources, children who suffer from ethnic discrimination by their peers, teachers and other segments of society experience a lower level of academic performance; when it comes to boys who suffer any form of racial bullying and other forms of ethnic discrimination have a higher level of psychological isolation than girls; this may lead to anger being built inwards, depression, violence, crime and hatred towards the society where they live. It can also lead to situation where they begin to join radicalized Islamic groups through conversions and taking the Quran very seriously. Some boys consider joining gangs and be with those with whom they feel identifies with their pain and suffering. Adult immigrant men who face economic discrimination by being denied jobs that are in harmony with their qualification also suffer from isolation and they built this anger inside of them, which leads to an extreme level of hatred towards to societies that have taken them in. People of immigrant and minority communities who face constant discrimination because of the color of their skin or ethnic background often end up struggling to be among the individuals who can have potentials to own their homes. Immigrant men who struggle to find jobs in the countries where they came and reside often tell their children that they do not belong to that country, their nationality is their skin color i.e. If an immigrant who lives in Norway struggles to find a job, despite his high skill at Norwegian and academic degrees, the frustration that it might bring in his life can lead him in situations where he tells his children that they are not Norwegians, even though they were born in Norway because Norwegian firms will not hire them for the jobs, which are in harmony with their education; the employer will often see their surnames and disqualify them because of what they are called or the color of their skin. He will not encourage their children to feel Norwegian or have Norwegian friends because of his painful experiences with the Norwegian society and the Norwegians themselves. This reflects on the economic exclusion and it exists across nations, tribes, family structures, gender, parental education, groups, cultural groups, ethnic lines and religious segments etc. However in countries like Norway, Denmark, Finland, Iceland, Luxembourg and other places adult men of color who are called all forms of racial slurs from groups of White nationalists from the Alternative Right and other similar groups end up in situation where they feel powerless to deal with such people. On one hand they are told to behave, but when it is the time for those immigrants of color to stand up for themselves, they are accused of all means things in the world because societies like the ones that

I have just mentioned like when immigrants of color act like subordinates and keep quiet about racism and discrimination. In the mind of many of the local population from the societies that I have just mentioned they believe that the more those groups of migrants of color shut up and keep quiet about discrimination, the better safe things would become, yet those are the same segments of those local populations that complain about their societies not dealing with integration and assimilation. I have said time after time in this book that Denmark is not a multicultural country; it is not a melting pot where you meet people of different races who say that they are Danes, I have always stated that Denmark is a homogeneous society that belongs to the Danes, and being Danish is about being connected to Denmark historically, culturally, emotionally and religiously; if you do not have anyone of these following, then you're not a Dane, sorry to tell you this, no matter how well integrated you are in the Danish society. Even Natasja Saad, a Biracial Sudanese-Danish singer who was born in Denmark was asked by ethnic Danes if she was adopted or if she came from India. Remember one of her songs "Give mig Danmark Tilbage"(Give me Denmark Back), it is a song where she explained her life in Denmark where she faced lots of racism and social exclusion. Let Norway be Norwegian the way the Norwegians have always known it during the ancient times, do the same for Finland, Iceland, Poland, Slovakia and other similar nations that want to remain in their bubble. Do not go there and act like a beggar; the authorities will be waiting on the other side, everyone will scream fire and things are going to be blown away. The locals from those countries do not dare say anything about other bubbles, they are waiting for their turn to close their own bubbles. Their magic tricks will work when the Alternative Right will take power and govern their nations, and then the Third Reich will rise again and the impure bubbles will be removed from the face of the Universe. No one will sing Kumbaya my Lord anymore; the backup plan works, their race must be pure again, their movement are now genuine, and then they are working on building pure bubbles where no dirty Third Worlder will show up. Did I forget something? Racial slurs are one of their most powerful weapons, they throw them at you like Nuclear Bombs, then they think you're trying, but you keep dancing, they believe that you're dying, but you keep walking on the lake of fire with a sense of pride on your chest. Kill the Liberals and eat their cakes for them. Otherwise our bubbles will turn to dirty bus stops where you have so many Mohammedan Jihadists, stop for a while: Did you just hear what you said? They will come to your house and kill you and your loved ones, be careful and just shut up; I do not want to be in trouble. That's why I love chemistry and physics; it is kind of an entertaining show where you speak your mind without being censored; the last stupidity experiment was worth a certain form of discouragement. Now back to the case; immigrants minorities color who experience social exclusion often to violence as their only resorts, some minorities of color see the level of their productivity falling into pieces. In countries like Norway and Denmark, there are not many immigrants from non-Western countries who own their homes, unless they have started their businesses. Home ownership among minorities of non-Western appearance is not that high in any Scandinavian country; I am not certain how it is in other Western countries. In the U.S. there is something called the American Dream, where people of different backgrounds can start from nothing and live the dream of their purpose, such a culture does not exist in Scandinavia - I do not know if this has a lot to do with something familiar, which I mentioned on this book earlier, the Law of Jante. The worse situation many of those minorities of color and immigrants often face some of the societies that I have mentioned is the desire to compete in the labor market for jobs, but when they get refusals from firms that do not want them, they do the jobs that their indigenous peers would not want to do, despite having similar qualifications; some of those minority communities feel like the societies where they put barriers on them on purpose so that they can give up looking for a job and live on public assistance. If that's the case, in my view it is also bullying; when you are stealing someone else's talent and psychologically damaging a person's ability to excel and expand, that makes you a bully; you judge a society on how it uses all its members' talents for its growth and the benefits that those talents bring to the next generations to come. There is also an area where some minorities and immigrants of color get things wrong; what they do not understand is that there should be no connection between multiculturalism and religion; you can live in a melting pot society and still be irreligious, multiculturalism is about culture and culture can be music, sports, movies, theaters, arts, traditions and so on; although religion has traditions, it has nothing to do with culture; religion is about believing in something/someone, which/who is greater than oneself, whether it is Christianity, Judaism, Islam,

Buddhism, Hinduism, Voodoo, Paganism and so on; these two topics should not be get mashed together so that religious zealots and their goats should be satisfied. Do you know, which other groups are stratified when you mixed these two different things together? Far Left and, especially the Far Right political parties who use both of these terminologies to talk about some of their stupid views by playing the politically incorrect card, trying to make sense out of their stupidity, whereas the Far Left is no naive that they just appease on everything, so let's just call it all multiculturalism. I was watching videos of a South African white man called R3NDi3R, whose real name is Renado Grouws; he makes videos about the circumstances about his country where he talks about the legacy of Apartheid and on how White South Africans are discriminated in South Africa by the current ANC government, I looked at some documentaries where I saw many Whites living in Shacks across many South African cities; Blacks and Coloreds who are not qualified for the jobs get them anyway because of the BEE(Black Economic Empowerment) policies. Many working class Whites, most of whom are Afrikaans speaking face the intense crisis in their country when they live in shanty towns face bullying and prejudice from their wealthy non-white South African peers, as well as non-whites foreigners who live in the country. More of 400.000 Caucasian South Africans live below the level of poverty, and those who live in squalors live for the US $30 a month, and there are around 80 of those White squalors across South Africa. There is no electricity, no running water, and every little food; there has been a similar situation in Zimbabwe where a same group of people had to give up their farms and landmass to make the incompetent locals satisfied. No matter what kind of a situation it is, I call it a systematic form of bullying; whether it is Apartheid in the RSA or racial segregation in the USA or any other form of oppression is systematic bullying. Countries like Norway, Denmark, Finland, Iceland and Sweden that have some of the most extensive daycare in the world struggle to achieve the possibility for immigrants to be dual-earners, this results in unemployment among immigrants and in many cases immigrants have a weaker participation in the labor force. Whereas the United States, the United Kingdom, Germany and Canada have have a much more successful job market for both immigrants and nonimmigrants than Scandinavian counterparts. Societies that ignore the importance of labor market attachment for households are looking at at potentials going to waste;

327

the consequences, which results to in the absence of earners and this increases the risk of poverty and social exclusion. This is even more so for immigrants and minorities of color in many Western nations. Norway is more successful at keeping the poverty rate low for its nonimmigrant residents, but when it comes to the immigrant population in that country, the incidence of poverty is about 60% . Although this is a serious problem, there are also many immigrants who do not want to work. The thing that I find surprising is that even Sweden has difficulties integrating some groups of immigrants in the labor market, but no matter where and which country it is in the Western world immigrants who are extremely poor have a higher struggle to integrate and assimilate in their new societies and their children will feel deprived of the life chances,which nonimmigrant children have; in my opinion it is a good idea that more efforts should be made so that immigrants can find jobs with decent wages, instead of encouraging them to receive public assistance from the government. Create policies that are more inclusive and beneficial for both the local citizens and those of immigrants backgrounds. Increased employment opportunities for both indigenous citizens and residents of minority and immigrant communities has a positive impact on financial situations and will facilitate integration and assimilation in other areas when it comes to some groups of immigrants. The immigrants who were born in the host countries will feel the sense of patriotism and nationalism when they have a high education and different kinds of achievements in various areas of their lives and pay taxes. This is not a Left wing issue, this is not a Right wing issue, this is not a Liberal issue, this is not a Conservative issue and this is not a Libertarian issue; this is a human issue. If natives and immigrants had equal opportunities the impact on the economy of their host countries would be enormous; when you have a population that has lower productivity you cannot expect a significant economic growth. On the other hand, immigrants have to make efforts to sell their products, which is themselves and bring arguments about why their employers.

CHAPTER 15

MY VIEW ABOUT TOMMY ROBINSON

To those of you who do not know Tommy Robinson,

I would recommend that you please read this book, The Enemy of the State where he explains how he is totally mistreated by the mainstream media, authorities, the political class and special interest groups for being a person who stands up for the survival of the values that have made his country, Britain, his continent, Europe and his civilization what they are. Unfortunately those valued are threatened by Islam, you heard me well; I did not say radical Islam, I said Islam, a religion, which imposes its will through the means of threats, violence, murder and bullying when it does not approve of the way people do things in non-Muslim nations or when it does not get its way. Stephen Christian Yaxley-Lennon was born on November 27th in 1982 in Luton, during that time there was only a single mosque in the town, in 2014 there were 30 mosques in the city, while countries like Saudi Arabia and other similar countries do not allow non-Muslims to practice their religions freely on equal footing with their majority Muslim members in their territories. This would not have been a problem if Muslims in Luton respected British values and stopped imposing their belief system and values on others in that town. Stephen Lennon, also known as Tommy Robinson has cousin who was groomed by Muslim men in Luton and the police did not care that much and took her for granted because she is a drug addict. At the time when Tommy went to school other cultures assimilated well in Luton, whether it is the Italians, the Chinese, the Jamaicans, the West Indians, the Indians, the Irish, the Ghanaians, the

Scandinavians, the East Europeans and other groups
of people blended in the British culture, but there was
a community that did not show the interest in
integrating into the British society and that is the
Islamic community. During the time that Tommy
went at school he had friends from different races;
most of Tommy's friends are non-whites, on the other
hand what they witnessed in their schools in Luton is
that the playground were segregated, not by race, but
by religion; there was a playground for Muslims and
there was another for non-Muslims, this meant that
Muslims did not want to mix in or play with non-
Muslims. It was not people like Tommy Robinson
who caused that division; it was the Muslim
community itself that made that decision to segregate
themselves from non-Muslims. Tommy had a friend
who was in love with an Asian girl and he was
violently attacked for it by a group of Asian Muslims.
Tommy Robinson was himself a victim of racial abuse
at the age of 12, and he was attacked by a group of
Pakistani and Middle Eastern Muslims in Luton when
he was returning home from swimming; the reason
why he was attacked it was because he is a Caucasian;
he was called a white pig by groups of those Asian
Muslims who were after him because he is a different
race than they are. Pakistani Muslims were throwing
bricks and stones at retirement homes where they
were many non-Muslim Britons, both whites, and
blacks to try to get the senior people living in that
particular area to leave either by going somewhere else
or leave the town. The police had not acted out of the

fear of being labeled as racists and Islamophobes. In that city there was a Jewish man who was beaten, bullied, racially abused and intimidated by a group of Muslims gangs and he had to explain to them why the State of Israel exists. This kind of savagery happened in 2014, and these are not things that Tommy Robinson has made up to get a sort of attention from society; these are people living real lives, dealing with real experiences. The British man who was attacked had to make plans to move to Israel for his safety because his only crime is being a Jew in a Muslim ghetto; Muslims view him as a Yid or a Kike Infidel that they just have to attack. The changes that Tommy Robinson and others have seen in their town, Luton and the rest of the United Kingdom are not benefiting the nation in which people like Tommy and his cousin Kevin have grown up and the nation that their family has always known. In Luton, there are even Muslims who do not want X-mas to be celebrated in the public because they believe that it is a sin, even though those Muslims are living in a majority Christian country with different sets of values from theirs. Tommy heard Sayful Islam, an al-Muhajiroun saying that the massacre of Russian children in Beslan in 2004 was justified and Saiful went further to say that he wishes that the same thing happened in England, in Luton, there have been racist attacks on Whites and Blacks by Muslim Pakistanis and other Muslims of other races. Tommy had also witnessed Muslim gangs celebrating the 9-11, already back then, people like Tommy and Kevin understood the mindset of those Muslim extremists; they knew their ideology, their values and knew how dangerous those people are. Not because they were sympathizing with those maniacs; they already knew back then that those radical Muslims did not have Luton's best interests. Both Pakistani street gangs and radical Muslims were after Tommy and others who were exposing their filthy agenda; the one thing that unites Pakistani street gangs and radical Muslim is their religion and a couple of stuff that also unites them, that's the hate that they have on Tommy Robinson, their desire for destruction and the drug business. When radical Muslims make protests, the police do not have to stop them and arrest them if they are involved in violence, but when Tommy Robinson and others complained, the police treated them wrongly and arrested them. It seems like the police walk on eggshells when it comes to the Muslim community, but when it comes to the people who own Britain, they treat their kind like dogs. At the time when Tommy Robinson did not know about politics, he joined the BNP (the British National Party), a far-right political party without even knowing what they are, their beliefs, and their policies; Tommy did not even know anything about Nick Griffin, nor did he know that Nick Griffin was a member of the National Front, another British far right White nationalist political party, to make matters worse, Tommy did not even know that that non-whites and Jews are not welcomed in the organization, they are not allowed to join the BNP because they are not Whites. A year later, Tommy left the British National Party, in 2009,

Tommy Robinson and others created a group UPL, United Peoples of Luton in response the way some Muslims were treating British soldiers returning home from Afghanistan. During the homecoming of those soldiers there was a parade in Luton and many British were paying respect to the soldiers who have sacrificed their goals, their times and their lives to defend the values that have made Britain what it is today. Those soldiers fought for the freedoms of the people of the UK and the rest of the civilized world. The first thing that Tommy and other Britons have witnessed is the presence of the police and some Muslims who were already making plans to cause trouble. That group of Muslims began to insult the soldiers, calling them baby killers, rapists and murders; they spat on the soldiers' faces and the police and council did nothing about it. The police and the council facilitated such a savage behavior from those Muslims who were involved in it. Tommy witnessed the attacks on British Armed Forces, other Britons who were there witnessed it as well. My question to you is this, what would you do if the armed forces of your country were attacked both physically, emotionally, verbally and psychologically by a group of Muslim radicals who do not respect the laws of your country? Tommy was always a target for Muslim Pakistani gangs and bricks and stones at his residence; that's why Stephen Lennon had to have different names to protect himself, his identity from those primitive savages. We all know what happens when you deal with radical Mohammedans; they threaten you, they abuse you, they intimidate you, they beat the crap out of you, they bully you and in the worst case scenario, they even kill you. It is part of their mindset; they have lost their humanity a long time ago when they made a decision to turn into violent beasts. Tommy Robinson is the co-founder of the English Defence League with his cousin, Kevin Carroll. Those of you who do not know the English Defence League, it is a street protest movement that is against the Islamization of Britain, Europe and the rest of the civilized world. The EDL is a movement where you have all forms of genders, ethnicities and cultures together; you find indigenous white Britons, you Blacks, Jews, Indians, Whites from other countries and other group of people, on the other hand this movement was hijacked by White nationalists from the British National Party, Anders Breivik, the National Front, the DPP, the NPD and other Neo-Fascists and Neo-Nazi organizations from different White majority countries. Another thing to take into account is that in many Western jails there are many radical Muslims who convert non-Muslims by forcing them to accept the Shahada and the number of converts in ordinary Western streets is rising among Whites and non-Whites from other religions, or those without any religion, it is increasing fast and radical Muslims are turning both indigenous and non-Muslim minorities from United States, France, Germany, Netherlands, Canada, United Kingdom, Sweden, Australia, Spain, Brazil, Argentina, Uruguay, Denmark, Norway, Finland and the rest of the civilized world. They even convert children from those countries without even their parents' consents - can you imagine radical Christian groups forcefully converting Muslim children without their parents' permissions? I think Muslims would go wild and they would be enraged. The concept of the EDL's nationalism is that everyone is welcome, whether you're Black, White, Mixed Race, Asian, Jew, gay, straight, man, woman, etc. Even if you're a Muslim who distances yourself from the political wing of Islam, you're welcome to the EDL, even if you're a Hindu and a Sikh. Tommy Robinson even faces threats from White nationalists who want to kill him because they see him as a Zionist who betrays his race. Most of us and even I included judge Tommy Robinson and the English Defence League through the headlines, and I also think that there is a double standard here when it comes to the EDL and radical Muslims. When Muslims are allowed to promote violence in the streets of the UK, the BBC does not report these things consistently, but when Tommy and the EDL take away Islamic flags from primitive savages, he is charged with assaulting a police officer or other charges in the book. Tommy Robinson has been convicted unfairly countless of times; he has been in jail countless of times because he has the guts to take a stand against a culture that is invading his country through the means of stealth jihad, sharia law, sexism, homophobia, misogyny, female genital mutilation, halal meat, anti-Semitism, racism and other forms of Islamic intimidations. While radical Muslims get away with a lot distresses, which they are causing on British streets. How much should

the British people continue to put up with radical
Muslims who do not want to respect British Laws and
British values, and continue to cause trouble in
Britain? Why is the British government allowing this
kind of barbarity to happen? Are they being corrupted
by wealthy Muslim countries that have an agenda for
their Islamic cause? Can you blame the EDL for
taking a stand against radical Muslims, illegal
immigration and the lack of assimilation from many
groups of minorities when the British government
walks on eggshells when it does not talk about these
kinds of things consistently and severely? Why isn't
the British government forfeiting the British
citizenship from Muslims who create violence and
distress in British society? Why isn't the British
government deporting those who have killed Lee
Rigby and send them back to Nigeria, where they can
pay for their stupidity? Don't talk to me about human
rights as a means of argument; when you create
trouble and cause distress, you are taking away other
people's rights, when you impose your religious beliefs
on others through means of threats and violence, you
are taking away other people's rights, why should I
give a damn about your rights? The Far Right segment
of the EDL has given the organization a bad name
and it has been portrayed as a racist organization by
the mainstream media, the political class and special
interest groups who do not have the courage to raise
complex topics. The EDL was sometimes violent, but
the point they were trying to make across is that the
mainstream media is protecting Islam from criticism,

the political elite are selling Western democracies to
Islamic nations like Saudi Arabia, Qatar and other rich
Muslim countries by allowing these nations to build
more mosques and madrassas in our part of the world
and bringing in hate Islamic preachers who hate our
way of life, which they find decadent and immoral.
Another reason why the English Defence League is so
aggressive it is because they feel like the leaders of the
Western world do not care about the survival of their
countries, they only care about open borders and
bringing more people who do not have what it takes
to integrate to the societies that have made them in, in
the first place; many of these so-called refugees are not
in Western societies to adapt and integrate, they are
here to replace the populations that have taken care of
them, given them food, clothes, shelter and
opportunities many of those people never had in their
countries. Real refugees do not come to Western
societies to declare a demographic war against the
populations that have taken them in; real refugees
realize that living in a Western country is not a right,
but a privilege, which they are determined to make the
most of, some of them also believe that once there is
peace in their countries, they are going to go back and
rebuild their own nations and some make plans to stay
and be part of the societies that have taken them, and
they are willing to use their skills to contribute to their
new homes. Tommy Robinson does not defend every
action of many EDL supporters, nor do I, but the
question you need to ask yourself is this, what would
you do if you see your culture, your identity and your

way of life eroded by Muslims who are creating sharia patrols, sharia courts and sharia law in your country? What would you do if you went through the things that both Tommy and Kevin have experienced in their lives with those Muslims creating distress in Luton and across the entire country? Already in London, white Britons are a minority in the capital city of Britain. No nation can put up with its own citizens being a minority in its capital or elsewhere; this emboldens racism, race tensions, xenophobia, cultural enclaves and so on. Do you think that the Turks will allow themselves to be a minority in Istanbul, Ankara, Izmir, Alanya and across their own country? What would happen if suddenly Greeks and Assyrians became a majority population in Istanbul, and Turks became a minority? Think about it for a second : Can you imagine South Africans, both Blacks, Whites, Coloreds, Indians and Malays allow populations of other African countries to become a majority in Johannesburg, Pretoria, Cape Town, Bloemfontein, Durban and other places in the country? Do you think that Han Chinese people are going to allow other types of Chinese to become a majority in China? Do you think that Malaysia will enable Christians to become a majority population in that marvelous country? Do you make that the Republic of the Congo will allow the citizens of the Democratic Republic of Congo and other African countries to become a majority population in this beautiful country? Do you think Iraq can allow Blacks to be a majority people in that Middle Eastern country? I do not believe so, do

339

you think that Syria will allow minorities of different
ethnicities and religions to become a majority
population in that country? People like Hillary Clinton,
George Soros and others who believe in open border
policies do not have any common sense in their heads;
I do not know if they are enough about the survival of
their nations or they want their nations to be Third
World countries. Sometimes I ask myself if those
people want to destroy their own countries by design
because the hate anything ideals about the nations that
have given so many opportunities that they would
never have, if they came from Third World "shitholes"
- We are giving too much power to countries that do
not like us by allowing them to decide the oil price and
import their oil, they are the same group of people
that use their oil revenues to put poison in the minds
of our citizens through the building of more mosques,
conversions, recruitment for jihadist activities,
terrorism, Sharia, Halal meat and other things that they
are using as weapons of wars against us because they
expect our destruction and we are stupid enough to
allow these things to happen, instead of learning from
countries like Russia and China on how they deal with
such maniacs. Once again, please do not talk to me
about their human rights; when you are at war against
someone who is being on your destruction, you are
not concerned about his human rights; you are
primarily concerned about your survival, and it is part
of our fundamental strategy. If you too concerned
about your enemy's human rights, despite his
willingness to destroy you, you will die like a headless

chicken that never paid attention to anything other than trying to reason with a monster. When I hear from organizations like Hope Not Hate and UAF(United Against Fascism) who protest against Tommy Robinson, calling him a racist, a hate monger for taking a stand against an ideology that treats women like lower intelligent animals, an ideology that advocates the stoning of adulterers,the killing of Jews, the execution of homosexuals, the prohibition of gambling, the murder of apostates, the death of both non-Muslims and Muslims who question Muhammad's character and the justification of killing infidels wherever they find them and then calling people like Tommy Robinson, Robert Spencer, Kevin Carroll, Brigitte Gabriel, Ayaan Hirsi Ali, Sean Hannity,Ted Cruz and others racists they have devalued the word racist and because of their own stupidity they have also devalued the words fascist and Nazi. Where are the Leftist organization like Hope Not Hate and the UAF when Muslim women in many Muslim countries are killed for dishonoring their families? Where are they when Anjem Choudary advocates replacing the British Constitution with the Sharia Law? Where are they when many British girls were raped for generations by Muslim Pakistani gangs because those girls happen to be Caucasians? Where are they when there is a high level of anti-Semitism in mosques? Where are they when Asian Muslims treat Blacks and others like scum? Where are they when Armenians cry for justice? I am sick and tired of those Leftists and anti-fascist groups fighting the wrong battle, I am sick and tired of them losing their moral authority by colluding with a religion that wants to suppress everything we all stand for; I would have more respect for these organizations if they stood up to fundamentalist Muslims who are trying to destroy their countries, I would have had more respect for them if they stood up to Christian and Jewish fundamentalists, I would also respect them if they used that energy to take a stand against organizations like the Danish Party, the Danish People's Party, the Norwegian Progress Party, the Finns, the BNP, the National Front, the Freedom Party of Austria and the extremists from other countries. Because both these imbeciles and Islamic radicals are two sides of the same coin and they do not deserve to have their ideas respected;both of those filthy vermins and disgusting cockroaches are clueless and dangerous; let us take for instance organizations like the Stormfront, the DPP, the Danish Party, the Identity Block, the DailyStormer, the BNP and other filthy rats like them who are cowards living in sewers: These movements share a lot of their ethos and rhetoric—things like"white genocide" —with charming people like Anders Behring Breivik, the far-right terrorist that killed 77 people in Norway in 2011.These so-called honorable citizens yearn for a return to a simpler time, one in which women knew their role as cleaning robots with built-in pleasure orifices; they put troublesome races in internment camps and those annoying black people weren't allowed to drink from the same water fountains as whites. Now let's talk about the other types of vermins, the radical Muslims who want to destroy the Western civilization from within with our miserable hands because those idiots want to bring back the Islamic Caliphate, which ended less than 100 years ago by Ataturk and Western powers. We all know that Islam discriminates against anyone who is not a Muslim and commands Muslims to hate non-Muslims. They believe that in order to bring peace in the world, they have to declare Jihad or the holy war against infidels worldwide so that we can be subjugated and killed if we do not convert to their religion. Those parasites believe in terrorism, intimidation and violence in order for them to get their way to the world. They also want to forbid music, sports, theater, arts, dance and they want to bring us back 1400 years, yet these are the imbeciles that the Liberal Left and those on the Far Left are defending and treating like victims, right? No wonder there are many nationalistic movements that are rising across many major countries, this is what happens when the Liberal Left and the Center Right swing problems with Islam under the carpet, instead of confronting the issues badly; this is what happens when many leaders from the European Union decide to take in up to more than 1 million refugees without the policies of extreme vetting and without knowing who those people are, what they believe and their motives. This is what happens when you take in the wrong kinds of individuals in your countries and encourage cultural enclaves, social cohesions, criminality, parallel communities and so on and so forth and this is what happens when you take in illegal immigrants in your shoes instead of sending them back to the nations where they come from. Stephen Lennon, alias Tommy Robinson is not an angel, neither am I; Tommy Robinson made a mistake when he traveled to the U.S. with someone else's passport and he ended up paying for it by going to an American jail. But I do not like the idea of him being placed in a prison area where there were groups of radical Muslims who wanted to kill him, what if they succeeded in killing him just like the animal that killed Theo Van Gogh in Holland in 2004 for being critical of Islam's view on women? The English Defence League has its flaws, and we all know it, but without them there would have been any attention on the problems that Islam brings in Britain and the Western world; without the English Defence League we would not have discovered anything about the Rotherham Scandal, which involved the sexual grooming of British white girls, white ladies, and white boys as young as twelve by Muslim Pakistani men who did it for racist reasons; I would like to pay tribute to the victims of such a barbaric conduct, and I also appreciate their bravery and the courage of those who have brought such an evil practice to light, this is the time for us to talk about tough situations because in my opinion the police, the social workers, the municipality and the government are as guilty as those maniacs that were involved in the rape for keeping such a story in the dark for decades out of the fear of being called intolerant in the name of diversity; these

victims have seen their lives being stolen from them
and they are not the same people anymore because
their government has failed them- in my opinion, what
happened to these women, girls and boys is a hate
crime and those Muslim Pakistani men should see
their British citizenship forfeited and they should go
and pass their jail time in Pakistan, and I do not care if
they face torture there, can you imagine if it was
Britons who were doing it to Pakistani or Middle
Eastern children in the Muslim world? Those Britons
would not be left alive would be left alive this garbage
is about having one standard for the Whites and
another for peoples of color; this is what I call the low
expectation narrative ,especially from those people
who claim to take a stand against Fascism, Nazism,
racism and other forms of hatred where do they stand
when indigenous British girls, women and boys had
been groomed by Muslim Pakistani men ? What did
the Muslims do to clean up their communities and
take responsibility for their crap, instead of blaming
everything on their host societies ? These kinds of
barbaric act and responses are the reason why the Alt-
Right and other nationalist groups are rising across the
United States, France, Germany, Sweden, Norway,
Denmark,Holland , Spain, Russia,Italy, Austria,
Hungary, Poland, Finland, Britain, Australia and other
major countries -Those who call organizations like the
EDL racists for reporting these facts are doing a
disservice to the victims of the Rotherham scandal and
ignoring the racism from the Muslim Pakistani
community and other types of Muslims who are

involved in this kind of savagery - the mainstream media has also failed these victims for failing to report the rape and the perpetrators as they are without being politically correct. We have seen this refusal to acknowledge reality and covering up of the truth, time and time again, in cases like this and Germany, Sweden, Austria, Switzerland, Finland and other European nations.Holding back information, merely because the perpetrator(s) was an immigrant in order to not appear racistly is vile, and a symptom of this cancer we call political correctness, and some people play the politically correct card to put more gas on burning trees ,but either way there are people who are paying for it -if we continue on that road, of course, if we are afraid that the Far Right is going to capitalize on these kinds of situations, then we are actually giving them the power to do so; let us deal with these matters courageously before they do and capitalize.It is one of the most stupid arguments that I have ever heard in my life, when you do not want to call spade for a spade because some far right vermins are going to profit from the situation to put all immigrants under the brush; you do not stop to a psychiatric hospital because there are some violent mentally ill people out there who have potential to do you harm; you do not hide the problems from a mental hospital out of the fear that the violent mentally ill individuals are going to capitalize on the problem; you deal with the issues as they are and find desperate solutions. I am not going to give up my way of life and defend my values out of the fear of not being called tolerant. It is not

people like Tommy Robinson, Dave Russell, Kevin
Carroll, Pamela Geller and other prominent
individuals who are responsible for the behavior that
many of these Muslim rape gangs chose to live by and
my question is this, when on earth will the Muslim
community put its house in order, instead of making
excuses for everything? This does not mean that all
Muslim men are involved in such savagery, but society
needs to speak out about these issues and confront
them consistently, many people in the Western world
are very frustrated about the way the political class
deals with illegal immigration, allowing the wrong
people to settle in their societies and putting with so
much crap from people who want to Islamize their
societies, and some of them do not want to class
themselves and Leftists or Rightists; they are tired of
being told to tolerate the intolerable, they are sick of
being told to endure the unendurable, they are sick of
being told to be patient and they are tired of being told
that everything is going to be ok, while things are
going in the opposite direction. The ignorance of both
the Liberal Left and the Center Right is pushing those
people to undesired political parties that are more
rigid, more aggressive and more derogatory; those are
the same individuals who see the political elite as
corrupt, untrustworthy and unable to lead, if these
problems continue to be ignored we will see the rise of
racist parties across the entire Western world and
racist attacks on minorities, whether they are Muslims
or not. My opinion about Tommy Robinson is that he
is not a racist; it is him who is viciously treated by the

police, the media, the political class and radical Muslims, while people like Anjem Choudary and his Islamist counterparts get away with a lot when they protest against Britain and they went the terrorist flag to run over the Buckingham Palace and Downing Street number 10; those are the same thugs who want the terrorist flag on the White House in America, they are more vile, more aggressive, more violent and their rhetoric is beyond distasteful. Those are the same people who are imposing sharia patrols and police in no-go areas across Britain, yet the government is not holding anyone of these sick people accountable; it is easy to take on Tommy Robinson because he is their natural prey and they have to do everything to destroy his character, his livelihood, his family, his chances of getting a career, his chances of getting lawyers who can defend him. At the same time the Muslim fundies who do not want to see democracy in Britain are living on benefits, cheating the system and making the people of their host society look like idiots. Believing in open border policies is very destructive for the First World.

CHAPTER 16

CONFLICTS BETWEEN THE POLICE AND MINORITY COMMUNITIES

Time after time we have witnessed and are still witnessing the conflicts between the police and minorities of color in the United States, in rural and suburban areas, this usually includes unjustified shootings, rough treatments, verbal abuse, racial violence and fatal abuse against people of color; I am not ignoring that Whites are more killed by the police by Blacks. However, this does not take away the fact that Blacks are twice as likely to be stopped by the police than Whites. I am going to focus on the police brutality on Blacks, Hispanics and Mixed-raced people in America, but I am also going to talk about the conflicts between the police and minority communities in other Western countries, such as Norway, Denmark, Austria and others. It is also important to take notice of how important it is to encourage each member to contribute to society and uses his/her talents to shine and find one's place in this journey, which we all call life; I am going to come back to this topic at the end of this chapter, but going back to the subject of police brutality on Blacks, this is nothing new; there have been brutality on Blacks by the police in the United States even during the times of racial segregation, racism is a system that is entirely based on what the color of your skin looks like, once again, I said based on what your color of skin looks like, not based on your religion or political movement; racism rewards the unworthy and the underserved based on something that one did not choose what one's color of skin will be and who one's parents will look like. Racism favors some groups over others and it is rooted in self-hatred, inferiority complex, insecurity, low self-esteem, low self worth, self destructive habits and the need to blame others for one's own personal problems or poor choices in life. The U.S. society knows what was done to the African Americans when they were treated like second and third class citizens, when they were called Colored people, when they were called Negroes and when they were called all vicious names in the book because those people were viewed as animals, monkeys and things that are less human and yet they are the ones who are to blame for a lot of bad things. What racism does to Caucasians mainly Caucasian men has not made the world a better place nor does it make Whites happy and give them a peace of mind. The problem between the police and minority/majority communities was also something that occurred in South Africa during the times of Apartheid and it was often encouraged by Whites and the police in the country, the reason why I use the terminology majority/minority it is because Black South Africans were treated like a minority, even though they represent the majority population in South Africa by a minority Caucasian Apartheid government and we all know much of the things the police back then did on Blacks there and things were not and are still not different from now. The problem with the police and minority communities creates a sense of anger, bitterness, violence and detachment from the societies where minorities live. The nature of grievances between the Black communities and the police in the United States is a product of various amounts of discrimination, which African Americans have dealt with since the times they were brought as slaves from the African continent to the United States and the contribution it has had on the unequal opportunities,to which racial segregation contributed. Abraham Lincoln who is one of the former President of the United States freed the former slaves and had lots of goals to include them in the American fabric, but we all know what happened to the man. Democrats are primarily responsible for the racial segregation that occurred in the United States, they were also responsible for denying Civil Rights to Blacks on the other hands, Republicans were not any better either, even though they claim to free the slaves. Democrats also created the Ku Klux Klan or the KKK, a White nationalist organization whose goal is to intimidate and kill Black people, just because they do not like African Americans. Many Whites naively think that just because racial segregation ended in America kids from inner cities have the same opportunities as their children, but that is not how it works; the truth is that kids from the inner cities may have the same potentials as kids from the suburbs, but they do not have the same opportunities; minorities whose children go to school do not have the same system as those who live in prominent suburbs, they do not have the same resources and the leadership that they have from their parents, teachers, religious authorities and other figures are not the same because of the legacy of racism, which the majority people, the Congress and even the Supreme Court approved during the times of segregation - you can ignore they way you want, you can try to switch this problem under the carpet, but it is something that will not go away. It was something that society condoned back then and to ignore the fact that people in the inner cities have higher hills and higher mountains to climb when it comes to reaching the same potential as their compatriots from the suburbs is to be complacent to such cruelty. When you take into consideration the fact that you where you come from determines the kind of education you will receive and how far you are going to go in your life, it 's hard to make a statement that we are all on equal footing in society. If you live in a poor neighborhood where resources for you are few and the education system is mediocre, that is all you are going to get. In inner cities you have some policemen who criminalize an individual behavior from Blacks than they would on the same behavior if Whites did it; a Caucasian kid who smokes dope is not criminalized the same way a Black kid does when he/she is in the same situation and does the same thing, a white man/woman who smokes pot has a higher chance of getting a college student loan than a black man/woman who does the same thing. I read a story about the times when Blacks were thriving during the 1920's and there was even an area somewhere in the U.S., which was known as the Black Wall Street...I think it was in one of the inner cities and Blacks owned businesses and had an excellent standard of living despite the high amount of racism and discrimination they faced that time. Some of the African Americans were even thriving better than their European American compatriots, but many European Americans did not like the fact that Blacks were thriving and making more progress than them, then they started to burn and destroyed everything those so-called Colored people owned and built. They killed the things that those African Americans worked hard to get and earn because of hate, jealousy, and envy. Why is Fox News and other media ignoring this part of history? I do not have any idea, I guess anyone who brings this subject to light is now a Liberal or a Leftist who wants White genocide. There are times when we are even ignoring that situations create violence; these riots do not come from nowhere, there is a history behind each one of those scenarios, this does not mean that I condone riotings or any kind of such a classless behavior because those who do the riotings are the same ones who pay for burning cars, supermarkets, shops and other staff and the rest of the community living in those suburbs pays for such frustrations and violence. It influences the African American and even Latino communities in those areas because those who were working in shops, stations, bookstores and other places find themselves in situations where they do not have a job, those who own those shops find themselves with nothing at all. On the other hand, why doesn't society mention the sport fans who riot when their teams lose a competition, a domestic championship and so on.; why doesn't society say college students who riot for no reason? Why is it that when people from inner cities protest for legitimate concerns, like for instance being murdered for looking at a cop or other reasons are suddenly criminals, freeloaders, thugs, less intelligent and violent savages? Ignore it the way you want - for all I care; it is true that African Americans cannot make eye contact with the police; those who do are called to the police car and searched. If you do not have an identity card, a State Card or anything similar, you could be in a situation where you could face jail time. The policeman can make up a charge against you, which usually includes disturbing peace; this does not happen in prominent Caucasian suburbs. It seems like there is a lower expectation narrative on Blacks and even Hispanics; it is racism, pure racism in its true colors. I would like to send my thoughts and sympathies to the victims who were killed by the police, and I would like to send my sincere thoughts to their loved ones, whether they are Black, White, Hispanic, Asian, Mixed-race and so on. One killing by the police is one too many. Wa also know that evil prevails when good men and good women are complacent about it, whether we are talking about the murder of civilians by the police or the killing of the police by the civilian population, that is why I also would like to send my thoughts and sympathies to every policeman and policewoman that has been killed by a group of insane civilians, my thoughts also go to their families and those whom they have left behind; let me explain why I think this way; not all policemen/policewomen have the desire to see dead Black and Latino bodies in inner cities and the impact that these kinds of horrific incidents can have on those left behind, those who are involved in such horrific tragedies have to face the harshest justices and face imprisonment for their brutal behavior, I can even go so far to say that policemen who are involved in unjustified murders of unarmed Blacks and Hispanics have to face death penalty and it must not take too many years for them to be put to death; I do not even care if there are states in America that do not have death penalty, they have to pay for their stupidity, the same needs to be said for thugs who shoot and kill the police, they have to suffer similar outcomes. The policeman's job is to protect the community and there has to be mutual respect on both sides, they risk their lives every single day to protect you and me from criminals and they also protect our rights to make demonstrations and express our discontent with society, in most cases when you call them, they do not ask you if you're Black, Biracial, White, Hispanic, Asian etc, before they come to your rescue. The conflicts between the police and minority communities, immigrants from non-Western countries or communities of color is not just a problem in the U.S.; it is also an issue in other Western nations, such as Norway, France, Russia, Italy, Germany, Sweden, Denmark, Spain, Portugal, Finland, Holland, Belgium, Austria, Hungary, Czech Republic, Poland, Switzerland, Luxembourg, Australia, New Zealand and even South Africa. There are ongoing conflicts between the police and the delinquents who are mostly Persians, Berbers, Arabs and Blacks in countries like: France, Belgium, Germany, Sweden, Norway, Italy, Spain, and Holland. In New Zealand it is the conflicts between the police and Maori communities, and also immigrants from non-Western countries who live there. In Australia it is a dispute between the police and both Middle Eastern and some Aboriginal communities in the country, in Canada, it is a conflict between the police and many different types of minorities of color. In France and other European countries most of these disenfranchised youth are from the

355

suburbs or inner cities of Paris, Lyon, Marseille, Rennes, Strasbourg, Bordeaux, Toulouse, Montpellier, Saint-Etienne, Calais and other cities, and town across the entire country. Both in France, Switzerland, Belgium and Luxembourg, the world banlieue refers to suburbs, but it is not always a reference to poor suburbs, but also wealthy suburbs. The terminology banlieues, which is in plural is often used to describe troubled suburban communities with a higher amount of unemployment and crime rates. Most of the residents living in those areas have foreign origins, mainly from former French colonies in Africa and the Middle East or the French overseas territories and departments. They are Berbers, Blacks, Biracials and Arabs; you can also find Asians, Jews and other communities in those areas. In Denmark, Austria, Norway, Finland, Iceland and Luxembourg, children of immigrants who were born in those countries are called second generation immigrants or just immigrants, and their children are called third generation immigrants; this means that the societies where they were taken do not consider them as Danes, Norwegians, Austrians, Luxembourgish, Finns, or even Icelandic and the term integration is used on them very often, even though they were born in those countries and even though the terminology of integration is applied to a newcomer who has to respect the laws of his/her host society, as well as its customs, not for someone who was born in the country, unless they do not respect the authorities, unless they do not value women, unless they do not value gender equality between men and females, unless they create no-go areas where the police cannot even enter, unless they do treat sexual minorities like undesirable beings and unless they impose religiopolitical systematic laws that are in conflicts with the values of their birth countries. My question to you who is reading this book is this...is it improper to ask someone who was born and raised in his/her country of birth to integrate into it? What is your own personal view about it? In France, minorities are both considered as French and foreign or the other, some indigenous French people do not think minorities living in France, having the French citizenship as French people, especially those from the Far Right because those minorities are not Caucasians. Children of minorities and communities of color feel torn between the cultures of their parents and the mainstream French culture, the situation depends on the experiences many of them have had with the French society; some of them feel both French and foreign, some do not feel French at all and there are many who feel like they belong to neither. Those of you who have read my books know that I was born in France and I am a French-born Congolese or a French-born of Congolese descent my world has always been about France, the Congo and the Democratic Republic of Congo when I was a child, even now as an adult, but things were far more different and a lot changed when I was 12 years old, but before I talk about it, I would just say that when I was between 9 and 10 years old, some of my aunts and uncles reminded me at time that I am not Congolese when I was in the Congo; I thought I always was, even though subconsciously without even knowing it, I felt French, I was told that Dennis Sassou Nguesso is not my president and back then my president was François Mitterrand, and they were not joking when they said about it. Some people around the area where we use to live called me Mr. Frenchman because I was not that good at speaking other local Congolese languages besides Lingala; I was quite awful at Lari, I was quite terrible at

Kituba and so on. Even though there were time when I did not feel French, it did not take long for me to reconnect with my Franco-Congolese nationalism. When I was 12 years old, I felt more French than Congolese, even though I was in the Congo because I questioned our abilities to run countries, when you see that no majority Black country has managed to become a First World country, besides Bermuda. The point that I am trying to make is not about it me, but looking at individual situations where I can sense some of their feelings, I am myself a child of a French suburb; I was born in Oullins, a suburb in the southern part of Lyon and to be honest with you if there is now a culture where I do not feel a sense of belonging, it is not the French culture, it is not the Congolese culture etc.; it is the Danish culture, I can do my best to abide the laws of the country, but I know that my frequency and the frequency of the Danish culture do not match and never will because the codes of conduct in this culture are not in harmony with my thoughts and way of thinking. In France and other Western countries, the main reason of alienation perceived by both the older and younger generations of minorities who live in inner cities and poor suburbs is the casual and the institutional racism; for a long time, countries like Denmark, Norway, Sweden and Finland have had difficulties dealing with the lack of integration of newcomers and their historical memories in it comes to their treatment of the Sami minorities and the Greenlanders, even Sweden that is the most experienced Nordic when it comes to integrating minorities of color deals with the same issues. My birth country on the other hand also struggles with its historical memories and the colonial past, especially during the times of the Second World War and the 1961 Massacre that took place in Paris, and other ongoing controversies. Children of minority communities, especially those who do not have a Western appearance claim that they frequently encounter racism, economic segregation and discrimination; those are the same people who have difficulties finding a job that is in harmony with their qualifications, they also happen to represent the populations with a lower home ownership, and some just struggle to make ends meet. In many Nordic countries when responding to job offers, African and Middle Eastern dissidents receive fewer responses, they even receive refusals; many companies in that part of the world know that it is illegal to discriminate someone based on their race, ethnicity, sexual orientation, gender and religious beliefs, but laws are not enforced in those countries and many of those societies also happen to be complacent about racism and discrimination, even when it comes to racial slurs on minorities of color. Many immigrants living in Scandinavia feel like the system is purposefully designed to put them on welfare for the rest of their lives or do what many call "ghetto jobs"; in other words, jobs that are not compatible with their educational qualifications, but at lower levels. Many of those minorities of color or immigrants from non-Western countries feel like the Danes, the Norwegians, the Swedes, the Finns, the Icelanders and the Faroese do not want them to excel and use their gifts to contribute to society; they feel the system works against them so that they can be targets of nationalist and far right political parties who are going to label them as lazy, inefficient, less intelligent, and unwilling to work. Those groups of people are also concerned about the future of their children and wonder of their children have a future in those countries, the nationalist and extreme parties from the right use these situations to score points in the elections, but they themselves do not offer any forms of solutions when it comes to integration and assimilation. Many immigrants from non-Western countries who live in Scandinavia feel like society treats them like small children who cannot reflect and think for themselves, they feel that they are often assisted like small children and dogs, who are talked down to because they feel like they are not expanding their horizons. If you are an immigrant who loves to work and pay taxes, the last thing that you would want is to be told by a Jobcenter what to do and how to live your life, another problem with Nordic countries is the way they describe minorities of color, either they just call them immigrants, first generation immigrants second generation and so on or bilingual people; I am going to tell you a story of a black man whose identity will not be revealed in this book by me or anyone else,at the place where he works in Denmark they told him that they are going to employ someone who is as dark skinned as he is- the black man who happens to be an employee in that particular company expected that he would meet another black man, but when they employer came to him, he represented the new Afghan employee to the black guy, and he wonders and asks himself lots of questions. The reason why the black employee was speechless, it was because when he heard from an employee that he would bring a dark skinned employer, he expected a black person; most black people are dark skinned - when he told me that story, I told him that Danes are idiots; I told him that the Danes are idiots because they cannot tell a difference between a Middle Eastern person, a Black person, a Biracial and an Indian because to them they're just all dark people. I told that black man that the Nordics are also idiots when they do not notice that Afghans and most of the Middle Eastern people are classified as

360

Caucasians, that means that the new Afghan employee who was introduced to the Black employee is a white man, not some "dark skinned" individual from the African continent, even though Middle Eastern people are not viewed as Caucasians by some regular Caucasians, then use your eyes to tell the difference between people of different ethnicities. In France, Belgium, Germany, Holland, Spain, Italy and Portugal unemployment in poor suburbs are very high; in France for instance, unemployment amongst people who live in poor suburbs is about 40% and sometimes higher in other places and the factor that explains such an insanity is the difficulties to find a job or even to start one's own business. There are political parties in the country that want those youth to lose their French citizenship and sent out of the France, and back to the countries of origins. There have been many abuses, both verbal and physical that were committed against the youth by the police, there have also been murders committed on the youth by the police; this feeds into the perception that the French police is above the law of the country when it comes to offenses against nonwhites - it leads more anger, frustration, rejection, alienation and other things that results to violence and insecurity. In countries like Poland, Hungary, Czech Republic, Slovakia, Romania, Bulgaria, Croatia and other East European nations there is a high level of police brutality against the Romani people and sometimes no arrests are made, even though some of those Romani people are beaten to death. In the Republic of the Congo, the police is brutal towards dissidents of the Democratic Republic of the Congo, I can go on and with cases in India, Egypt, Morocco, Turkey, Greece, Ivory Coast, Brazil, Argentina, United Arab Emirates, Saudi Arabia and so on and so forth; the point that I am trying to make is that wherever there is police brutality, ill-treatment cannot be avoided, I am going to come back to this topic, where I am going to talk about the responsibility, which many of these communities need to take and why do I still think that there has to be law and order, but right now I am going to focus on a movement in the U.S., known as the BLM or Black Lives Matter and what is behind that movement, I am looking forward to deal with both perspectives by giving my honest view about the situation. The Black Lives Matter movement is an activist movement, which started in the African-American community; the purpose of their movement is to campaign against violence, systematic racism and discrimination against black people in the United States. They also protest against against racial profiling, police brutality and unequal opportunities in the United States, especially when it comes to the criminal justice system across the country. This movement started after the passing of the African-American teenager, Trayvon Martin who was killed by a Hispanic man, George Zimmerman. Since that time, the BLM has been recognized as a street movement nationally, following the passings of more and more African American people killed by the police, such as Michael Brown, Eric Garner, Freddy Gray, Jonathan Ferrel, John Crawford, Laquan McDonald, Akai Gurley, Tamir Rice, Eric Harris, Walter Scott and many other African American victims who were killed by the police in the U.S. To be honest with you, those who undermine the BLM's frustrations and anger by trying to propose a ban on them fail to miss a point; you cannot just sit by and shut up when the police kills members of your community, you cannot just sit and stay silent; if you are treated badly, both physically, verbally, emotionally and psychologically, and continue to create what you believe is going to be a perfect atmosphere in your environment to avoid being abused racially, physically and so on, you are not doing yourself a favor, in fact, you are rewarding your bully's behavior. The behavioral psychology, which I am talking about is called the "Law of Effect", this law reveals that behaviors as functions of their consequences. If the police who abuse Blacks expect black people to be nice to them, all the time, then the abusive police will continue to treat blacks like animals, take into account that you need to encourage positive behavior and discourage offensive behavior. If someone treats you badly, do not smile and pretend that it is ok; draw the line, pretending s if it is ok is not the teachings of Christianity, even Jesus himself was setting some people straight, he also drew the line and let them know that their behaviors were not in line; this is not coming from someone who is religious, but an Atheist. There times when you have to use forceful language to the intimidator, just like I do in this book without making any form of apology for it. If the abusive police understood the law of cause and effect, things would be done differently and they would not have killed so many African Americans and others, on the other hand, the police have the right to protect themselves against armed gangs and armed thugs, no matter what race they are. The trouble with the BLM movement is that they are not to be found when Black gangs and drug dealers kill our fellow brethren in inner cities, making the rest of the community unsafe across America, both the BLM and the New Black Panther Party do not demonstrate when both Democrats and Republican mayors from inner cities have ignored them for decades and just use their votes to get to excell in government offices and say to them "See You in 4 Years". The BLM and

the New Black Panthers Party do not demonstrate when
Blacks are treated like slaves and possessions in many Middle
Eastern countries. They do not protest when some Nordic
person in Denmark or Norway uses the N-word on Black
people in their local languages. They do not demonstrate when
governments from different African countries do not treat
their own citizens well. Another thing that I condemn is the
fact the some BLM supporters chant "What do we want? Dead
cops! What do we want? Dead cops! What do we want? Dead
cops! What do we want? Dead cops! What do we want? Dead
cops!" I do not like this chant, nor do I like it when many
BLM supporters say that they say pigs in a blanket and fry
them like bacons, the reason why I am against such a rhetoric,
which in my view is misplaced on the police, instead of it being
placed on the Far Right ultranationalist groups who would fit
in this description very well and I would include extremist
Muslims and others on that list pigs in the blanket. The police
are there to protect us, most of them do not care about your
race, your color, your ethnicity, your religion, your political
views, your social class and so on; they just want to protect you
and I, and those policemen and policewomen who are racists
and attack African Americans and others for no reason other
than racial do not deserve their jobs and they have to face the
toughest justice, which the law possesses; the same needs to be
said if a Black policeman or policewoman attacks a Caucasian
or a Hispanic or any other non-black person just for racial
reasons because we are all equal under the law and there
should not be any form of special demands. I sometimes need
to agree with Dr.Ben Carson on the fact that at times, the
BLM distracts from what matters most, the real problem here
is not the police; young African Americans cannot find jobs,

young Hispanics cannot find jobs and the violence that tears neighborhoods in inner cities have higher impact on the minority communities living in that area than others. I am not saying that we should undermine police brutality for the wrong reasons, what I am saying is that there is a bigger problem in the black community and many black Americans feel that they have been ignored by both the Republicans and Democrats for decades after decades; in my opinion Black Americans do not want the government to feed them, they do not want the government to clothe them, they do not want the government to pay their bills, they want their honor and they want their dignity. The same can be said about Hispanic Americans and others, I can draw a parallel to this with integration problems in Nordic countries and the rest of Europe and my message to the Danes, the Norwegians and others is that most of the immigrants from non-Western countries do not want to be fed by your governments, they do not want to be clothed by your governments, they do not want you to pay their bills and assist them like small children, they want their honor, pride, and dignity; they have been ignored by you for far too long for many decades; you have created a system where you have encouraged a culture of passivity and the culture of leniency;take ownership for it and learn from the situation; if you cannot give it to them, then do not complain about your minority communities not integrating into your societies. Do not complain about the failure of your integration policies when you haven't realized that the things that you are doing are not working, and when they don't, then you cannot expect your minority communities to assimilate in your way of thinking. Your integration policies have failed, yet you want to bring more migrants in your societies and "integrate" them into the community, what do you guys think the impact is going to be? Congratulations for your insanity. On the other hand the immigrant gangs who are selling drugs and running streets are not doing themselves a favor by killing each other because one of you wants a portion of the drug market in a particular neighborhood have lost the meaning of common sense because they are also responsible for other crimes and the conflicts with native mobs, it seems like they really lack a sense of awareness about themselves and who they are. The same goes to a group of immigrants who cheat the welfare system and are involved in theft; alienation is not an excuse to do the crime, racism is not an excuse to take part in illegal activities. There is something affirmative that minority communities, people of color, immigrant communities can do, instead of waiting for someone to do things for us; this is not about oversimplifying the issues when it comes to racism, hatred, discrimination and the denial of opportunities.But we need to lift each other's spirits up by encouraging one another to start our businesses, help ourselves to send our children to the best schools, have respect for our elderly people and learn from their life's experiences, I also recommend that those who do not have the skills to compete against the locals need to prove the system wrong, for how should the system continue to have power over them? They need to take their power back and set things straight; the violence that rises in our quarters does not have to represent who we are, it does not have to represent our values, those who have those values need to question their mindsets. Bullets, gun violence, criminality, street violence and death do not have to be the images of us, let us remember that it has an influence on our communities and the next generation is going to pay for our miserable decisions, but it does not have to be like this. Whether it is happening in the United States, Canada, Sweden, France, Czech Republic, Denmark, Hungary, Portugal, Brazil, Norway, Finland, Argentina, Chile, Mexico, Australia, South Africa, New Zealand, Spain, Russia, Israel, Greece, etc.; whether we are Black, Hispanic, Romani people, East Europeans, Mixed Race, Arabs, Jews, Persians, Berbers, Indians Malays, Amerindians or whether we belong to any minority group from any other country, we have to march on local education boards to prove our worth and find our places in the societies where each one of us has an address. We must now allow our school systems to fail the coming generations like it failed the old generations; if our communities are put in bilingual schools because little expectation narratives about us, then it is up to us to make them shine, it is up to us to let those schools shine for every single pupil and student that studies in those schools. No one can give us our honor, no one can give us our dignity, no one can give us our self-worth; we have to dig in and find those values within ourselves and within each other. Each one of us needs to confront the media in our respective or residential societies who characterizes us as bandits, uneducated, unskilled, unable, less intelligent, idiots, inferior human beings, unable to learn, unable to reflect logically and so on and so forth. We in some countries, which you have often seen me mention on this many times in a harsh manner; we have to confront the comedians who humiliate and bully us and stop this madness and tell them the truth about their stupidity. Many politicians on the Left and on the Right talk about our integration to the mainstream cultures and they speak about making poverty history in our inner cities and inner towns, but it seems like poverty is winning the minds of many minorities, peoples of color, and immigrants from non-Western countries, apparently, their policies have not worked and, you cannot vote for the same people who keep doing the same things and expect different results. We need to shame members of our communities who are selling drugs and destroying our reputation in the name of stupid choices, we have to humiliate them and let them know that they will not do their crap in our name. There are many problems in our inner cities that have been ignored for far too long; minority communities who speak out against those kinds of problems are scorned and shun from others. This is not about oversimplifying the issues when it comes to racism, discrimination, unequal opportunities, rejection, racial abuse and so on, those things can kill us, but we do not need to use them as excuses to live on public assistance or steal from someone else's home or even rape a woman from a mainstream society because of the racism from that particular mainstream society and such things need to stop - we need to remember that at the end of the day, each one of us is responsible for our own actions and decisions and those decisions have consequences for better or worse, and we must not accept radical Muslims to try to impose their system of beliefs in inner cities also - the system also has a choice and with those choices come multiple consequences that can have either positive or negative impacts on different communities. The failure of the system to realize that we also exist is killing us, but not as quick as a bullet; it is killing us softly by tearing our lives apart little by little until we begin to lose our lives in the inside, this quote is an inspiration from Dr.Ben Carson, although it is not the exact quotation from him. Failure can kill you like a bullet if you let it control you and influence your life,

if we want to be success, we need model fruitful and
productive people, we need to admire them; we do not have to
admire what they do, nor do we have to approve of their
behavior, but focusing on the model that has led them where
they are. No one can make us succeed, this has to come from
us alone and it is up to us to make things work and create our
own legacy. Education is the key,but it must be coupled with
actions and common sense, this a quotation from Brigitte
Gabriel who is the founder and the president of the American
Congress for the Truth, also known as ACT for America. If
you have a good education and couple it with action, you can
ride high, no matter what you race is. When slavery was at its
pick, it was illegal to teach a slave because the evil masters
feared that an educated slave is a free man, and that was
something that the evil masters did not want. We need to talk
about billions of resources that we have and turn them into
profits and get everyone at work, we are in control of our lives
and start dealing with things that matter in our communities. It
is also critical that we respect the police and the law, fathers
who kill their daughters in the name of honor need to see the
citizenship of their host countries be revoked from them and
face deportation to their countries of origins, immigrant men
who rape women because the way those women are or because
of the way those women dress also have to be in situations
where they need to be incarcerated back to their countries of
origin and they have to lose their Western citizenships. We
need to send a message of order and civility, both for native-
born citizens and new arrivals. It is not healthy to assist people
too much to a point where they become too dependent or
satisfied on public assistance from the government; this is
something, which both the Left and the Right have not

ignored in the United States and many other Western or other majority white countries for decades after decades. Minorities, peoples of color and immigrants from non-Western countries are not asking governments to built up social housing for them; they want to buy their houses, they want to buy their cars, they want to choose the right schools for their children, and they want to climb the ladder. Nations rise and fall based on the character of their populations, their leadership and the values that they represent, especially when they choose to accept corruption at the highest levels of politics, governments and even special interest groups who do not have any interest in the well-being of the societies that have made them who they are, they are the ones who have the willingness to destroy the same societies by sacrificing millions of lives for the sake of their ideals. They are the same people who conquer to divide because they enjoy seeing us killing one another and drive ourselves under graveyards, it seems like we are going in that direction when we choose incompetent people to run the fabric of our societies, by taking the train of course. We are in trouble, and they do not care about what is happening with our jobs, they do not care about the everyday man, they do not care about the ordinary woman, and they do not care about generations to come. They finance wars and make profits from buffing other nation's natural resources and leaving many of the locals in poverty. George Soros and other Special Interest Groups are taking advantage of the BLM's situation for their own causes; they do not care about African Americans, they just view them as unintelligent people with no means to make it the next day. You know that one of the former Presidents of the United States once said that when a government refuses to allow a peaceful revolution, violent revolution is inevitable.

There times when governments in many countries, whether developed or developing experience rigged elections so that they or their opponents can stay in power; we all know that power corrupts if you have for the wrong motives. Many people who are governing us these recent moment do not serve us, but the super rich, may they are using voting machines from George Soros and other who have desires to destroy the sovereignty of nations. These are the same people who want to destroy mankind by trying to start World War 3 between NATO allies and Russia, they even do not care if there is a nuclear war and millions or perhaps billions of lives being lost. To be honest with you, the special interest group only cares about money and power for the wrong reasons, whatever stands between their evil purpose and the survival of nations, they are against it because Globalism is the language, which they speak and they believe in unlimited immigration from Third World countries to First World countries so that they can start social unrests, cultural enclaves, racial tensions, national conflicts, genocides and so on. Those people have blood in their hands and open borders means chaos. Both George Soros and many other elites have multiple control over major news network and the mainstream media, they make donations to empower the New World Order and on the hand, they tell call those who are against their Globalist agenda conspiracy theorists; those who do not learn from history are doomed to repeat it, just because World Wars happened in the past, it does not mean that they cannot happen again; major that cost millions of lives occur because there are many individuals and nations who do not choose to act. They first came for freethinkers, I did not want to speak up because I am not a freethinker and then they came for the Patriots, I did not want speak up because I am not a patriot and they came for the destruction of nations, I did not want to talk up because I am not proud of my country, then they came for Third World populations, I did not want to speak up because I am not from the Third World and when they came for me, there was no one left to speak for me. Those elites view themselves as deities and creators of everything, let me make something clear to you; there are times and situations where each one of us is an author of our experiences and realities, and if we want different experiences, it is up to each one of us to create them; there are those who use their power to create for good purposes, and then there are those who use their power to create for evil purposes. George Soros and his puppets are against the progress of nations as we know it, especially countries that are great democracies, they are also against the right of nations to maintain their self-determination and to have an opposition against imperial rule. In my view, George Soros is a Globalist and an elitist who is among the evil 1%, this sounds controversial from me who admires both fruitful and rich people and I want to make it clear; I have said that if you want to be successful in life, you need to model successful people and rich people; you do not have to like all of them, nor do you have to like their behaviors and I am going go further with this detail later. Admiring the rich does not mean accepting responses from elites who want to destroy national and cultural identities through the means of unlimited immigration, both George Soros and many other elites have had their hands on many international conflicts, civil unrests, state coups, political instability and they have overthrown many governments and have been involved in many assassinations. The purpose that the elite have is to depopulate the planet and I do not even know if I believe in climate change, I wonder if it is a scam from the political elite. I would have anything against George Soros and the other elites if they used this model to destroy the OPEC, the Muslim Brotherhood and Muslim countries that are funding terrorism and building thousands of mosques and madrassas in the Western world and the rest of the non-Muslim world for that matter, instead of treating Blacks like less intelligent groups of cattle by financing Black Lives Matter and approving of the riots and civil unrests that paralyze communities who want nothing more than improving their lives, sending their children to school and live their lives in peace, instead of supporting the Neo-Nazis in Ukraine who are the same people who would turn on him and other Zionists had they had things going their way, my view of this man and others is that they are evil elites and evil Zionists; if your goal is to conduct financial warfare and currency speculations, then I don't know what to say about you -when you are destroying the national economic structures to maintain the rates by centralizing everything in international monetary organization, you are robbing those nations of their independence. It is because of the Maastricht Treaty that most of the EU members do not have their currencies anymore, include my birth country; there should be not be a United States of Europe, there should not be a United States of Africa, there should not be a United States of Asia, there should not be a United States of Latin America and there should not be a United States of Australasia; There is only one United States, and that is the United States of America, an independent country, which is in the Americas, an independent state with its constitution, just like any other nation on earth. In any country we talk about who is going to be president and who is going to win the elections, even in the main democracies, while in some nations there are different forms of dictatorships, but no matter what if those who are leading their countries are not puppets, their lives are going to be taken away from

them because the goals of the Special interest groups
is to cultivate a world empire and monopolize its
economy, this is a plot to destroy national sovereignty,
this is why the Hungarian government views people
like George Soros and other Zionists as a threat to
their national security, excuse me for this language and
rhetoric and explanation for the "Zionist" language,
but this is what happens when you have idiots
destroying other people's lives and those are the same
fools who give Jews a bad name, again this has
nothing to do with supporting Israel, by the way, not
all the people who are involved in such imbecilic plots
are Jews; you find many different kinds of individuals
who are involved in such evil purposes, I want to
make that clear and the Western mainstream media is
not bringing these things in the open, yet they talk
about fighting for the freedom of the press; looking
back, I think I made a mistake when I wrote
"Freedom of Press: The Sitting Duck, a book of
poetry that I published in 2009 that talks about
journalists being persecuted for doing their job, when
I look back, I think I made a terrible mistake doing
that, and I sincerely regret it. The topic that I am
raising about the evil special interest groups who have
blood in their hands has nothing to do with trying to
say that rich people are bad, although some are - you

also find poor and middle-class individuals who are evil, but this does not excuse the way the New World Order elitists who do not want immigrants where they live in their mansions, but they want open borders and let immigrant from Third World countries in unlimited amounts so that they can destroy their same countries that have given them opportunities to be as wealthy as they are, while they live in safe mansions and villas, the average citizen in many countries is threatened by Islamic terrorist attacks, criminality and other forms of violence - what kind of value do they add to our lives? Their policies are destroying nations, cultures, identities, law and and order, constitutions, national governments, languages, economies, education systems, infrastructures and the worst of all-they are taking lives of people who have nothing to do with the exponent of their evil agenda. To the New World order elitists, the common man has no value so they can keep torturing the word they way they like without any form of impunity; their arrogance is in thinking that they can decide on other people's lives. This is what I call systematic bullying because these goons want more human enslavement for their own gain, on the other hand there are many 1% people who are patriots and love their nations, many of them do the best they can to contribute to the well-being of their countries, I know that this is a very controversial thing to say, but you and I have the ability to join the 1% and do things differently by using our wealth to turn complaints into opportunities; if we just stick to the claims, then we are not helping the masses; there is no difference between you, me and the 1%; the difference between us and them is the model they all of them have chosen to follow and apply, you and I have the ability to do the same thing because now that we have brought the size of the complaints, we can now start focusing on the size of us so that we can contribute and influence other people for the better by adding value to their lives, and by treating them dignifiedly, but we first have to overcome our personal obstacles and be optimistic people. If you and I want to do better than the 1%, let me tell you this; if you can't beat them, join them and we want to transform the lives of the 99%, we need to modify our beliefs and change our frequencies, by doing that, we can start taking inspiring actions that will bear lots of fruits; we can help them lift themselves up and restore their honor, instead of us doing everything for the 99% and assisting them with small children or groups of cattle. Remember that charity starts at home, not abroad; I am not trying to ask for a creation of a utopia where the world is problem free, anyone who thinks like that is mistaken, we live in a world of contrast and dualities and issues are always going to pop up on the surface; if you know a world where things like that do not exist, please give me a call or send me an e-mail, I would like to know more about it and how it operates. Back to the theme of the BLM movement; I would like to say to them that Black people suffer more in places like the Middle East, Russia, China, India, Pakistan, Japan, other East European countries, in other words, places where there is more racism on Blacks than in the U.S. not to undermine the racism that exists in America and the suffering of African Americans, but it is not an excuse to burn other people's personal belongings, assets and equities; it is not an excuse to paralyze neighborhoods and make things difficult for one's own community. We cannot afford to allow other people's negative opinion of us to become our lives' experiences, we must never give anyone a permission to disrespect us and make us feel inferior - the way, which we can make ourselves credible is to take a stand against racist police brutality, but also against gangs that are destroying inner cities and killing thousands and thousands of our brethren; we are not respecting ourselves when we do not condemn the thugs who are giving us a bad image and poisoning our minds with drugs, crime, systematic violence and systematic bullying - no one is telling those drug dealers not to have a job; they have made decisions not to want to contribute to the fabric of your country, which is a beacon of life for mankind, despite its faults. This message is not just to my fellow African American brethren, but also my brethren who live in the suburbs of my country of birth, France and others who live in England, Netherlands, Belgium. Sweden, Germany, Canada, Spain and other nations; it is also a message to other kinds of minorities, this is not about us trying to earn respect of those who believe that we cannot pass their gates because they put hoofs through, which we cannot jump because they want to create an environment in which they feel it is ok to treat people like crap, on the other hand when we do not respect ourselves, we cannot expect others to respect us, I have said it in chapter 8 that we are our worst enemy because we refuse to listen and take ownership of the issues that are affecting our communities negatively until it is too late - we do not even value ourselves, but expect others to appreciate us - you get what you give. If we want our communities to be successful and regain our honor and dignity, we have to take responsibility for ourselves and for one another - no one can give you your honor, no one can give you your dignity, no one can give you your pride, no one can give your your self-worth; you have to swim towards the ship and get it there by yourself. The conditions that are influencing the inner cities and the suburbs negatively are reflections of the way we think about ourselves and about each other; It is up to us first of all to walk on the first stepping stones to be better and strengthen our communities. Of course, politicians in Western countries from both the Left and the Right have failed to embolden the battle of ideas that makes the Western world what it is to many minority populations and other groups of people who are vulnerable; if you go back to the times when the U.S. was segregated, African Americans were treated like second class citizens and they were treated like inferior human beings and called satans by the mainstream U.S. society, the consequences of this horrific situation has led some African-Americans to convert to Islam because they saw Christianity as the White man's religion, not that Islam is a better religion, but I hope you get my point; if you don't, then we are witnessing the same scenarios today, not just in the USA, but in France, Netherlands, Belgium, Spain, Norway, Denmark, Sweden, Italy, Canada, Australia, Finland, New Zealand, Hungary, Greece and other countries; when the academia, the political elite, the special interest groups, the multinationals and others do not embolden the battle of ideas about what makes their values better than Islam, that's when radical Muslims win the minds of the most disconnected, the vulnerable and the sad ones. They gain by poisoning their minds and converting them to Islam, and we are allowing ourselves to struggle to deal with those radical Muslims who often hate preachers, Salafists and others financed by our so-called allies from Middle Eastern countries - in the name of freedom of religion, tolerance, and diversity, we are allowing our communities to be fall into the ruins by allowing the nations that sponsor terrorism to build more mosques, madrassas, and Middle Eastern study departments; Islamic radicals take advantage of those who have faced rejection from society and those who have been left behind, those people manipulate painful and angry minds by radicalizing those individuals and once they hold radical views, they can plan their mission against the Western world,but also against Western interests and other non-Muslim countries, which they also see as infidel lands or Western subordinates. They oppose everything that defines the West and wants stringent Islamic laws worldwide. Islamic terrorist turns their radicalized elements by taking away their humanity and turning them into beasts, the marginalized are recruited on the internet, mosques, madrassas and Islamic street propaganda and one they become fundamentalists, then they go to suicide missions in the Western world and elsewhere; many of them are individuals who were born in Western countries. Many Western governments have to take responsibility for this because of their cowardice and submission to the people at the top who also contribute to the destruction of their societies; the responsibility also lies to the communities in inner cities and elsewhere that are allowing the rise of radical Islam in their neighborhoods, schools, universities, colleges, trade unions and so on. There are also people, regardless of their wealth and economic security who are attracted to the propaganda of the Islamic radicals, they make a choice to join those evil beasts - that is why I would like to come back and say that at the end of the day, we are responsible for ourselves and our lives, the sooner we are aware of it, the chances are that we are able to create the lives that we want for ourselves, our communities and our nations. That's said, I would like to include that the area where Sheriff David Clarke has a point is when he states that the BLM movement does not demonstrate when cops are killed by thugs who want nothing but crime, destruction, and anarchy in their communities The BLM movement is not taking a stand against rappers who have misogynistic view of women and degrading views of Blacks, whether those rappers are black or white, I guess there is a double standard here; in my native France we are witnessing violence, and against cops by delinquents and as someone who is a child of a suburb, I do not accept any violence against cops, nor do I accept any form of murder on cops because such behavior is not part of the values that France and the United States represent. We all know that there are some racist cops out there, but I feel the need to say it again and again; most cops have our best interests and they are putting their lives on the lines to protect our lives from criminals and gangs who do not care about our way of life, our laws and order. Cops who like anyone regardless of race, ethnicity, religion and so on and they are not getting the respect that they deserve; you do not get your point across by killing and destroying, you do not beg an oppressor for justice. In France and other Western countries, the conflict between the police and minority communities has been going on for a long time. I think the anti-cop rhetoric needs to stop, there is no place for hateful ideologies in modern societies, whether it is the Black Panthers, the Alternative Right, the KKK, the Islamic political ideology, White nationalists, Black nationalists, Jewish nationalists, tribalists, far right ultranationalists, far left anarchy and so on and so forth. This madness has gotten out of control and the rhetoric, whether it is coming from cops or any community in any country, whether it is in the U.S., France, Britain, Holland, Hungary, Poland, Sweden, Canada, Norway, Finland, Germany, Austria, Australia, Russia, Hungary, Portugal, Switzerland, Estonia etc. I do not care if some people think that I am walking on both lines; this is not an either or situation, you may criticize me the way you want, but the truth is that I am seeing unfair treatment on both sides and it is not benefitting anyone, but creating sectarian communities; before you play the Liberal or the Leftist card on me, save your breath; this is not time to play the Left and Right game when we are seeing people losing their lives on both sides and what we are witnessing a decline of our societies in our lives and we are more divided than ever. The solution to the conflicts between the communities and the police is a creation of the truth and reconciliation commission where groups of people can come and give statements about their experiences, whether it is a bad experience from a cop or a cop being mistreated by a member of a community. I also recommend that perpetrators on both sides give a testimony and request amnesty from criminal prosecution, hearing and inquiries have to take place on both sides where the two parties can tell their stories and find a path to a possibility to heal. There have to be reparations for the crimes and rehabilitations, so that they can be used as lessons from, which we can draw and do things differently. There have to be consequences to those who abuse cops; I suggest that those who are abusive to cops and those who go so far to even murder cops have to be sent to labor camps for 25 years or they have to face the death penalty. Cops who someone or people from people from a particular community have to also placed in labor camps or face harsher laws of justice, even the death penalty. The purpose of these propositions is to send a powerful message to those who do not respect the law and and feel the need to create anarchy and destruction, they have to know that any form of crime has consequences and the consequences are harsh. I am not a pedagogue or a Sunday school teacher who will sit around and start philosophizing the systematic causes of crime, if there is someone from whom we can get some inspiration when it comes to dealing with criminals, I suggest that we get some inspiration from Sheriff Joe Arpaio from Arizona in the USA; Joe Arpaio is known for being tough and sending a strong message to criminals that think the world is all about them and his policies are effective. Now some of you might wonder what foreign policy has to do with crime in our domestic inner cities and ghettos, to tell you the truth there is something to it because we are too busy trying to save the world with policies that are not working, those are the same policies that are coming back to bite us hard, yet we keep making the same mistakes over and over again. This is not about not talking with anybody and isolate ourselves, but the truth some of the nations that we consider allies are in fact contributing to the end of our existence with our miserable hands. We are spending trillions and trillions of Dollars and Euros in the Middle East without any form of useful results; we could have used those sums of money to rebuild our communities, our schools, our hospitals, bridges, foster homes, retirement homes, veterans, homeless people and we could also have used those trillions of Euros to invest in small businesses. Some people would say that they are trying to bring democracy in the Middle East and the rest of the world, let me tell you that the priority of the United States, France, Germany, Italy, Spain Canada and other nations are the need of their citizens; it is not the job of the United States to bring democracy in four corners of the world, if those nations want freedom, they have to begin to question their system of values and ways of thinking first, then they have to make up their minds if they want democracy or not, we are spending trillions on foreign aid and many of the nations that receive aid have not seen the conditions of their peoples improve because of corruption. Not every country in the world thinks that the system of democracy is a good idea and they like things the way they are there. Our nations are in debt, and we have no direction, we have no imagination, and we have no strategies, but we want to invest trillions of Dollar rebuilding other countries, and on Foreign Aid, while communities and the police cannot get along, this is resulting in a vacuum, from which the Islamic radicals are profiting, the same do to Far Right and the Far Left; I say that Black Lives Matter, Native Lives Matter, Caucasian Lives Matter, Blue Lives Matter, Asian Lives Matter, Jewish Lives Matter, Albino Lives Matter, Eastern Lives Matter, Straight Lives Matter, Gay Lives Matter, Women's Lives Matter, Men's Lives Matter, Children's Lives Matter and so on, and so forth; the point that I am trying to make here is this...All Lives Matter, when we value all lives it means that we are all people and each one of us is equal under the law; we are all made of the same organisms, and we are on this journey, which we know as life.

IN CLOSING

The problem with the international elites is that they have been in the habit of denying facts out of the concerns that by accepting the fact, they think they are going to welcome unpleasant beliefs that can influence their deep pockets, their destinies the way the want to live. It has something to do with not trying to focus on the things that you do not want out of the theory that says that the more you concentrate on the things that you do not want, the more you give it power and the more of the same comes to you. The international elite thinks that by dealing with the issues that our societies are facing we are using our energies to focus on the wrong things, although it is important to focus on what you want, the problems that our nations are facing have nothing to do with us surviving for a short term, but surviving for a long time by finding solutions that that work, after identifying the problems, instead of sugarcoating them. It is true that if we want our external world to better better, our internal world has to improve first, but one of the way for it to improve is for us to take inspired actions, which can influence both ourselves and our environments in better ways, some it requires that swamps are to be drained harshly. Maybe some of you think that I am controversial, outspoken, aggressive and like calling the issues as I see them, but history has taught us that you need to identify the forces of evil by their names if you want to attract solutions that will defeat them. I have never pretended to be a Sunday school teacher or a Jesuit, I like confronting issues and raise concerns about topics of our lifetime, this requires that you do not run for a popularity contest and try to make everyone happy because it's not my goal; sometimes you have no choice, but generalize when there are general problems and from now on statements that I made in this book reveal that I am screaming for solutions. We cannot ignore the fact that the Western civilization and the rest of the non-Muslim world is at war against the political wings of the Islamic faith; those who believe in the strictest forms of Islamic laws must not be taken lightly because they do not mince words; they mean what they say, the values, which Islamists hold are not compatible with civilized values that have defined and shaped advanced societies, as they believe that those fundamental values are manmade; the greatest danger to peace is to drag the world into destruction, wasting too many trillions of Dollars, Euros, Pounds and other currencies on wars that have been undeclared. Those wars lead us nowhere, especially in Middle Eastern countries, this is something that we have faced for many years, while our nations have problems of their own already. Despite many people from civilized countries making efforts to promote fundamental values in the Middle East and elsewhere, this has not worked, and we are not even questioning those policies, I personally do not believe that the idea of democracy works for all countries of the world; some nations are used to the system that they have and some populations think that the Western world is imposing it system of government on others, people in some parts of the world value security over other fundamentals and those in the developing countries have to work really hard to provide to provide a sense of safety where wealth can be granted. Whether we like or not political systems are based on cultures, system of values, traditions, beliefs and the way specific populations feel about themselves; a transition to new fundamentals requires that specific populations need to start taking responsibility by questioning some of their values and by being prepared to change their mentalities; if you want to get new fresh fruits, you have to get rid of old and evil roots, maybe they need to get themselves pruned first and adopt new principles. The idea that the Western world is spreading democracy around the world is some mythology, if you expect all nations to take this system; it works for other non-Western nations, for some, it has not worked, it looks like major countries are focusing too much on fighting the wrong battles, instead of finding strategies that work; a stable state is active, modern and has a population that follows the rule of law, a population that holds its

390

government accountable. If a particular population wants democracy, it has to be up to them to decide to know what it is; they also have to be willing to reject corruption and adjust their culture. Many of the citizens of different nations are less interested in politics, religion and how their governments function; they just want to wake up and find work, send their children to school and plan their own future. In some parts of the world, we have seen dictators being replaced by religious fundamentalists who want to take all over the world by subjugating those who do not believe and worship the way do, they want to suppress those who do question their doctrines and ways of thinking and in the worst case scenario, they want to kill anyone who does not worship their god and prophet, while bringing the world back to the 7th century; those are the same people who are causing problems in the streets of Germany, France, Netherlands, United States and Canada because they are bringing their own problem with them in nations that have given them refuge, yet these are the same fools who want to turn the world into an Islamic colony. Those ignore these kinds of issues are apologists for evil; if you are willing to tolerate the intolerable in the name of diversity, compassion, humanity, brotherhood, unity and so on, you are not doing for those virtues; you are doing it for contributing to the destruction of your country. If you are a citizen of the world, you are a citizen of nowhere, and you do not have a country, and you do not have any basis of the meaning of having a country, having your origins and having your lineages. If you think having a country is a rhetoric from far-right nationalists, then you need to examine your level of consciousness; having a country does not mean that you have hate over another person, it only means that you value your nation's sovereignty and borders, and you willing to do what it takes to defend it, just as ultra-nationalism contributes to wars and genocides, so does the concept of world unity; just take a look at history and ideologies that contributed to millions of lives being lost in the name of ultra-nationalism and the idea of the global unity; this means that any immoderation is harmful. If you believe in open borders where you expect the rich Western world to take in the complete misery of developing countries and if you believe in unlimited immigration, you think that what belongs to nobody belongs to everybody, this means you are contributing to racism and prejudices among peoples. The thing that gets on my nerves is that places like China, Nigeria, Peru, and India see themselves more as world citizens than the citizens of their countries, it seems like they do not see themselves as attractive people. If the concept of Globalism is about ending the existence of national states, then I do not see myself entering the Globalism Train; we live on our beloved planet Earth, but the Earth is not a country, we are all human beings and our lives on Earth is not eternal, it is very important to treat our fellow man with respect and dignity, but there is nothing wrong with defining different humans by their cultural, ethnic, racial, national and original

ties and this includes boundaries, this does not mean
rejecting enlightenment values, but enforcing it by
being secure about oneself and one's identity. On the
other hand, it is a terrible judgement to play the
language police card by setting up schemes that troll
people viciously, there should not be any place for
bullies and thugs in any civilized society; the point that
I am trying to make here is that many people on the
Far Right, ultranationalist groups, ultra-religious
groups and others confuse political incorrectness with
vulgarity or bigotry, I wonder what kind of people
waste their time playing games with semantics; playing
the politically incorrect card makes it easy dismiss
reliable information by writing all the data off as the
project of bigots, using racial slurs, tribal slurs, ethnic
slurs on minorities and any other group of people is
not about tearing down taboos, what I think the
extreme right is doing is systematic bullying and they
do this to cover up for racists or their racist remarks;
they cover up for anti-Semites, racists, sexists,
homophobes, tribalists, chauvinists and extreme
Feminists; this is also a tactic, which fundamentalist
Muslims use when they impose the values of the
political and religious wings of Islam to those of us
who do not have any interest in them whatsoever. It
feels like when rats bite your feet and begin to devour
it, you will not notice a thing, until you wake up, and
your foot is finally gone. It is not worth the drama,
trying to reason with someone who believes that you
do not have the moral courage and the pure intellect
to honestly answer questions that make you feel like

arguing with an idiot who thinks you are talking in circles. One of the messages that I have been sending in this book is that when you run your mouth by calling other people vicious names, don't whine when someone does the same things to you, I couldn't care less about your nationality, your race, your religion, etc.; your right to free speech does not mean careless talk and you are responsible for the choices that you make - once you make a decision to cross the line of civility by using a language that you use in bars, pubs, and other similar places because you believe that one cannot be accountable for your stupidity because you are free, you are not free; you are in bondage, and someone needs to come to you and tell you that. When you say that you are free by dehumanizing others, you're not free; you're toxic and your level of toxicity is polluting your own environment, one way or the other, someone out there is paying for your own stupidity; think of me the way you like, Liberal, Leftist, immigrant lover etc.; I do not have anything to prove to you, I do not have to crack head to be a Conservative by trampling over bodies that are less suited to me,this has nothing to do with Conservatism. On the other hand, there is no question that criticizing Islam and Muslims has nothing to do with racism, anyone who thinks it does need to examine the meanings of words, you've got to be bullheaded not to realize that Islam is a religion, not a race; a religion is an idea; Muslims are not a race, just like Christians and Buddhists are not a race, but followers of their respective faiths - in my view all religions have to be subjected to critique and opposition because that is how you bring ideas into light. I want a better word where people and other living beings can live safely and in peace; I want a better world where people can prosper in many ways they define prosperity and live the lives of their purpose, but you start first by carrying about a group in your nation before you make plans to "save" the world. There is nothing wrong with questioning the fact that many rich Westerners are saving African children in Third world countries, rather than providing for the people of their nations; charities begin at home and end abroad, just because I am black it does not mean that we should not question the way many black majority countries function today and why do many of those societies struggle, what will it take for those societies to own to our misfortunes. I am not beholden to anybody, whether it is the Danes, Norwegians, Russians, Muslims, Atheists, Liberals, Conservatives, Libertarians and any other group of people and I am not going to allow myself to be bullied into submission by anyone of these groups or anybody else for that matter; I rise from ashes and beyond the horizon.

BALTHAZAR RODRIGUE NZOMONO-BALENDA

ABOUT THE AUTHOR

Balthazar Rodrigue Nzomono-Balenda [prounced:
Szómóno-Balenda]; commonly referred to as
Rodrigue, Rod, Rodwell, Bal or Balthazar (born:
August 29th, 1981) is a French-born self-published
author who has published several books of poetry;
including books, such as the Depth of My Soul and
Far Beyond the Horizon. He was born in Oullins, a
suburb in the southern part of Lyon and has also
grown up in Brazzaville, Kinshasa, and Pretoria.
Rodrigue is originally a French-born Congolese; he has
his origins in the Republic of the Congo and the
Democratic Republic of Congo. He studied BA in
Business Language & IT at the University of Southern
Denmark, and later he carried on with Multimedia
Design at the Nordic Multimedia Academy. Both
Colleges are situated in Kolding, Denmark. By nature,
Rodrigue is a very private man, conservative and
philosophical; at first, he doesn't allow himself to be
an open book. Rodrigue has a tendency to be
unapologetic about who he is and where he comes
from, whether it is France, the Congo, the Democratic
Republic of Congo and other countries where he has
his lineages. Besides his native French, Rodrigue
speaks English, Lingala, Danish, Norwegian and some

German. Rodrigue is an Atheist; his religious views has evolved as being detached from his former religion, Christianity in 2008. Between 2007 and 2009, Rodrigue was a member of the International Society of Poets, an organization owned by the International Library of Poetry. Rodrigue has had various amounts of jobs, including occupations such as a wareshouse employee, a marketing coordinator, a production employee and a translator for the Danish National Police.

www.ingramcontent.com/pod-product-compliance
Lightning Source LLC
Chambersburg PA
CBHW060232290526
45789CB00001B/13